University Texts in the Mathematical Sciences

Textbooks in this series cover a wide variety of courses in mathematics, statistics and computational methods. Ranging across undergraduate and graduate levels, books may focus on theoretical or applied aspects. All texts include frequent examples and exercises of varying complexity. Illustrations, projects, historical remarks, program code and real-world examples may offer additional opportunities for engagement. Texts may be used as a primary or supplemental resource for coursework and are often suitable for independent study.

Md Aquib

Fundamentals of LaTeX

Springer

Md Aquib
Department of Mathematics and
Statistics, College of Science
Imam Mohammad Ibn Saud
Islamic University (IMSIU)
Riyadh, Saudi Arabia

ISSN 2731-9318 ISSN 2731-9326 (electronic)
University Texts in the Mathematical Sciences
ISBN 978-981-96-9317-7 ISBN 978-981-96-9318-4 (eBook)
https://doi.org/10.1007/978-981-96-9318-4

Mathematics Subject Classification: 68U05, 68N15, 00A66, 68U35, 00A35, 97U50, 65Y99

This Springer imprint is published by the registered company Springer Nature Singapore Pte Ltd.
The registered company address is: 152 Beach Road, #21-01/04 Gateway East, Singapore 189721, Singapore

To my beloved mother,
whose unwavering support and prayers have been my strength,

and to the memory of my late father,
whose guidance and values continue to inspire me every day.

Foreword

In an age where the presentation of ideas holds as much weight as the ideas themselves, the art of document preparation is more than just a technical skill, it is a medium of clarity, structure, and precision. LaTeX has stood the test of time as the preferred typesetting system for producing high-quality documents, particularly in the realms of academia, science, and engineering. Its unparalleled ability to handle complex mathematical expressions, bibliographies, and large structured documents has made it indispensable to students, educators, researchers, and professionals worldwide.

This book, *Fundamentals of LaTeX*, was born out of years of teaching, mentoring, and observing how new users approach LaTeX, often with curiosity, sometimes with frustration, but always with the desire to create something professional. While many excellent resources exist, beginners frequently find themselves lost in scattered documentation or overwhelmed by technical jargon. This book aims to fill that gap by offering a clear, structured, and accessible introduction to LaTeX, beginning with the basics and gradually leading to advanced topics such as mathematical typesetting, document customization, graphical integration, and reference management. The book is meticulously organized, reflecting the author's deep understanding of the topic. Each chapter builds confidence by combining clear explanations with practical examples. The reader is not simply told what LaTeX can do, they are shown how to do it, step by step, with real applications that highlight the system's strengths.

What sets this book apart is its clarity of instruction and thoughtful progression through topics. Early chapters introduce the LaTeX environment, document classes, and essential commands with clarity. As the book unfolds, readers encounter more advanced content, including the intricacies of mathematical environments, floating objects, tables, the use of packages, and even the design of complex documents like theses and presentations. Special attention is paid to the integration of graphics, bibliography management, and the creation of custom document structures, all these being essential skills for academic authors.

With hands-on examples, practical tips, and progressive learning paths, the goal is to enable readers to move from writing their first line of LaTeX code to confidently preparing articles, theses, reports, and presentations. Whether the reader is a student writing their first paper, a graduate student preparing a dissertation, a researcher submitting an article to an academic journal, or a professional creating technical documentation, this book offers both a strong foundation and an enduring reference. It invites you not only to learn LaTeX but also to appreciate its philosophy: that beautiful documents are not only possible but achievable through structured thought and disciplined expression.

I have no doubt that *Fundamentals of LaTeX* will become a staple on the bookshelves of academics, engineers, computer scientists, and writers around the world. It is a guide that not only informs but inspires, encouraging readers to produce their best work in the most suitable format.

National University of Science and Technology Politehnica Bucharest
Department of Mathematics and Informatics
Bucharest, Romania
May 20, 2025

Gabriel-Eduard Vîlcu

Preface

In the world of academic and scientific writing, precision and structure are paramount, and LaTeX has long stood as the standard for producing high-quality, publication-ready documents. Whether used to prepare research papers, dissertations, technical reports, or instructional materials, LaTeX offers a level of typographic control and consistency unmatched by conventional word processors.

Fundamentals of LaTeX is the first of a two-volume series that introduces users to the foundational elements of LaTeX. It is written for beginners, students, and professionals who are new to the system or who wish to deepen their understanding of its essential features. This volume begins with the core concepts of LaTeX, including document structure, formatting, text handling, and the creation of simple but structured documents. From there, it leads readers through topics like typesetting mathematical expressions, managing figures and tables, handling references, and customizing document layouts.

Each section of the book is designed to build both conceptual understanding and practical skill. With code examples, output illustrations, and real-world scenarios, readers are equipped not just to read about LaTeX but to write with it confidently. The book is meant to be hands-on, clear, and friendly, while remaining comprehensive enough to serve as a long-term reference.

This first volume lays the groundwork for more advanced topics covered in the second volume. It is our hope that readers will come away with a solid command of LaTeX fundamentals and a sense of readiness to explore its more sophisticated features.

LaTeX is a living tool, evolving through the collaborative effort of a global community of developers and users. This book is inspired by that spirit of sharing, and we thank the LaTeX community whose contributions and insights have made this work possible.

Riyadh, Saudi Arabia Md Aquib

Acknowledgments This work is the result of many years of learning, teaching, and refining ideas. I am deeply thankful to my students, whose questions and curiosity constantly challenged me to explain concepts more clearly and practically. Their feedback shaped much of the structure and flow of this book.

I also want to acknowledge the invaluable contribution of the global LaTeX community, developers, package authors, and documentation writers, whose efforts continue to keep LaTeX alive, modern, and user-friendly. This book leans heavily on their work, and I am honored to pass on their knowledge in a pedagogical format.

To my colleagues and friends in academia who encouraged me to write and believed in the value of a well-structured beginner's guide: thank you. And to my family, whose patience and quiet encouragement supported me through long hours of writing, editing, and revising, this book would not have been possible without you. Finally, I would like to thank Prof. Gabriel-Eduard Vilcu for writing foreword for this book.

Competing Interests The author has no competing interests to declare that are relevant to the content of this manuscript.

Contents

Chapter 1

Introduction to LaTeX

Contents

Md Aquib, *Fundamentals of LaTeX*, University Texts in the Mathematical Sciences,
https://doi.org/10.1007/978-981-96-9318-4_1

Abstract: This chapter provides a foundational overview of LaTeX, a high-quality typesetting system widely used for producing technical and scientific documents. It begins by introducing LaTeX, tracing its historical development from Donald Knuth's creation of TeX to Leslie Lamport's enhancements that led to LaTeX as we know it today. The chapter highlights the advantages of using LaTeX over traditional word processors, including its superior handling of mathematical notation, structured formatting, and cross-referencing. Practical applications in academic writing, publishing, and technical documentation are discussed. Readers are guided through the process of installing LaTeX on various platforms and setting up a working environment. The chapter concludes with an introduction to the basic structure of a LaTeX document, preparing readers for more advanced topics in subsequent chapters.

Keywords: LaTeX, Application of LaTeX, Installing LaTeX, Markup language, TeX

1.1 What Is LaTeX?

LaTeX `Lay-tech` or `Lah-tech` is great for documents that contain mathematical symbols, scientific symbols, or advanced formatting. Imagine it as a way to create professional-looking papers without worrying about layout and design.

Word processors like Microsoft Word or Google Docs are very popular, and you can click and drag most things around. There is something different about LaTeX. Instead of pointing, you instruct LaTeX on what your document should look like by typing commands into a text file. You write the thing in LaTeX, and when you are done with it, it generates a gorgeous PDF.

Think of what you could build with LEGO bricks. In your final document, including LaTeX commands is like building bricks into the house. Do you want the section title to be a bit longer? That is something you can do with a command. Would you like to insert a math equation? For that, too, there is a command. And never have to worry about messing up fonts or margins because LaTeX just makes everything look perfect.

LaTeX is widely used by researchers, scientists, and academics because it can do equations, citations, and bibliographies better than word processors. In essence, it can be applied to any document needing accuracy and shape, such as books, reports, and presentations.

LaTeX is not a word processor; it is a document preparation system. When you give LaTeX instructions, it creates your document. At first, it seems kind of weird to be writing directions instead of editing a paper. Despite this, once you learn LaTeX, you get more control and you get better results, particularly if you write longer documents.

1.2 History and Development of LaTeX

To understand where LaTeX comes from, let's take a step back and talk about how people used to write and format documents.

In the 1970s, a computer scientist called *Donald Knuth* grew tired of how hard it was to produce good mathematical books and papers. At the time, it was hell to produce technical documents with complicated equations and exact formatting. So, Knuth decided to invent a new system, called *TeX* (pronounced "tech"). TeX allowed users to write documents using commands that described how the text should look, focusing on beautiful typesetting, especially for mathematical content.

Although TeX was very, very good, it was also a little hard to use, since it needed to be commanded with just the right words. That is where *Leslie Lamport* comes in. In the 1980s, Lamport created *LaTeX* (which stands for "Lamport TeX") to make TeX easier to use. He extended TeX, incorporating pre-written templates and macros that took care of common procedures such as laying out sections, adding lists, or inserting figures and tables. This made it much easier for regular people, especially academics, scientists, and engineers, to write professional documents without needing to know every technical detail of TeX.

Gradually, LaTeX became the standard for anyone who wanted to produce a document with fancy formatting, such as a scientific paper, thesis, or book. Since it is built on top of TeX, LaTeX continues to generate some of the most pleasingly typeset documents, particularly for mathematical and technical writing.

One reason LaTeX has remained popular for so long is that it is free and open source, meaning anyone can use it or improve upon it. The LaTeX community has developed tens of thousands of packages, add-ons that add functionality to LaTeX. For example, if you want to write a chemistry paper, there is a package for drawing molecular structures. If you are a musician, there is a package for writing music notation.

In the time since its invention, LaTeX has expanded to handle just about any kind of document, from books, articles, and presentations to Web pages. Today, people use LaTeX for everything from simple reports to highly technical books and research papers, making it an essential tool for anyone working in academia or science.

1.3 Why Use LaTeX? (Advantages and Applications)

You might ask, "Why would I want to use LaTeX when I can just use a normal word processor like Microsoft Word or Google Docs?" Great question! So let us see what it is about LaTeX that so many professionals, particularly in academia and science, adore.

1.3.1 Professional-Looking Documents

One of the best things about LaTeX is that it makes your documents look really nice. Whether you are writing an article, a book, or a scientific paper, LaTeX handles the layout and design for you. It also makes damn sure everything is clean and uniform from your section headings to your margins. With LaTeX, you do not need to worry about screwing up page breaks, or misaligning images by accident.

1.3.2 Best Choice for Mathematics and Science

If you do any writing where you might want to write equations, scientific symbols, or technical stuff, LaTeX is the way to go. It was specifically built from the ground up to deal with complicated formulas and notations, and thus it became the mathematicians', scientists', and engineers' tool of choice. Rather than trying to format equations into a normal word processor, you can write equations in LaTeX in a few lines of code, and LaTeX will make sure they come out beautifully. Here is a basic example:

Basic Example

LaTeX Code:

```
\[
E = mc^2.
\]
```

Output:

$$E = mc^2.$$

For more complex formulas, such as fractions, roots, and summations, LaTeX is the best tool available:

Complex Formula

LaTeX Code:

```
\[
\frac{a}{b}
\]

\[
\sqrt{x^2 + y^2}
\]

\[
\sum_{n=1}^{\infty}
\frac{1}{n^2}
\]
```

Output:

$$\frac{a}{b}.$$

$$\sqrt{x^2 + y^2}.$$

$$\sum_{n=1}^{\infty} \frac{1}{n^2}.$$

1.3.3 Automation of Tedious Tasks

LaTeX is great at doing things that you would have to spend a long time doing in a word processor. Have to number all your sections, figures, tables, and equations? LaTeX does that for you. Generate a table of contents automatically or a list of figures. It comes in particularly handy when dealing with large documents, such as research papers, dissertations, or books, since it would be a pain to try and keep track of all the information by hand.

1.3.4 Consistent Formatting

Have you ever sat there for hours trying to make your fonts/margins/headings be the same in every section of a document? In LaTeX, this is never a problem. You set the general style once, and LaTeX insists that every part of your document is written in the same style. It makes your papers look professional and clean, without you having to do anything.

1.3.5 Customization with Packages

LaTeX has a huge ecosystem of packages; these are like add-ons that give you extra tools and features. There are packages for just about everything: making complex tables, writing musical scores, creating high-quality graphs, or even formatting documents to meet specific journal requirements. If you need something special in your document, chances are that there is already a LaTeX package for it.

1.3.6 Perfect for Large Documents

Writing a large document, such as a thesis or a book, can be a challenge in regular word processors because they tend to slow down or become difficult to manage. LaTeX handles large documents with ease. You can break your document into smaller pieces, manage each section separately, and then let LaTeX put everything together. This modular approach makes it simple to work on big projects.

1.3.7 Free and Open Source

Another big plus: LaTeX is completely free! No need to purchase software or deal with licenses. It is also open source, free software, and so the LaTeX community is constantly trying to improve it, add new features, assist users. Even better, it is available on all the popular platforms (Windows, Mac, Linux) and can even be done in your Web browser using online LaTeX editors like Overleaf.

1.3.8 Applications of LaTeX

LaTeX is used in a wide range of fields and industries. Here are just a few examples:

1. *Academic Publishing*: The language of scientific papers in many scientific disciplines is the LaTeX code. In mathematics, physics, and computer science, most journals are open to submissions in LaTeX, largely due to its capacity for sophisticated content.

2. *Books and Theses*: LaTeX is the standard for writing books, theses, and dissertations. It can handle big papers, references, and citations, which is exactly what one needs as an academic writer.

3. *Presentations*: With a LaTeX package called Beamer, you can even design professional-looking slides for presentations, so it is also a very useful tool.

4. *Technical Reports*: LaTeX has become the standard for technical writing, particularly in fields such as engineering and software development, where it is important to have precise formatting and mathematical material.

1.4 Installing LaTeX and Setup

Before you start using LaTeX, you need to install the right tools on your computer or use an online editor. There are a few different ways to work with LaTeX, depending on your preferences and operating system.

1.4.1 Installing LaTeX on Your Computer

If you want to work offline, you can install a LaTeX distribution on your computer. A LaTeX distribution is a collection of software tools that allows you to compile `.tex` files into output formats like PDF. Here are some popular options:

- *Windows*: You can install *MiKTeX*, which includes all the tools you need to work with LaTeX. It comes with a basic editor, but you can use more advanced editors as well.
- *Mac*: *MacTeX* is the recommended distribution for Mac users. It includes the TeXShop editor, which is a great tool for writing LaTeX.
- *Linux*: Many Linux distributions have LaTeX packages available. The most common is *TeX Live*.

Once you have installed the distribution, you can write your LaTeX code in any text editor, but there are specialized LaTeX editors that make things easier.

1.4.2 Online LaTeX Editors

For those who prefer a more accessible and collaborative writing environment, online LaTeX editors provide an excellent alternative to traditional offline installations. These cloud-based platforms allow users to write, compile, and share LaTeX documents in real time without requiring any software installation. Among these platforms, *Overleaf* is widely regarded as one of the most user-friendly and powerful tools for LaTeX document preparation.

One of the biggest advantages of Overleaf is that it does not require users to install any software on their computers. Unlike traditional setups, where users must download and configure a LaTeX distribution such as `TeX Live`, `MiKTeX`, or `MacTeX`, Overleaf operates entirely in a Web browser. This eliminates compatibility issues and ensures that users can work on their documents from any device with an Internet connection.

Another key feature of Overleaf is its real-time collaboration capability. Multiple users can edit the same document simultaneously, making it an ideal tool for co-authored research papers, academic reports, and large-scale projects. Changes made by one collaborator are instantly visible to others, reducing the need for version control and back-and-forth email exchanges. This makes Overleaf particularly useful for students and researchers working in teams.

Overleaf also automates the document compilation process, allowing users to see a live preview of their document as they type. Traditionally, compiling a LaTeX document requires running a sequence of commands manually, such as `pdflatex` or `biber`. Overleaf simplifies this process by providing automatic compilation and error detection, making it especially helpful for beginners. If a syntax error occurs, Overleaf highlights the issue and provides suggestions for resolving it.

In addition to its ease of use, Overleaf provides a vast collection of templates tailored for different document types, including research papers, theses, CVs, presentations, and even scientific posters. Many of these templates conform to the formatting guidelines required by academic journals and institutions, saving users significant time and effort. The platform also supports integration with reference management tools such as *Zotero*, *Mendeley*, and *BibTeX*, enabling seamless citation management.

To begin using Overleaf, users simply need to visit Overleaf's website and create an account. Once logged in, they can start a new project by selecting a template, uploading an existing `.tex` file, or creating a blank document. The editor provides a split-screen interface, displaying the LaTeX source code on one side and the compiled PDF output on the other. Users can also share their documents by generating a unique link, allowing collaborators to either edit or view the document, depending on the permissions set by the owner.

Beyond Overleaf, several other online LaTeX editors offer similar functionality. *Papeeria* provides a minimalistic interface with cloud storage integration, making it a suitable choice for those who prefer a lightweight experience. *Authorea*, designed specifically for academic writing, supports LaTeX alongside Markdown and HTML, allowing for a more flexible writing experience. *ShareLaTeX*, which has now merged with Overleaf, originally functioned as a standalone collaborative LaTeX editor and continues to provide the same real-time editing capabilities.

Online LaTeX editors have transformed the document preparation process, making LaTeX more accessible to a wider audience. Whether used for research papers, professional reports, or collaborative projects, these platforms streamline the writing experience while maintaining the powerful typesetting capabilities of LaTeX. With no installation required, automatic compilation, and seamless collaboration features, tools like Overleaf have become indispensable for modern LaTeX users.

1.4.3 Choosing a LaTeX Editor

Once you have installed LaTeX or signed up for an online editor, you will need an editor to write your `.tex` files. Some editors come with the LaTeX distribution, but there are other options that can make writing LaTeX easier.

Here are a few popular LaTeX editors:

- *TeXworks* and *WinEdt* (Windows, Mac, Linux): A simple, user-friendly editor that is included with many LaTeX distributions like MiKTeX

- *TeXShop* (Mac): A great editor that comes with the MacTeX distribution

- *Visual Studio Code* (Cross-platform): A versatile code editor that can be set up for LaTeX with the LaTeX Workshop extension

- *Overleaf* (Online): The easiest option for getting started quickly, with no installation required

1.4.4 Compiling a LaTeX Document

Once you have written your `.tex` file, you need to compile it to get the final output, usually a PDF. Here is the step-by-step guide to compile your LaTeX document:

1. If you are using a desktop editor like TeXworks or TeXShop, you will see a "Compile" or "Typeset" button. Click this button, and the editor will generate the PDF from your `.tex` file.

2. If you are using a desktop editor like Winedt, click the button PDFTeXify or just use combination of

keys *Shift + Ctrl+ P* and the editor will generate the PDF from your `.tex` file.

3. If you are using Overleaf, your document automatically compiles every time you save, and you can download the output PDF directly.

In most cases, LaTeX editors provide error messages with line numbering if something goes wrong during compilation, making it easier to fix problems in your document.

1.5 Basic Document Structure

When you write a LaTeX document, it follows a specific structure. Understanding this structure will help you create organized and well-formatted documents. In this section, we will cover the basic parts of a LaTeX document and how they work.

In fact, to create a LaTeX file, we need at least three commands:

1. `\documentclass{}`.
2. `\begin{document}`.
3. `\end{document}`.

Remark 1.5.1 *1. All the commands in LaTeX are preceded by the \ (backslash) symbols.*

2. Commands in the LaTeX are case sensitive.

The first line in a LaTeX document specifies the document class. This tells LaTeX what kind of document you are writing (e.g., an article, book, or report).

The main content of your document starts after the `\begin{document}` command. Everything you write after this point will appear in the final output. This command tells LaTeX that the actual document content is starting.

Finally, you end your LaTeX document with the `\end{document}` command. Anything you write after this command will be ignored by LaTeX. This tells LaTeX that the document is finished.

1.5.1 Creating the First LaTeX File

Here is a simple example for creating a LaTeX document:

Latex Document

LaTeX Code:

```
\documentclass{article}

\begin{document}
I am    writing    my

First LaTeX
document.
\end{document}
```

Output:

I am writing my First LaTeX document.

Remark 1.5.2 1. *Article document class is suitable for most of the writing projects.*

2. *LaTeX ignores most of the extra spaces in a file. Blank line (or lines) tells LaTeX to start a new paragraph. The situation can be analyzed in the above example.*

Exercises for Chap. 1: Introduction to LaTeX

1.1 What Is LaTeX?

1. *Describe LaTeX in Your Own Words*: Write a short paragraph explaining LaTeX and its purpose in typesetting documents. How does it differ from typical word processors like Microsoft Word?

2. *Key Components*: List three key features of LaTeX that make it a powerful tool for typesetting technical and academic documents.

3. *True or False*: LaTeX is primarily word processing software. Justify your answer.

1.2 History and Development of LaTeX

1. *Timeline of LaTeX*: Research the history of LaTeX and create a timeline of its key developments, starting from its origin with Donald Knuth's TeX system to the modern versions we use today.

2. *Historical Figures*: Who are the key figures behind the development of LaTeX? Briefly describe their contributions.

3. *Difference Between TeX and LaTeX*: In what ways do TeX and LaTeX differ? Provide at least two distinct differences.

1.3 Why Use LaTeX? (Advantages and Applications)

1. *Advantages of LaTeX*: List five advantages of using LaTeX over other typesetting or word processing tools.

2. *Application Areas*: Provide examples of at least three fields where LaTeX is commonly used and describe why it is preferred in these fields.

3. *Research and Report*: Find an academic or research paper that was written using LaTeX. Describe the types of formatting or features used in the paper that make LaTeX ideal for such work.

1.4 Installing LaTeX and Setup (Overleaf, TeXShop, etc.)

1. *Installation Walkthrough*: Install LaTeX on your own system (or use an online platform like Overleaf) and document each step you took, including any challenges faced during installation.

2. *Comparison Exercise*: Compare at least two LaTeX editors (e.g., Overleaf, TeXShop, MiKTeX). What are the key differences in their features, and which one would you prefer to use for your own projects?

3. *Setup Practice*: Create a simple LaTeX document using your chosen editor. The document should contain a title, author, date, and a short paragraph about any topic of your choice.

1.5 Basic Document Structure

1. *Document Structure Identification*: Write down the basic structure of a LaTeX document. Label the document body and any necessary commands (e.g., `documentclass`, `begin{document}`, `end{document}`).

2. *Create a Simple Document*: Write a simple LaTeX document that includes a few paragraphs. Compile the document and ensure it runs without errors.

Chapter 2

Document Structure and Formatting

Contents

Md Aquib, *Fundamentals of LaTeX*, University Texts in the Mathematical Sciences,
https://doi.org/10.1007/978-981-96-9318-4_2

Abstract: A well-structured document is essential for clarity, readability, and professionalism, whether you are writing an academic paper, a thesis, a technical report, or a book. LaTeX provides a rich set of tools to organize and format your content logically and consistently, allowing you to focus on writing while ensuring a high-quality visual presentation.

Keywords: LaTeX formatting, Sections and subsections, Document classes, Preamble, Lists in LaTeX, LaTeX environments

This chapter introduces the fundamental components that define the structure of a LaTeX document. It begins with an explanation of document classes, packages, and the basic preamble setup. We then explore hierarchical elements such as chapters, sections, subsections, and paragraphs, which help organize content into meaningful divisions. Alongside structural elements, this chapter also covers formatting tools including line spacing, page layout, font styles, text alignment, indentation, and the use of environments for quotations, lists, and other textual elements.

Additionally, you will learn how to use custom titles, headers, and footers, as well as how to manage white space and breaks in a document. These techniques not only improve the aesthetics of your work but also enhance the user experience for your readers.

By the end of this chapter, you will be equipped to construct documents that are not only technically sound but also typographically elegant and structurally coherent.

2.1 Creating a Basic LaTeX Document

Now that we have familiarized ourselves with the overall structure of a LaTeX document, it is time to put theory into practice. This section provides a hands-on walkthrough of building a basic LaTeX file from scratch, intended for users who are just beginning their journey with this powerful typesetting system.

The aim here is to establish a solid foundation in constructing simple yet well-formatted documents. We will begin by defining the document class, a required step that determines the overall layout and style of the document. Then, we will progressively add content such as plain text, sections and subsections, and a simple mathematical formula using LaTeX's intuitive syntax.

Along the way, you will become familiar with important structural elements like the preamble, environments, and commands that govern how content is interpreted and rendered. The examples provided in this section are chosen to be minimal yet illustrative, helping you quickly grasp how different parts of a LaTeX document fit together.

By the end of this section, you will be able to independently create a basic document that includes structured text, formatted paragraphs, and inline or displayed mathematical expressions. This will serve as the starting point for more advanced topics covered in later chapters, such as document customization, typesetting complex mathematics, creating tables and figures, and referencing external content.

2.1.1 Document Class

In every LaTeX document, the very first step is to declare the type of document you are writing. This is done using the `{\documentclass}` command, which specifies the overall layout and structural behavior of your document. Depending on whether you are creating a research article, a book, a thesis, or a formal letter, LaTeX offers various predefined document classes to suit your needs.

The general syntax for declaring a document class is:

```
\documentclass[options]{class}
```

Here, the `class` could be something like `article`, `report`, `book`, `letter`, or `beamer`, and `options` may include page size (e.g., `a4paper`), font size (e.g., `12pt`), and others.

For instance, a typical document starting an article might look like this:

Basic Article Class Declaration

```
\documentclass[a4paper,12pt]{article}
```

This command sets up an A4-sized document using a 12-point font under the `article` class, which is suitable for short documents like academic papers, essays, and articles.

Another common class is the `beamer` class (See Chap. 7), used for presentations. Its declaration appears nearly the same but results in a very different output structure:

Beamer Class Declaration

```
\documentclass{beamer}
```

In more extensive documents such as dissertations or technical reports, the `report` class is often preferred. It introduces chapter divisions and a more formal layout.

Basic Report Structure

```
\documentclass[12pt]{report}
\title{Sample Report}
\author{John Doe}
\date{\today}
\begin{document}

\maketitle
\tableofcontents
\chapter{Introduction}
This is the first chapter.

\section{Background}
\section{Objective}

\chapter{Methodology}
\chapter{Conclusion}

\appendix
\chapter{Additional Data}
\end{document}
```

In this case, the document is organized into chapters and sections. Notice how the use of `\chapter` is a distinctive feature of the `report` class. Additionally, the `\appendix` command allows the creation of appendices, automatically formatting them with the correct labels.

If you are preparing a book, the `book` class provides even more structure, including support for front matter, such as a preface or table of contents, and back matter like bibliographies or indices. Here is an example:

Basic Book Structure

```
\documentclass[12pt]{book}

\title{A Comprehensive Guide to LaTeX}
\author{Dr. LaTeX}
\date{\today}

\begin{document}

\frontmatter
\maketitle
\chapter{Preface}

\mainmatter
\chapter{Introduction}
\section{Why Use LaTeX?}

\chapter{Formatting Documents}
\chapter{Mathematical Typesetting}

\backmatter
\chapter{Appendix A: Installation Guide}

\end{document}
```

The `book` class enhances document structure with commands such as `\frontmatter`, `\mainmatter`, and `\backmatter`, which help distinguish different parts of a traditional printed book. Furthermore, chapters in the `book` class always begin on a new right-hand page, a stylistic choice consistent with published books.

For shorter, more formal correspondence, the `letter` class offers a minimal and professional layout. Instead of sections and chapters, it includes constructs specific to letters:

Example: Writing a Formal Letter

```
\documentclass{letter}

\usepackage{hyperref}

\signature{Dr. LaTeX}
\address{123 Main Street \\
City, Country}

\begin{document}

\begin{letter}{Jane Smith \\
456 Elm Street \\
Another City, Country}

\opening{Dear Ms. LaTeX,}

I hope this letter finds you well. I am
writing to formally introduce myself and
discuss a potential collaboration.

LaTeX provides an excellent way to format
professional letters efficiently.

\closing{Sincerely,}

\end{letter}

\end{document}
```

This layout handles formatting elements like sender and recipient addresses, greetings, and signatures, making it ideal for professional communication.

Feature	`report`	`book`	`letter`
Chapters	Yes	Yes	No
Table of contents	Yes	Yes	No
Appendices	Yes	Yes	No
Front and back matter	No	Yes	No
Letter formatting	No	No	Yes

Table 2.1: Comparison of `report`, `book`, and `letter` Classes

Comparison of Document Classes

Choosing the right document class is crucial for ensuring proper structure and formatting. Each class offers unique features that cater to different document requirements (Table 2.1).

2.1.2 The Preamble

Before the main body of any LaTeX document begins, there is a critical configuration area known as the *preamble*. This section appears before `\begin{document}` and serves as the foundation for defining the document's layout, functionality, and stylistic features.

The preamble typically begins with the `\documentclass` declaration, which sets the overall structure of the document. Following that, one or more `\usepackage` commands are included to load external packages, each extending LaTeX's capabilities in a specific way. These packages might enable image inclusion, improve mathematical typesetting, define hyperlink behavior, or customize fonts and colors.

Consider the following basic preamble:

Example: A Minimal Preamble

```
\documentclass{article}
\usepackage{graphicx}
% Allows image inclusion
\usepackage{amsmath}
% Enhances mathematical formatting
\usepackage{hyperref}
% Adds hyperlinks

\begin{document}
```

In this example, the document class is set to `article`, which is well-suited for shorter documents such as journal articles, essays, and reports. Three commonly used packages are then loaded. The `graphicx` package provides support for including external image files using the `\includegraphics` command. The `amsmath` package, developed by the American Mathematical Society, enhances LaTeX's mathematical environments, making it easier to write aligned, multiline, and complex mathematical expressions. Lastly, the `hyperref` package allows for hyperlinking within the document (such as clickable references) and to external sources like websites and DOIs.

Though the example above is simple, it illustrates the modular nature of LaTeX: only the necessary tools are loaded, keeping the document efficient and lightweight. As your documents grow more complex, your preamble may include custom macros, layout definitions, bibliographic configurations, or even language support. For that reason, it is good practice to keep the preamble well-organized, grouping similar settings together and adding brief comments for clarity.

In larger projects, especially collaborative ones, a clean and thoughtfully structured preamble ensures that the document remains easy to maintain and adapt over time. It is often the first place others will look when trying to understand or modify how the document behaves.

2.1.3 The Document Environment

In every LaTeX document, there is a clearly defined boundary that separates the preamble, the configuration, the and setup area, from the body of the document itself. This boundary is created using the `document` environment, which is delimited by the commands `\begin{document}` and `\end{document}`. Only the content placed within this environment is interpreted as the main material to be typeset; anything outside it is either ignored or used for setup purposes.

The structure is simple but crucial:

Code Snippet: The Document Environment

```
\begin{document}

% Your content goes here

\end{document}
```

This environment is where all elements of the document, titles, sections, paragraphs, equations, figures, tables, citations, and so on, are placed. When LaTeX encounters `\begin{document}`, it begins processing the content for output, applying the rules and formatting that have been specified in the preamble. The command `\end{document}` marks the end of the typeset material. Anything that appears after it will be ignored by the compiler, even if it is syntactically valid.

For example, a minimal working document might look like this:

Example: Minimal Document Structure

```
\documentclass{article}

\begin{document}

Hello, world!

\end{document}
```

In this example, the preamble contains only the document class declaration. The phrase *Hello, world!* is placed inside the `document` environment, and therefore, it is what appears in the final PDF output.

The discipline of separating configuration from content is one of the key principles that gives LaTeX its strength in document preparation. It ensures that authors can focus on writing and structure without being distracted by layout considerations, which are handled separately. This structure also allows for reusable templates where content can be changed independently of formatting, making it ideal for collaborative, academic, or long-term projects.

2.1.4 Adding a Title, Author, and Date

A well-structured document often begins with a clear title, the author's name, and the date of creation. In LaTeX, this is achieved using a set of dedicated commands:`\title`, `\author`, and `\date`, which are declared in the preamble. These commands define the metadata for your document, and their output is rendered on the page only when `\maketitle` is used inside the `document` environment.

The process is intuitive. First, define the title, author, and date at the top of your file, after specifying the document class and any necessary packages. Then, within the body of the document, call `\maketitle` to typeset this information on the first page.

Consider the following example:

Example: Title Page with Author and Date

LaTeX Code:

```
\documentclass{article}

\title{Introduction to LaTeX}
\author{Dr.~LaTeX}
\date{\today}

\begin{document}

\maketitle

\end{document}
```

Output:

Introduction to LaTeX

Dr. LaTeX

July 6, 2026

In this example, the `\title` command sets the document's main title, while `\author` identifies the writer. The `\date` command can be manually specified (e.g., `\date{April 2025}`) or dynamically generated using `\today`, which inserts the current date at the time of compilation.

The command `\maketitle` is what triggers LaTeX to typeset the provided title information. Without it, the document will compile normally, but the title, author, and date will not appear. It is typically placed right after `\begin{document}`, ensuring the title appears on the first page.

If you are writing a letter or using classes like `beamer`, the title generation process differs slightly, but in most standard document classes, such as `article`, `report`, and `book`, this pattern remains consistent. Using this structure not only provides a professional appearance to your document but also helps automate features like metadata extraction when generating PDFs.

2.1.5 Sections and Structuring Content

One of the great strengths of LaTeX lies in its ability to structure long and complex documents using hierarchical sectioning commands. This structure not only makes the document easier to read and navigate but also ensures that elements such as the table of contents, headers, and cross-references are generated automatically and consistently.

To organize content, LaTeX provides a built-in set of commands that define progressively smaller divisions of a document: `\section`, `\subsection`, `\subsubsection`, `\paragraph`, and `\subparagraph`. These commands are designed to reflect the logical structure of your text, much like headings and subheadings in a book or article.

Let us examine a typical example:

Example: Structuring a Document

```
\documentclass{article}

\begin{document}

\section{Introduction}
This is the opening section of the
document.

\subsection{Background}
Here, we provide context and historical
background.
```

```
\subsubsection{Development Timeline}
Details of major developments are listed
here.

\paragraph{Further Explanation}
This paragraph offers elaboration on the
timeline.

\subparagraph{Technical Note}
A brief remark on technical specifics.

\end{document}
```

Rendered Output

1 Introduction

This is the opening section of the document.

1.1 Background

Here we provide context and historical background.

1.1.1 Development Timeline

Details of major developments are listed here.
Further Explanation. This paragraph offers elaboration on the timeline.
Technical Note. A brief remark on technical specifics.

In this example, each command introduces a different level of heading. The `\section` command creates a primary division in the document and is numbered automatically. Inside it, the `\subsection` and `\subsubsection` commands create sublevels, each indented further in the hierarchy.

Interestingly, `\paragraph` and `\subparagraph` behave slightly differently than the higher-level sectioning commands. Rather than producing a vertical break followed by a heading, they create inline bolded labels, immediately followed by the corresponding text. This makes them suitable for minor subtopics or brief annotations that do not require much visual separation.

Using these commands properly contributes to the semantic clarity of your document and allows you to automatically generate a table of contents with `\tableofcontents`. It also ensures your document is well-structured for PDF navigation and accessibility tools.

Each document class handles sectioning slightly differently. For instance, the `article` class does not support chapters, so `\chapter` is unavailable unless you switch to the `report` or `book` classes, where chapters act as top-level divisions. In these classes, `\section` becomes a secondary-level heading beneath chapters.

Ultimately, careful use of sectioning commands ensures your content is not only visually structured but logically organized, an essential feature when preparing documents for academic, technical, or professional purposes.

Remark 2.1.1 *In LaTeX, sectioning commands such as* `\section` *and* `\subsection` *are designed to automatically number headings by default. However, there are cases, particularly in prefaces, appendices, or standalone documents, where numbered sections may not be desirable. In such situations, an asterisked version of the command can be used. For example, to create an unnumbered section or subsection, you can use* `\section*{}` *or* `\subsection*{}`*, respectively. These commands suppress the numbering and still format the headings with the appropriate styling.*

It is important to note that LaTeX follows a strict hierarchy in its sectioning structure. A `\subsection` *must always follow a* `\section`*. Attempting to use a subsection* *without first defining a section will result in incorrect formatting or errors. Think of LaTeX's sectioning system as a tree: branches like* `\subsection` *and* `\subsubsection` *must grow from a defined trunk, which is typically the* `\section` *command. This ensures logical organization and structural consistency across the document.*

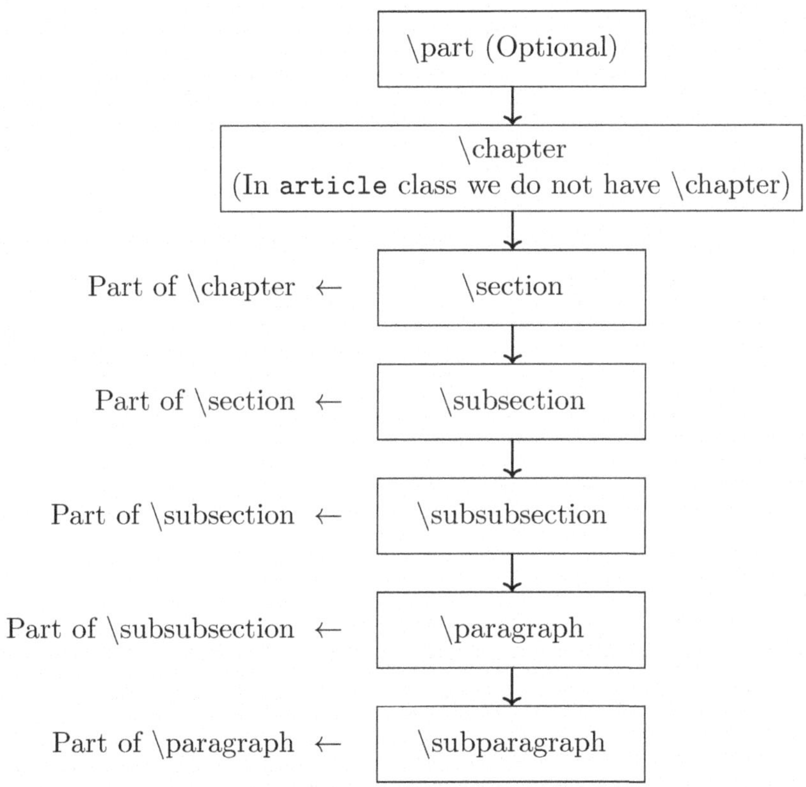

2.1.6 Complete Example

Let's put everything together. Below is a complete example of a basic LaTeX document.

Example

```
\documentclass{article}
\usepackage{amsmath}
\title{My First LaTeX Document}
\author{Your Name}
\date{\today}
\begin{document}
\maketitle
\section{Introduction}
This is the introduction to my first LaTeX
document.Here, I will explain what the
document is about.
\subsection{Purpose}
The purpose of this document is to learn the
basics of LaTeX.
\section{Mathematical Expressions}
In LaTeX, writing mathematical expressions is
simple. For example, Einstein's famous
equation is written as:
\[
E = mc^2
\]
\end{document}
```

The LaTeX will display:

My First LaTeX Document

Your Name

June 5, 2025

1 Introduction

This is the introduction to my first LaTeX document. Here, I will explain what the document is about.

1.1 Purpose

The purpose of this document is to learn the basics of LaTeX.

2 Mathematical Expressions

In LaTeX, writing mathematical expressions is simple. For example, Einstein's famous equation is written as:

$$E = mc^2$$

In this example, the document begins with the declaration of the `article` class, which is one of the most commonly used classes in LaTeX for writing academic papers, short reports, and articles. The preamble also includes the `amsmath` package, which is essential for writing mathematical expressions and symbols with enhanced formatting capabilities.

The title of the document is specified using the `\title{}` command, and it is displayed at the beginning of the document with the `\maketitle` command. The structure of the content is organized using sectioning commands. It consists of two main sections: one titled "Introduction," which contains a subsection called "Purpose," and another titled "Mathematical Expressions." These structural commands help divide the content clearly and hierarchically.

Within the body of the document, a well-known equation from physics, $E = mc^2$, is typeset in mathematical notation using LaTeX's math mode. This showcases the utility of LaTeX in presenting mathematical content in a clean and readable format, demonstrating both its power and elegance in technical typesetting.

2.2 Formatting Text (Bold, Italics, Underline, and Font Sizes)

In LaTeX, formatting text is simple yet highly customizable. Whether you want to emphasize a word with italics, make your headings stand out in bold, or adjust the font size to suit your document, LaTeX gives you easy-to-use commands for all these tasks. In this section, we will cover the most common ways to format text in LaTeX, including bold, italics, underline, and font size adjustments.

2.2.1 Bold Text

Let us start with bold text. You can make text bold in LaTeX by using the `\textbf{}` command. This is useful for emphasizing headings, important terms, or any text that needs to stand out.

Here is how you do it:

```
\textbf{This text is bold.}
```

Bold Text

LaTeX Code:

```
This is normal text.
\textbf{This text is
bold.}
```

Output:

This is normal text.
This text is bold.

2.2.2 Italic Text

To italicize text in LaTeX, use the `\textit{}` command. Italics are often used for emphasis, technical terms, or book titles.

Here is the syntax:

```
\textit{This text is italicized.}
```

Italic Text

LaTeX Code:

```
This is normal text.
\textit{This text is
italicized.}
```

Output:

This is normal text.
This text is italicized

Remark 2.2.1 *You can also use* `\emph` *command to produce to italicize text. The same* `\emph` *command can also be used to non-italicize text in a italic section.*

2.2.3 Underlined Text

While underlining is not as common in LaTeX documents, it is sometimes useful. To underline text, we use the `\underline{}` command.

Here is the syntax:

```
\underline{This text is underlined.}
```

Underlined Text

LaTeX Code:

```
This is normal text.
\underline{This text
is underlined.}
```

Output:

This is normal text.
This text is underlined.

2.2.4 Combining Text Formatting

You can combine different formatting commands to create more complex effects. For example, you can make the text both bold and italicized at the same time:

```
\textbf{\textit{This text is bold
and italicized.}}
```

Bold and Italic Text

LaTeX Code:

```
This is a normal text
\textbf{\textit{
This text is bold and
italicized.}}
```

Output:

This is normal text.
This text is bold and italicized.

Adjusting Font Size

Typography plays a vital role in shaping how information is perceived in a document. In LaTeX, you can adjust the font size semantically, using predefined commands rather than numeric sizes. These commands allow for scalable and consistent formatting that aligns with the document class settings.

LaTeX provides a hierarchy of font size commands ranging from very small to very large. These commands include `\tiny`, `\scriptsize`, `\footnotesize`, `\small`, `\normalsize` (the default), and then increasingly larger sizes such as `\large`, `\Large`, `\LARGE`, `\huge`, and `\Huge`. These size adjustments are relative to the base font size specified in the document class, typically 10pt, 11pt, or 12pt.

The following Table 2.2 offers a quick overview of LaTeX's font size commands and their visual effect:

Font size command	**Example output**
`\tiny`	This is tiny text
`\scriptsize`	This is script-size text
`\footnotesize`	This is footnote-size text
`\small`	This is small text
`\normalsize`	This is normal text
`\large`	This is large text
`\Large`	This is larger text
`\LARGE`	This is even larger text
`\huge`	This is huge text
`\Huge`	This is the hugest text

Table 2.2: Font size options in LaTeX

To use these font size commands in your document, you enclose the desired text in curly braces following the command. This localizes the effect and prevents unintentional resizing of the rest of the document. Consider the following example that demonstrates how different font sizes affect content within the same section:

Using Font Size Commands

LaTeX Code:

```
\Huge{This is a very
large heading.}
\large{This is slightly
larger text.}
\normalsize{This is
normal text.}
```

Output:

This is a very large heading.
This is slightly larger text.
This is normal text.

These font size commands are typically used within paragraphs, headings, figure captions, or footnotes. It is important to remember that they do not affect spacing between lines or sections, only the size of the characters themselves.

Additionally, if you wish to apply a different size to a longer block of text, you can wrap it in a group using braces or apply the size command within an environment. For instance:

```
{\small This entire paragraph will appear in
small font size.}
```

This grouped formatting ensures clarity and prevents unintended size changes beyond the intended scope.

Text Alignment: Centering, Left, and Right

While LaTeX defaults to fully justified text, producing a neat, column-like appearance, there are times when you may want to override this and apply a different alignment. This is especially useful in cover pages, letters, signatures, or when formatting text for visual emphasis. LaTeX provides a set of environments that allow you to manually align blocks of text to the left, right, or center.

To align text to the left, one uses the `flushleft` environment. Similarly, for right-aligned text, the `flushright` environment is used. If you wish to center the content, the `center` environment provides the appropriate structure. Each of these environments wraps a block of text and overrides the default justification behavior within its scope.

The following example demonstrates all three alignments using their respective environments. The left column presents the LaTeX code, while the right column illustrates the corresponding visual output:

Example: Aligning Text in LaTeX

LaTeX Code:

```
\begin{flushleft}
This text is aligned
to the left.
\end{flushleft}

\begin{flushright}
This text is aligned
to the right.
\end{flushright}

\begin{center}
This text is centered.
\end{center}
```

Output:

This text is aligned to the left.

This text is aligned to the right.

This text is centered.

Each alignment environment starts on a new line and ends its effect at the environment's closing tag. Unlike regular justified paragraphs in LaTeX, which attempt to fill the entire line width by adjusting spacing between words, these environments maintain a ragged edge on the opposite side, preserving the selected alignment precisely.

It is also worth noting that these environments are primarily intended for short blocks of text. Overusing them in long passages may disrupt the visual rhythm of the document. However, when used selectively, they offer an effective tool for fine-tuning the structure and visual presentation of your writing.

Customizing Fonts

In LaTeX, selection of the appropriate font family can significantly enhance the clarity and tone of a document. Whether you are writing prose, mathematical exposition, or technical documentation, LaTeX provides several built-in font families that can be applied either locally to a phrase or globally to entire sections.

Three primary font families are available by default in LaTeX: serif (roman), sans-serif, and monospaced (typewriter). The default font in most document classes is the serif family, which gives a formal and traditional appearance. However, you can switch to a different font family to suit different contexts. For instance, sans-serif fonts are often preferred for section headings or presentations due to their clean, modern look, while monospaced fonts are commonly used for code snippets or inline technical content.

The following example illustrates how to use these font families in practice. On the left, you will see the LaTeX code, and on the right, the resulting visual output:

Example: Switching Between Font Families

LaTeX Code:

```
\texttt{This is
typewriter font.}

\sffamily
This is sans-serif
font.
\rmfamily
Back to roman font.
```

Output:

`This is typewriter font.`
This is sans-serif font.
Back to roman font.

Each font family can be invoked in two ways: by using a specific command that changes only a block of text (e.g., `\texttt{...}` for inline typewriter font) or by switching the entire environment using a declaration like `\sffamily` or `\ttfamily`. The latter affects all subsequent text until the family is reset, such as returning to roman using `\rmfamily`.

When selecting fonts, it is helpful to consider readability and the purpose of the text. Serif fonts are easier to read in long blocks of body text, while sans-serif fonts work well in slides or short bursts of information. Monospaced fonts are ideal when precision and alignment matter, such as in coding documentation or tabular data.

It is worth noting that these default families can be extended by loading font-related packages or using compilers like XeLaTeX or LuaLaTeX, which allow system font usage via the `fontspec` package, though such customization lies beyond the basic scope and will be explored in later sections.

Handling Special Text Elements

LaTeX provides a rich set of tools for typesetting special textual content such as code snippets, small capitals, and strikethrough text. These features are essential when you need to convey syntax, technical terminology, or editorial notes clearly and with stylistic accuracy.

One of the most important tools for typesetting raw code or commands without interpretation is the `verbatim` environment. This environment preserves all characters, including special LaTeX symbols like \, { and }, exactly as they are typed. This is especially useful when documenting LaTeX itself, writing tutorials, or displaying command-line input.

Example: Displaying Raw Code with `verbatim`

LaTeX Code:

```
\begin{verbatim}
\textbf{This text
will appear exactly
as typed.}
\end{verbatim}
```

Output:

```
\textbf{This text
will appear exactly
as typed.}
```

Unlike other environments, the `verbatim` environment disables all LaTeX formatting within its scope. As a result, even commands like `\textbf` are rendered as plain text. When you need inline verbatim text, the \`verb` command is also available for short, inline code snippets.

Another useful feature is the ability to apply small capitals. This can be achieved using the `\textsc{}` command, which converts its content to small capital letters, a style often used for acronyms, proper names, or emphasis in headings.

Example: Using Small Capitals

LaTeX Code:

```
\textsc{This is Small
Capitals Text.}
```

Output:

THIS IS SMALL CAPITALS TEXT.

In certain editorial contexts, you might need to show deletions or corrections. For this purpose, LaTeX provides the ability to apply strikethrough formatting. This is enabled via the `ulem` package, which includes the command `\sout{}` for striking through text. However, one should exercise caution: loading `ulem` alters the default behavior of `\emph{}` from italicizing to underlining, which might affect emphasis throughout your document.

Example: Applying Strikethrough with `ulem`

LaTeX Code:

```
\usepackage{ulem}
\sout{This text is
strikethrough.}
```

Output:

~~This text is strikethrough.~~

If you wish to avoid the side effects of `ulem` but still want to use strikethrough text, you may consider using the `cancel` or `tikz` packages for more targeted control.

2.2.5 Best Practices for Text Formatting

While it is easy to use these formatting commands, you should avoid overusing bold, italics, and underlining, as it can make your document look cluttered. LaTeX is designed to produce professional-looking documents, so use formatting sparingly and purposefully. Keep in mind: *Bold* is often reserved for section headings and very important terms, *italics* are commonly used for emphasis or technical terms, and underlining is rarely used in formal documents but can be useful for specific situations like hypertext links or educational materials.

2.3 Lists (Itemized, Enumerated, and Description Lists)

Lists are an essential part of almost any document, helping to organize content clearly and concisely. Whether you are creating bullet points, numbered steps, or describing a list of terms, LaTeX provides flexible environments for each. In this section, we will explore three common types of lists in LaTeX: itemized lists, enumerated lists, and description lists.

2.3.1 Itemized Lists (Unordered Lists)

An itemized list is useful when you want to list items in no particular order, similar to bullet points. In LaTeX, itemized lists are created using the `itemize` environment. Each list item is prefixed with the `\item` command, which generates the bullet point.

Here is a basic example of an itemized list:

```
\begin{itemize}
    \item First item
    \item Second item
    \item Third item
\end{itemize}
```

Itemized List

LaTeX Code:

```
\begin{itemize}
\item LaTeX makes professional
```

```
              typesetting easy.
\item You can create complex
        mathematical formulas.
\item It's widely used in
cademic and scientific writing.
\end{itemize}
```

Output:

- LaTeX makes professional typesetting easy.
- You can create complex mathematical formulas.
- It's widely used in academic and scientific writing.

2.3.2 Enumerated Lists (Ordered Lists)

Enumerated lists, also called ordered lists, are useful when the sequence of items matters. In LaTeX, you can create an enumerated list using the `enumerate` environment. Just like the itemized list, each item is preceded by the `\item` command, but the numbers will be added automatically.

Here is how to create a basic enumerated list:

```
\begin{enumerate}
    \item First step
    \item Second step
    \item Third step
\end{enumerate}
```

Enumerated List

LaTeX Code:

```
\begin{enumerate}
\item Install LaTeX on your
      computer.
\item Write your document
      using LaTeX syntax.
\item Compile the document to
      generate a PDF.
\end{enumerate}
```

Output:

1. Install LaTeX on your computer.
2. Write your document using LaTeX syntax.
3. Compile the document to generate a PDF.

2.3.3 Description Lists (Term and Description)

A description list is useful when you need to define or describe a series of terms. In LaTeX, you can create a description list using the `description` environment. The format allows you to specify a "term" and then provide its "description."

Here is how to create a description list:

```
\begin{description}
    \item[Term 1] Description of term 1.
    \item[Term 2] Description of term 2.
    \item[Term 3] Description of term 3.
\end{description}
```

Description List

LaTeX Code:

```
\begin{description}
\item[LaTeX] A typesetting system widely
used for technical and scientific
documents
\item[TeX] The typesetting engine that
LaTeX is built on
\item[Overleaf] An online LaTeX editor
that simplifies writing and
collaboration
\end{description}
```

Output:

LaTeX A typesetting system widely used for technical and scientific documents.

TeX The typesetting engine that LaTeX is built on.

Overleaf An online LaTeX editor that simplifies writing and collaboration.

2.3.4 Nesting Lists (Combining Itemized, Enumerated, and Description Lists)

One of the powerful features of LaTeX is the ability to nest lists within each other. You can create an itemized list inside an enumerated list, or any combination of lists, by simply adding the relevant environment inside another.

Here is an example of a nested list:

```
\begin{enumerate}
    \item First step
    \begin{itemize}
        \item Sub-item 1
        \item Sub-item 2
    \end{itemize}
    \item Second step
    \item Third step
\end{enumerate}
```

Nested List

LaTeX Code:

```
\begin{enumerate}
\item Set up your LaTeX environment.
\begin{itemize}
\item Install a LaTeX distribution
(e.g., MiKTeX or TeX Live).
\item Choose a LaTeX editor
(e.g., Overleaf or TeXShop).
\end{itemize}
\item Start writing your document.
\item Compile and review
the output.
\end{enumerate}
```

Output:

1. Set up your LaTeX environment.
    - Install a LaTeX distribution (e.g., MiKTeX or TeX Live).
    - Choose a LaTeX editor (e.g., Overleaf or TeXShop).
2. Start writing your document.
3. Compile and review the output.

2.3.5 Customizing List Labels

You can customize how the labels in ordered lists appear. LaTeX allows you to change the numbering style in an enumerated list by adding optional arguments to the `enumerate` environment.

For example, to use Roman numerals or letters instead of numbers:

Roman Numeral

LaTeX Code:

```
\begin{enumerate}[I.]
    \item First item
    \item Second item
    \item Third item
\end{enumerate}
```

Output:

I. First item
II. Second item
III. Third item

You can also use letters:

Lettered List

LaTeX Code:

```
\begin{enumerate}[a.]
    \item First item
    \item Second item
    \item Third item
\end{enumerate}
```

Output:

a. First item
b. Second item
c. Third item

2.3.6 Customizing Bullet Points and Numbering Styles

By default, itemized lists use bullets, and enumerated lists use Arabic numerals. These can be modified using the `label` option in `enumitem`.

Changing Bullet Styles in Itemized Lists

You can change the default bullet shape using:

```
\begin{itemize}[label=$\star$]
    \item First item
    \item Second item
\end{itemize}
```

Other options include:

- `label= $\diamond$` for a diamond bullet
- `label=$\blacktriangleright$` for a filled triangle

Customizing Numbering Styles in Enumerated Lists

The numbering style of an ordered list can be modified as follows:

```
\begin{enumerate}[label=\alph*)]
    \item First item
    \item Second item
\end{enumerate}
```

Other numbering styles include:

- `label=\arabic*)` for Arabic numerals (1, 2, 3, ...)
- `label=\Roman*)` for uppercase Roman numerals (I, II, III, ...)
- `label=\roman*)` for lowercase Roman numerals (i, ii, iii, ...)
- `label=\Alph*)` for uppercase letters (A, B, C, ...)
- `label=\alph*)` for lowercase letters (a, b, c, ...)

2.3.7 Adjusting Spacing Between List Items

The `enumitem` package also allows customization of spacing between list items and margins.

Reducing Vertical Space Between Items

By default, LaTeX adds some vertical spacing between list items. You can reduce it as follows:

```
\begin{itemize}[noitemsep]
    \item First item
    \item Second item
\end{itemize}
```

For even tighter spacing, use:

```
\begin{itemize}[noitemsep, topsep=0pt]
```

Increasing Space Between Items

To increase spacing between items:

```
\begin{enumerate}[itemsep=10pt]
    \item First item
    \item Second item
\end{enumerate}
```

2.3.8 Nested Lists with Custom Labels

LaTeX supports nested lists, where an itemized or enumerated list is placed inside another.

Nested Enumerated Lists with Custom Labels

You can define custom labels for each level of nesting:

```
\begin{enumerate}[label=\arabic*., itemsep=5pt]
    \item Main point 1
    \begin{enumerate}[label=\alph*)]
        \item Sub-point 1
        \item Sub-point 2
    \end{enumerate}
    \item Main point 2
\end{enumerate}
```

Aligning Lists Within Text and Tables

Sometimes, you may need lists inside tables or text blocks. The `paralist` package provides inline lists.

```
\usepackage{paralist}
```

To create a compact inline list:

```
This sentence contains
\begin{inparaenum}[1)]
    \item First point,
    \item Second point, and
    \item Third point.
\end{inparaenum}
```

2.3.9 Best Practices for Using Lists

While LaTeX makes it easy to create different types of lists, it is important to use them appropriately: *Itemized lists* are great for points that do not have a specific order, *enumerated lists* should be used when the order of items matters, such as steps in a process, and *description lists* are perfect for definitions or clarifying terms.

Avoid excessive nesting of lists, as this can make your document difficult to read. Instead, try to keep lists simple and straightforward to improve readability.

2.4 Special Characters and Symbols

In LaTeX, dealing with special characters and symbols is both powerful and flexible. However, some characters that are commonly used in writing (such as %, $, &, or #) have special meanings in LaTeX. Additionally, LaTeX provides easy ways to insert symbols that are not part of the regular keyboard, such as mathematical symbols, Greek letters, and more.

In this section, we will explore how to:

1. Escape special characters so they can be used as normal text.

2. Insert common symbols and characters, including Greek letters and special symbols.

This will be discussed in detail in the next chapter.

2.4.1 Special Characters in LaTeX

When working with LaTeX, you may encounter certain characters that have a predefined meaning within the typesetting system. These characters serve special functions such as defining commands, mathematical operations, and structural elements within the document. As a result, attempting to use them directly in text may lead to errors or unintended formatting.

The following characters are considered special in LaTeX:

, $, % , & , _ , { , } , ~ , ^ , \

Each of these symbols is reserved for specific internal functions. For example, the percent sign (%) is used to introduce comments in a LaTeX document, while the ampersand (&) is used for column alignment in tables. If you need to display these characters as regular text rather than invoking their special meaning, they must be "escaped" using a backslash (\) before the character.

Escaping Special Characters

LaTeX uses a number of characters that have special meaning within its syntax. These characters include symbols like the percent sign, ampersand, dollar sign, and others that serve as command triggers, delimiters, or control characters. Attempting to use these characters as plain text without properly escaping them will often result in errors or unintended behavior. Therefore, it is important to know how to "escape" these symbols so that they appear in the document as literal characters, rather than being interpreted as LaTeX instructions.

To display a special character as part of your document's content, you must precede it with a backslash (\). For instance, if you want to write the percent sign % (which normally begins a comment in LaTeX), you must write \%. Similarly, the dollar sign $, which is used to enter math mode, must be written as \$ to appear in regular text.

The following example demonstrates how to write all common special characters correctly:

Example: Escaping Special Characters

LaTeX Code:

```
\# \% \& \_ \{ \} \$
\textbackslash
\textasciitilde
\textasciicircum
```

Output:

% & _ { } $ \ ~ ^

Each of these characters has a specific role in LaTeX's processing engine:

The hash symbol (#) is used internally to represent parameters in macro definitions. To print it, escape it with \#.

The dollar sign ($) delimits inline and display math environments. To include it as a monetary symbol in running text, use \verb|$|.

The percent sign (%) indicates that the rest of the line is a comment. It is ignored during compilation unless escaped with \%.

The ampersand (&) is used to separate columns in tabular environments. To print it as part of a phrase like "Research & Development," write \&.

The underscore (_) creates subscripts in mathematical expressions. In standard text, you must use _ to print an actual underscore.

Curly braces ({}) group content and are vital in many LaTeX commands. To show them as characters, use \{ and \}, respectively.

The tilde (~) creates a non-breaking space, typically used to prevent line breaks between words. If you wish to display an actual tilde character, use `\textasciitilde`.

The caret (^) is used for superscripts in math mode. To include it in normal text, write `\textasciicircum`.

The backslash (\) is perhaps the most essential character in LaTeX, as it initiates every command. Displaying a literal backslash requires the command `\textbackslash`.

Understanding how to correctly escape these characters is crucial for writing error-free documents, particularly when including programming code, command-line instructions, or syntax that relies on these symbols.

In contexts such as writing technical manuals, software documentation, or academic papers with code excerpts, it is often more efficient to use the `verbatim` environment or the `listings` package, which allows you to include content with special characters without manually escaping each one. However, for ordinary prose and inline explanations, escaping is the most appropriate solution.

Handling Special Characters in Verbatim Mode

In normal LaTeX mode, many characters, such as #, $, %, &, _, {, }, ~, ^, and `\textbackslash{}`, carry special syntactic meaning. Attempting to include these characters in your document without escaping them will result in compilation errors or unintended behavior. However, when the goal is to display these characters exactly as they are written, for instance, when presenting source code or command-line input, it is both cumbersome and impractical to escape every symbol.

To address this need, LaTeX provides the `verbatim` environment, which treats all content within it as literal text. In other words, LaTeX bypasses its usual parsing of commands and symbols and reproduces the characters exactly as they appear in the source file. This makes the `verbatim` environment ideal for displaying code blocks, configuration snippets, or any text containing special symbols.

The following example demonstrates its usage:

Verbatim Code Example

LaTeX Code:

```
\begin{verbatim}
This line includes:
# $ % & _ { } ~ ^ \
\end{verbatim}
```

Output:

```
This line includes:
# $ % & _ { } ~ ^ \
```

Notice how all special characters are rendered plainly in the output without any errors or modifications. There is no need to use backslashes to escape the characters; LaTeX simply reproduces the raw content. Additionally, line breaks, spacing, and indentation within the environment are preserved as written in the source.

It is important to mention that because the `verbatim` environment disables command parsing, you cannot use LaTeX commands inside it. Anything beginning with a backslash, whether it is a genuine command or not, will be shown as is.

This environment is invaluable when writing technical documentation, software manuals, or educational materials where displaying exact syntax is required. In situations where inline verbatim text is needed (such as a code fragment within a paragraph), you can use the `\verb|.....|` command. For example, the inline expression `\verb|x =`

`a + b|` will render exactly as typed, maintaining spacing and symbol accuracy.

By utilizing the `verbatim` environment thoughtfully, you can present complex technical content in LaTeX documents cleanly and accurately, without the overhead of escaping every individual character.

Using `textcomp` for Additional Symbols

While LaTeX includes a robust set of default symbols, certain typographic and textual symbols, such as currency marks, old-style numerals, upright Greek letters, and additional punctuation, require extended support. The `textcomp` package addresses this need by offering a broader range of text-mode symbols that are not covered by the base LaTeX distribution.

To make use of this extended symbol set, you begin by including the package in your document preamble with the following line:

Package Inclusion

LaTeX Code:	Purpose:
`\usepackage{textcomp}`	Activates support for additional symbols such as upright Greek letters, currency symbols, and accents not available in standard LaTeX

Once loaded, the package enables the use of various typographic elements that are especially useful in scientific writing, multilingual text, and documentation involving measurements or currencies. For instance, it makes it possible to use properly formatted tildes and carets as characters rather than control symbols, something that would otherwise require verbose workarounds.

The following example illustrates the effect of using some of these symbols in a document:

Using textcomp Symbols

LaTeX Code:

```
\documentclass{article}
\usepackage{textcomp}
\begin{document}
Tilde:
\textasciitilde{}
Caret:
\textasciicircum{}
Degree symbol:
25\textdegree C
Euro: \texteuro
\end{document}
```

Output:

Tilde: ˜ Caret: ˆ
Degree symbol: 25°
C Euro: €

The `textcomp` package is particularly important when working with multilingual documents or writing that requires specialized characters that align typographically with the surrounding text. Unlike math-mode equivalents, the symbols provided by `textcomp` are designed for use in text mode, preserving the document's font consistency and stylistic integrity.

Additionally, this package supports font encoding features that improve compatibility with modern font packages and document classes. As such, it often complements other foundational packages like `fontenc` and `inputenc`, especially when combined with T1 font encoding for European languages.

2.4.2 Using Mathematical Symbols

Mathematical typesetting is one of the most compelling features of LaTeX, providing a structured and consistent way to represent equations, symbols, and notations. Unlike conventional word processors, where formatting mathematical expressions can be tedious and inconsistent, LaTeX ensures clarity and precision in mathematical documentation.

Mathematical content in LaTeX is enclosed in what is known as *math mode*. This mode allows for seamless integration of mathematical symbols and expressions into documents. There are two primary ways to enter math mode: inline math mode, which is useful for short expressions within a paragraph, and display math mode, which is used for standalone equations. The inline mode is activated by enclosing expressions between dollar signs (`$...$`), while display mode is achieved using double dollar signs (`$$...$$`) or the `equation` environment.

For example, the well-known Euler's identity:

$$e^{i\pi} + 1 = 0$$

is produced in display mode, ensuring it stands out separately in the text.

Basic Mathematical Notation

LaTeX provides commands for writing standard mathematical expressions such as fractions, exponents, roots, and logarithms. A fraction is created using the `\frac{}{}` command, where the first argument represents the numerator and the second the denominator. For example:

$$\frac{a+b}{c-d}$$

Exponents and subscripts are fundamental in mathematical notation. Superscripts are created using the caret symbol (^) and subscripts using the underscore (_). Consider the expression:

$$x^2 + y^3 = z^n$$

For roots, LaTeX provides the `\sqrt{}` command. The square root of x is written as:

$$\sqrt{x}$$

while a cube root can be written using an optional argument:

$$\sqrt[3]{x}$$

Summation, Integration, and Limits

Mathematical series and calculus operations are neatly typeset in LaTeX. The summation symbol is represented by `\sum` and is typically accompanied by subscripts and superscripts:

$$\sum_{i=1}^{n} i^2 = \frac{n(n+1)(2n+1)}{6}$$

Similarly, definite integrals are written using `\int`. For instance, the integral of a sine function over the interval $[0, \pi]$ is expressed as:

$$\int_0^{\pi} \sin x \, dx = 2$$

Limits are also fundamental in mathematical writing and are handled using the `\lim` command:

$$\lim_{x \to \infty} \frac{1}{x} = 0$$

Differential Equations and Operators

Differential equations frequently appear in scientific and engineering literature. Derivatives can be represented using standard notation:

$$\frac{dy}{dx} = 3x^2 + 2x - 5$$

Partial derivatives are expressed as follows:

$$\frac{\partial u}{\partial x} + \frac{\partial u}{\partial y} = 0$$

Higher-order derivatives, such as second-order differentials, are typeset in a similar manner:

$$\frac{d^2y}{dx^2} + 4\frac{dy}{dx} + 4y = 0$$

For compact representations, the `\nabla` command provides the gradient operator:

$$\nabla \cdot \mathbf{F} = 0$$

Advanced Equations: Navier-Stokes and Maxwell's Equations

Beyond basic mathematics, LaTeX excels at handling complex mathematical models such as the Navier-Stokes equations, which describe fluid dynamics:

$$\frac{\partial \mathbf{u}}{\partial t} + (\mathbf{u} \cdot \nabla)\mathbf{u} = -\nabla p + \nu \nabla^2 \mathbf{u} + \mathbf{f}$$

This equation governs fluid motion, where $\mathbf{u}$ represents velocity, p denotes pressure, ν is viscosity, and $\mathbf{f}$ is an external force.

Maxwell's equations, fundamental to electromagnetism, are another example of complex mathematical expressions typeset effortlessly in LaTeX:

$$\begin{aligned}
\nabla \cdot \mathbf{E} &= \frac{\rho}{\varepsilon_0}, \\
\nabla \cdot \mathbf{B} &= 0, \\
\nabla \times \mathbf{E} &= -\frac{\partial \mathbf{B}}{\partial t}, \\
\nabla \times \mathbf{B} &= \mu_0 \mathbf{J} + \mu_0 \varepsilon_0 \frac{\partial \mathbf{E}}{\partial t}.
\end{aligned}$$

2.4.3 Special Symbols

Apart from standard mathematical symbols and Greek letters, LaTeX offers a rich collection of special symbols used across various disciplines, including physics, engineering, and statistics. These symbols are essential for writing equations, scientific expressions, and precise technical documentation.

One of the most commonly used special symbols is the *degree symbol*, which is frequently seen in temperature measurements and angular notation. In LaTeX, the degree symbol is written using the command `^\circ`. For example, to represent an angle of 90 degrees, one would write:

$$90^\circ$$

which is encoded as:

```
90^\circ
```

Another commonly used symbol is the *plus-minus symbol* (±), which represents uncertainty in scientific measurements or alternative solutions in mathematical equations. The corresponding LaTeX command is `\pm`. It is frequently used in expressions such as:

$$x = 5 \pm 0.2$$

which can be written in LaTeX as:

```
x = 5 \pm 0.2
```

In calculus and physics, the *infinity symbol* (∞) is widely used to denote limits, improper integrals, and concepts of boundlessness. This symbol is generated in LaTeX using the command `\infty`. An example is the improper integral:

$$\int_0^\infty e^{-x}\, dx = 1,$$

which is written in LaTeX as:

```
\int_{0}^{\infty} e^{-x} \,dx = 1.
```

In differential equations, the *partial derivative symbol* (∂) is commonly used to represent derivatives of functions with multiple variables. In LaTeX, this symbol is invoked using the command `\partial`. For instance, the expression for the partial derivative of a function $f(x, y)$ with respect to x is:

$$\frac{\partial f}{\partial x}$$

which is written in LaTeX as:

```
\frac{\partial f}{\partial x}.
```

Beyond these fundamental symbols, LaTeX supports a vast range of specialized symbols, including logical operators, set notations, and physics-related symbols. For example, the *nabla symbol* (∇) used in vector calculus is written as `$\nabla \cdot \mathbf{F}$$`, which renders as $\nabla \cdot \mathbf{F}$.

Similarly, the *hbar symbol* ($\hbar$) representing the reduced Planck's constant is given by `$\hbar = \frac{h}{2\pi}$`, which produces $\hbar = \frac{h}{2\pi}$.

The availability of these symbols makes LaTeX an indispensable tool for scientific and mathematical writing. Whether documenting fundamental physics equations, technical engineering expressions, or precise mathematical derivations, these special symbols enhance the clarity and readability of the content. Their correct usage ensures that equations are both visually accurate and consistent with professional publishing standards.

2.4.4 Common Symbol Tables

Here's a quick reference Table 2.3 for some commonly used symbols:

Symbol	Command	Output
Plus-minus	`\pm`	$\pm$
Degree	`^\circ`	90°
Infinity	`\infty`	∞
Approximately	`\approx`	$\approx$
Element of	`\in`	$\in$
Subset	`\subseteq`	$\subseteq$
Integral	`\int_a^b`	$\int_a^b$
Summation	`\sum_{i=1}^n`	$\sum_{i=1}^n$
Partial derivative	`\partial`	∂

Table 2.3: Common symbols and their LaTeX commands with output

This table gives you a quick way to recall the commands for common symbols.

2.4.5 Best Practices for Special Characters and Symbols

Always use math mode ($...$ or `\[...\]`) for mathematical symbols and expressions. Escape special characters like %, &, or $ by placing a backslash (\) in front. Keep a reference table of commonly used symbols and their LaTeX commands for quick access while writing.

Exercises for Chap. 2: Document Structure and Formatting

2.1 Creating a Basic Document (Sections, Subsections, and Paragraphs)

1. *Basic Document Creation*: Create a simple LaTeX document that includes a title, author, and date. Add at least two sections, each with subsections and multiple paragraphs.

2. *Section and Subsection Practice*: Write a LaTeX document with three sections. In each section, include at least one subsection and a short paragraph discussing a different topic.

3. *Compile a Document*: Explain the role of the `\section`, `\subsection`, and `\paragraph` commands in structuring a document. Provide a simple example of how these commands work.

2.2 Formatting Text (Bold, Italics, Underline, and Font Sizes)

1. *Text Formatting*: Create a LaTeX document that demonstrates the use of bold, italics, and underline. Include examples of how each of these formatting options can be applied to text.

2. *Font Size Practice*: Create a document that showcases all the available font sizes in LaTeX, from `\tiny` to `\Huge`, and explain when it is appropriate to use each.

3. *Formatting Challenge*: Write a paragraph that contains text in bold, italics, and underline, along with different font sizes. Ensure that the formatting appears consistent and easy to read.

2.3 Lists (Itemized, Enumerated, and Description Lists)

1. *Creating Lists*: Write a LaTeX document that contains an itemized list, an enumerated list, and a description list. Demonstrate how to nest lists within one another.

2. *Customizing Lists*: Modify an enumerated list to start at a number other than 1. Change the labels of an itemized list to use custom symbols, such as dashes or stars.

3. *List Practice*: Create a description list that defines key LaTeX terms (e.g., `documentclass`, `section`, `textbf`). Provide a brief description of each term.

2.4 Special Characters and Symbols

1. *Escape Special Characters*: Write a LaTeX document that contains all special characters such as #, \$, %, &, _, {, }, ~, and ^. Show how to escape each of these characters so they appear correctly in the output.

2. *Using Math Symbols*: Create a LaTeX document that includes at least ten commonly used mathematical symbols (e.g., `\alpha`, `\sum`, `\pi`). Explain how to include these symbols in both inline and display math modes.

3. *Special Character Practice*: Write a paragraph that includes at least five special characters and symbols, ensuring they appear correctly in the compiled document.

Chapter 3

Working with Mathematical Content

Contents

Md Aquib, *Fundamentals of LaTeX*, University Texts in the Mathematical Sciences,
https://doi.org/10.1007/978-981-96-9318-4_3

Abstract: Mathematics is at the heart of countless academic and scientific disciplines, and one of LaTeX's most celebrated capabilities is its unparalleled support for high-quality mathematical typesetting. Whether you are composing lecture notes, academic articles, textbooks, or technical reports, LaTeX provides a powerful, elegant, and consistent system for writing mathematical expressions, from basic algebraic equations to sophisticated multiline formulas, matrices, and integrals.

Keywords: Mathematical typesetting, Mathematical symbols, Matrices and arrays, Theorems and proofs, Math environments

This chapter serves as a comprehensive introduction to incorporating mathematical content into your LaTeX documents. We begin by distinguishing between inline and display math environments, exploring how to write equations both within a paragraph and as standalone, centered expressions. We then delve into mathematical symbols, operators, and functions that are commonly used in scientific writing, including Greek letters, set notations, derivatives, and summation notation.

Further sections will cover aligning multiple equations, using the `amsmath` package for advanced formatting, and integrating numbered and labeled equations for cross-referencing. We also examine the construction of arrays, matrices, and multiline equations, which are essential for fields like linear algebra and physics.

By the end of this chapter, you will have a strong foundation in mathematical typesetting with LaTeX and the skills to format your mathematical content with clarity, precision, and typographic finesse.

3.1 Inline and Display Math Mode

One of LaTeX's greatest strengths is its ability to beautifully format mathematical expressions. Whether you are working with simple equations or complex formulas, LaTeX makes it easy to include math in your document. There are two primary ways to include math in LaTeX: *inline math* and *display math*.

3.1.1 Inline Math Mode

Mathematics is an integral part of scientific and technical writing, and LaTeX provides a robust way to format mathematical expressions. In many cases, mathematical expressions appear within the body of a sentence rather than as standalone equations. These expressions are best rendered using the inline math mode, which ensures they seamlessly integrate with the surrounding text without disrupting the flow of the document.

To enter inline math mode, mathematical expressions are enclosed within dollar signs ($...$). Everything placed between these symbols is treated as mathematical content and formatted accordingly. For example, if we wish to describe the area of a circle, we can write:

Inline Math

LaTeX Code:

```
The area of a circle is
given by $A = \pi r^2$,
where $r$ is the radius
```

Output:

The area of a circle is given by $A = \pi r^2$, where r is the radius.

Inline math is great for simple equations that fit within the flow of a sentence, like $E = mc^2$ or $x^2 + y^2 = z^2$.

Inline math mode is particularly useful for simple expressions such as equations, symbols, and notations that do not require special emphasis or alignment. For example, the famous Einstein equation relating energy and mass, $E = mc^2$, or the Pythagorean theorem, $x^2 + y^2 = z^2$, can be neatly incorporated within a sentence using this mode.

An alternative notation for inline math in LaTeX is to use `\(...\)` instead of dollar signs. The following two lines produce the same result:

```
    The force exerted is given by $F = ma$.

The force exerted is given by \(\ F = ma \ \).
```

Although both methods function identically, enclosing expressions within dollar signs is generally more common.

While inline math mode is ideal for short equations within sentences, it is not suitable for complex expressions that require additional formatting, alignment, or emphasis. For longer equations, especially those that need to be displayed on a separate line, display math mode (covered in the next section) should be used.

To maintain readability and ensure proper spacing, inline mathematical expressions should be kept concise. Overly long equations in inline mode can disrupt the natural flow of a sentence and make the text harder to read. For such cases, breaking the equation into a display-style format improves clarity.

Inline math mode in LaTeX is a powerful tool for embedding mathematical symbols and expressions within textual content while maintaining the overall document structure. Understanding when to use inline math versus display math is essential for producing well-organized and readable mathematical documents.

3.1.2 Display Math Mode

Display math mode is used for larger, more complex equations that need to be centered and set apart from the rest of the text. This mode is also preferred for multiline equations. In LaTeX, display math mode can be triggered in two ways:

1. Using `\[ ...\]` for unnumbered equations
2. Using the `equation` environment for numbered equations

Unnumbered Display Math

LaTeX Code:

```
\[
E = mc^2
\]
```

Output:

$$E = mc^2$$

Numbered Display Math

LaTeX Code:

```
\begin{equation}
E = mc^2
\end{equation}
```

Output:

$$E = mc^2 \qquad (1)$$

3.1.3 Display Math Mode

Mathematical expressions in LaTeX are not limited to appearing inline within a sentence. In many cases, equations require additional space and must be emphasized by displaying them separately. Display math mode is used for such scenarios, allowing complex mathematical expressions to be centered on their own lines, providing greater readability and clarity.

Using Display Math Mode To render an equation in display mode, LaTeX provides two primary methods: using bracketed notation or employing the equation environment.

The simplest approach is to enclose the mathematical expression between the delimiters `\[ ...\]`. This method produces an unnumbered display equation:

Unnumbered Display Math

LaTeX Code:

```
\[
E = mc^2
\]
```

Output:

$$E = mc^2$$

This notation is useful for cases where numbering the equation is unnecessary, such as when displaying a standalone formula in a document or when a number reference is not required.

In contrast, when equations need to be referenced elsewhere in the text, the `equation` environment should be used. This environment automatically assigns a number to the equation:

Numbered Display Math

LaTeX Code:

```
\begin{equation}
E = mc^2
\end{equation}
```

Output:

$$E = mc^2 \tag{1}$$

This numbering allows the equation to be cited later using the `\ref` command, as in:

```
Equation~\ref{eq:einstein} expresses the
relationship between energy and mass.
```

Multiline Equations and Alignment When working with equations that span multiple lines, the `align` or `gather` environments from the `amsmath` package provide structured formatting. For instance, a multiline equation with proper alignment can be written as:

```
\begin{align}
    E &= mc^2 \\
    F &= ma
\end{align}
```

This results in:

$$E = mc^2 \tag{3.1}$$

$$F = ma \tag{3.2}$$

The alignment operator (&) ensures that equal signs and other mathematical elements are aligned, improving readability and maintaining a consistent visual structure.

When to Use Display Math Mode Display math mode is ideal for equations that require emphasis, clarity, or reference. It is commonly used in scientific papers, research articles, and textbooks where equations play a crucial role in explaining concepts. While inline math mode is suitable for brief mathematical expressions within a paragraph, longer equations should be presented in display mode to improve legibility.

By properly utilizing display math mode, authors can ensure that equations are neatly formatted, numbered when necessary, and well-integrated within the logical flow of a document.

3.1.4 Key Differences Between Inline and Display Math

Mathematical expressions in LaTeX can be formatted using either inline math mode or display math mode, depending on the complexity and importance of the equation within the document. Understanding the differences between these two modes is essential for properly structuring mathematical content.

Inline math mode is used when a mathematical expression needs to appear as part of a sentence without disrupting the text flow. This mode is enclosed between dollar signs (`$...$`) and is useful for short formulas, variables, or simple calculations that integrate naturally within a paragraph. For example, the quadratic formula is given by $x = \frac{-b \pm \sqrt{b^2 - 4ac}}{2a}$, which appears within the sentence without excessive spacing.

In contrast, display math mode is used when equations require emphasis or need to be presented more clearly on a separate line. This mode ensures that mathematical expressions are centered and properly spaced, making them easier to read. It is particularly useful for complex equations, summations, or integral representations. Display math mode can be activated using the notation:

```
\[
  x = \frac{-b \pm \sqrt{b^2 - 4ac}}{2a}
\]
```

which results in:

$$x = \frac{-b \pm \sqrt{b^2 - 4ac}}{2a}$$

One of the key distinctions between inline and display math mode is how mathematical symbols and operators are formatted. In inline math mode, summation and integral limits appear beside their respective symbols, such as $\sum_{i=1}^{n} i^2$. However, in display math mode, these limits appear directly above and below the summation or integral sign:

$$\sum_{i=1}^{n} i^2$$

This formatting distinction is important when presenting equations that involve multiple terms or complex notations. Display mode provides a more readable format by avoiding compressed mathematical expressions that might otherwise clutter a paragraph.

3.1.5 Common Mistakes in Math Mode

When using math mode in LaTeX, authors often encounter common errors that affect the readability and correctness of their documents. One frequent mistake is forgetting to close the math environment, leading to compilation errors or improper rendering. Since inline math is enclosed between single dollar signs, and display math uses double dollar signs (deprecated) or brackets (`\[ ...\]`), it is essential to always ensure proper closing of these environments.

Another common issue is choosing the wrong mode for an equation. While it is technically possible to place com plex expressions in inline math mode, doing so can break the layout of the surrounding text, making it difficult to read. Consider the expression:

```
$x = \frac{-b \pm \sqrt{b^2 - 4ac}}{2a}$
```

In an inline setting, this fraction may appear cramped, whereas using display math mode improves its clarity:

```
\[
  x = \frac{-b \pm \sqrt{b^2 - 4ac}}{2a}
\]
```

The second approach is preferable when writing technical or scientific documents where precise mathematical notation is crucial.

3.2 Common Mathematical Symbols and Operators

In mathematics, symbols and operators are crucial for expressing formulas and equations. LaTeX provides a vast collection of predefined symbols and operators to make writing these expressions as smooth and professional as possible. In this section, we will cover some of the most commonly used mathematical symbols and operators that you will likely encounter in your work.

3.2.1 Arithmetic Operators

Arithmetic operations form the foundation of mathematical notation, and LaTeX provides a clear and structured way to represent these expressions. When writing arithmetic expressions in LaTeX, it is important to differentiate between standard operators, such as addition and subtraction, and those that require specialized commands, such as multiplication and division. These operations can be used in both inline and display math modes depending on their complexity.

The **addition** and **subtraction** operators follow standard notation and can be inserted directly into equations. For example, the expression $x + y = z$ represents addition, while $a - b = c$ represents subtraction. These operators require no special formatting in LaTeX and appear as expected in mathematical expressions.

For **multiplication**, LaTeX provides multiple options depending on the desired notation. The most commonly used symbols are the multiplication sign ($\times$) and the centered dot ($\cdot$), each suited for different contexts. The $\times$ symbol is typically used in arithmetic operations or vector products, while $\cdot$ is preferred in algebraic and scalar products. The expressions $a \times b$ and $x \cdot y$ are both valid representations of multiplication, but the choice of notation depends on convention and clarity.

Division can be represented in different ways depending on the formatting needs of the equation. The simplest method is the forward slash (/), which is commonly used in inline math mode to represent simple ratios such as a/b. However, for more structured fraction notation, LaTeX provides the `\frac` command, which formats expressions as fractions with a numerator and denominator. For example, the expression:

```
\[
\frac{a}{b}
\]
```

renders a properly formatted fraction that is easier to read, especially in display mode. This format is preferred when writing mathematical documents, particularly in cases where fractions involve complex terms or multiple variables.

Examples and Application

The use of arithmetic operators extends to various mathematical and physical applications. Consider Newton's second law of motion, which states that the force acting on an object is the product of its mass and acceleration:

$$F = ma$$

Here, the multiplication operation is implied without an explicit symbol, a convention frequently used in physics and engineering. However, when representing explicit calculations, it is common to use either $a \times b$ or $a \cdot b$ to clarify the multiplication process.

Similarly, in probability theory, the likelihood of independent events occurring together is determined by multiplying their individual probabilities:

$$P(A \cap B) = P(A) \cdot P(B)$$

In this context, the centered dot notation provides a clear distinction from the cross product or scalar products used in vector mathematics.

3.2.2 Relational Operators

In mathematical expressions, relational operators are used to define relationships between quantities, allowing us to compare values and establish conditions for equations and inequalities. LaTeX provides a comprehensive set of relational operators, which can be used in both inline and display math modes to express mathematical statements clearly.

The most fundamental relational operator is the equality operator ($=$), which asserts that two expressions represent the same value. This operator is widely used in equations, such as the classic Pythagorean theorem:

$$a^2 + b^2 = c^2$$

Beyond equality, we often encounter expressions of inequality, which are used to indicate that one value is greater than, less than, or not equal to another. LaTeX provides specific commands to express these relationships. The not equal to operator is represented by $\neq$, written in LaTeX as:

$$x \neq y$$

This notation states that x and y are distinct values, meaning they do not hold the same numerical or algebraic value.

For comparisons involving magnitude, we use the greater than ($>$) and less than ($<$) operators. For example, the statement:

$$x > 5$$

indicates that x is strictly greater than 5, while:

$$y < 10$$

implies that y is strictly less than 10. In situations where equality is also a possibility, we use the greater than or equal to ($\geq$) and less than or equal to ($\leq$) operators, which allow for inclusivity in mathematical conditions. These are written in LaTeX as:

$$a \geq b, \quad c \leq d$$

Relational operators are extensively used in a wide variety of mathematical disciplines. In calculus, for instance, inequalities define domains and constraints for functions. In optimization problems, constraints like:

$$f(x) \leq g(x)$$

help determine feasible solutions. In set theory, inequalities are employed to describe bounds on numerical sets, while in physics and engineering, they are crucial for defining tolerances and operational limits.

By correctly employing relational operators in LaTeX, one can create professional-quality mathematical documents that clearly communicate relationships between values. This ensures that mathematical logic is conveyed effectively, making it easier for readers to interpret results and follow derivations.

Rational Operators

LaTeX Code:

```
The inequality
$x \neq y$ means that
$x$ is not equal to
$y$, and $x \leq y$
means $x$ is less
than or equal to $y$.
```

Output:

The inequality $x \neq y$ means that x is not equal to y, and $x \leq y$ means x is less than or equal to y.

3.2.3 Set and Logic Operators

LaTeX provides a rich collection of symbols that are especially well-suited for expressing concepts in set theory and mathematical logic. When writing mathematical documents involving set relations or logical connectives, having access to properly rendered symbols greatly enhances both the readability and the formality of the exposition.

For instance, suppose we want to express that a certain variable belongs to a given set. In LaTeX, the membership symbol is written using the command `\in`, and it produces the familiar notation $x \in A$. Similarly, inclusion relations between sets, such as subset and superset, are denoted using `\subseteq` and `\supseteq` , respectively. These commands generate the symbols $\subseteq$ and $\supseteq$, commonly used in mathematical writing.

Logical operations are also fully supported in LaTeX. The conjunction (logical AND) is represented by the command `\land`, which produces the symbol $\wedge$, while the disjunction (logical OR) is written using `\lor`, giving $\vee$. These are often used in formal proofs, logic programming, and discrete mathematics to connect propositions.

To illustrate how LaTeX handles such notations, consider the following example, which demonstrates the use of set membership and inclusion within a formal sentence.

The code snippet appears on the left and the output on the right:

Set and Logic Example in LaTeX

LaTeX Code:

```
For all
$x \in \mathbb{R}$,
we have that
$A \subseteq B$
if everyelement of
$A$ is also in $B$.
```

Output:
For all $x \in \mathbb{R}$, we have that $A \subseteq B$ if every element of A is also in B.

In this example, the `\in` symbol is used to express that x belongs to the set of real numbers $\mathbb{R}$, and the `\subseteq` command denotes a subset relation between two arbitrary sets A and B. Notice that by enclosing these expressions within dollar signs, we place them in inline math mode, seamlessly integrating them into the surrounding text.

LaTeX's set and logic operators not only support proper symbolic representation but also uphold typographic consistency with the surrounding mathematical content. This makes them indispensable for producing high-quality documents in mathematical sciences, theoretical computer science, and logic-heavy disciplines.

We summarize some common mathematical symbols in the following Table 3.1.

Symbol	Command	Symbol	Command
$\emptyset$	`\emptyset`	$\bigcup$	`\bigcup`
$\in$	`\in`	$\bigcap$	`\bigcap`
$\notin$	`\notin`	$\setminus$	`\setminus`
$\subset$	`\subset`	$\approx$	`\approx`
$\subseteq$	`\subseteq`	$\doteq$	`\doteq`
$\supset$	`\supset`	$\neq$	`\neq`
$\supseteq$	`\supseteq`	$\geq$	`\geq`

$\cup$	\cup	$\leq$	\leq
$\cap$	\cap	$\sim$	\sim
$\div$	\div	$\times$	\times
$\pm$	\pm	$\circ$	\circ
$\cdots$	\cdots	$\ldots$	\ldots
$\vdots$	\vdots	$\ddots$	\ddots
$\leftarrow$	\leftarrow	$\rightarrow$	\rightarrow
$\Leftarrow$	\Leftarrow	$\Rightarrow$	\Rightarrow
$\leftrightarrow$	\leftrightarrow	$\Leftrightarrow$	\Leftrightarrow
$\cong$	\cong	∞	\infty
∂	\partial	$\prime$	\prime
$\ast$	\ast	$\cdot$	\cdot
$\star$	\star		

Table 3.1: Mathematical symbols and their LaTeX commands

3.2.4 Common Greek Letters

Greek letters are an essential part of mathematical notation and are widely used across various disciplines, including physics, engineering, and statistics. In LaTeX, Greek letters are represented using simple backslash commands, making it easy to incorporate them into mathematical expressions.

Greek letters are categorized into lowercase and uppercase forms. While many uppercase Greek letters resemble their Latin counterparts
(such as $A, B, E, K, M, N, O, P, T, X, Y, Z$), some retain distinct mathematical meanings, such as Γ (Gamma), Δ (Delta), and Ω (Omega).

Lowercase Greek letters such as `\alpha`, `\beta`, and `\pi` are commonly used in scientific notation, such as angles, variables, and coefficients in equations. However, uppercase Greek letters such as `\Pi` and `\Sigma` are frequently used in advanced mathematical contexts such as summations, matrices, and probability theory. Some uppercase Greek letters have unique meanings in various fields.

Greek Letter

LaTeX Code:

```
The area of a circle
is calculated as $A =
\pi r^2$, and $\Sigma$
is often used to
represent a summation.
```

Output:

The area of a circle is calculated as $A = \pi r^2$, and Σ is often used to represent a summation.

Here is the list of Greek symbols and the command to generate them (Table 3.2).

Greek letter	**Lowercase symbol**	**Lowercase command**	**Uppercase symbol**	**Uppercase command**
Alpha	α	`\alpha`	A	–
Beta	β	`\beta`	B	–
Gamma	γ	`\gamma`	Γ	`\Gamma`
Delta	δ	`\delta`	Δ	`\Delta`
Epsilon	ϵ	`\epsilon`	E	–
Zeta	ζ	`\zeta`	Z	–
Eta	η	`\eta`	H	–
Theta	θ	`\theta`	Θ	`\Theta`
Iota	ι	`\iota`	I	–
Kappa	κ	`\kappa`	K	–
Lambda	λ	`\lambda`	Λ	`\Lambda`
Mu	μ	`\mu`	M	–
Nu	ν	`\nu`	N	–
Xi	ξ	`\xi`	Ξ	`\Xi`
Omicron	o	`o`	O	–
Pi	π	`\pi`	Π	`\Pi`
Rho	ρ	`\rho`	P	–
Sigma	σ	`\sigma`	Σ	`\Sigma`
Tau	τ	`\tau`	T	–
Upsilon	υ	`\upsilon`	Υ	`\Upsilon`

Phi	ϕ	\phi	Φ	\Phi
Chi	χ	\chi	X	–
Psi	ψ	\psi	Ψ	\Psi
Omega	ω	\omega	Ω	\Omega

Table 3.2: Greek symbols and their LaTeX commands

3.2.5 Mathematical Functions

In LaTeX, common mathematical functions like trigonometric, logarithmic, and exponential functions have predefined commands. These functions are formatted correctly and set apart from variables automatically.

Mathematical Function

LaTeX Code:

```
The sine of an angle
is written as
$\sin(\theta)$, and
the natural logarithm
is represented as
$\ln(x)$.
```

Output:

The sine of an angle is written as $\sin(\theta)$, and the natural logarithm is represented as $\ln(x)$.

Some basic functions are summarized in the following Table 3.3.

Functions	Commands	Functions	Commands
sin	\sin	sinh	\sinh
cos	\cos	inf	\inf
tan	\tan	sup	\sup
log	\log	min	\min
exp	\exp	max	\max
ln	\ln	arcsin	\arcsin
lim	\lim	arcos	\arccos
lim inf	\liminf	arcten	\arctan

lim sup	`\limsup`	det	`\det`
arg	`\arg`	ker	`\ker`
dim	`\dim`	hom	`\hom`

Table 3.3: Functions and their LaTeX commands

3.2.6 Delimiters

Sometimes we require to produce a large delimiter. Large delimiter can be produced with the commands `\left` and `\right`. For example, if we want to produce:

$$\left(\frac{5}{6}\right),$$

then with normal keyboard input:

```
$(\frac{5}{6})$
```

the output will look like:

$$(\frac{5}{6}).$$

But, with the `\left` and `\right` commands, that is:

```
$\left(\frac{5}{6}\right)$
```

the output will be:

$$\left(\frac{5}{6}\right),$$

that is what we wanted to produce.

NOTE:

1. The `\left` and `\right` commands always occur in pairs.

2. If you have single delimiters (e.g., if you want to produce large { for cases like piece-wise functions) only, then write the command as

```
\left\{ \ldots\ldots \right.
```

3. We can also increase the size of parentheses, square bracket, curly bracket, etc., using the commands `\big`, `\big\big`, `\Big`, etc.

   For example, to produce $\big(\frac{5}{6} \big)$ instead of using `$\left( \frac{5}{6} \right)$`, we can use `$\big( \frac{5}{6} \big)$`, and we will have the desired output $\big(\frac{5}{6} \big)$.

Some common delimiters are listed in the following Table 3.4.

Delimiter	Command	Delimiter	Command
(	`\left(`	)	`\right)`
[	`\left[`	]	`\right]`
{	`\left\{`	}	`\right\}`
|	`\left|` or `\right|`	||	`\left\\|` or `\right\\|`
⌊	`\lfloor`	⌋	`\rfloor`
⌈	`\lceil`	⌉	`\rceil`

Table 3.4: Delimiters and their LaTeX commands

Remark 3.2.1 *To produce the curly braces* { }, *you need to use the command* `\{ \}`.

3.2.7 Summation and Integral Operators

Mathematical notation frequently involves summation and integral operators, which are essential in various fields such as calculus, algebra, and mathematical analysis. LaTeX provides robust support for representing these operations with clarity and precision.

Summation Notation

Summation is used to represent the sum of a sequence of terms, often indexed by an integer variable. The summation symbol, denoted by $\sum$, is commonly used in discrete mathematics and series representations. In LaTeX, the summation operator is written as:

$$\sum_{i=1}^{n} x_i$$

where the lower limit ($i = 1$) is placed as a subscript using _ and the upper limit (n) is written as a superscript using ^.

For instance, the sum of the first n natural numbers is represented as:

$$\sum_{i=1}^{n} i = \frac{n(n+1)}{2}$$

Summations are widely used in mathematical proofs, numerical methods, and statistical computations. A more complex example is the sum of squares:

$$\sum_{i=1}^{n} i^2 = \frac{n(n+1)(2n+1)}{6}$$

which frequently appears in physics and engineering when analyzing moments of inertia.

Single Integrals

Integration is the continuous counterpart of summation and is fundamental in calculus. The integral symbol $\int$ is used to compute areas, solve differential equations, and describe physical phenomena. In LaTeX, an integral is written as:

$$\int_a^b f(x)\,dx$$

where a and b are the limits of integration, defining the range over which the function $f(x)$ is integrated. A common example is the evaluation of a definite integral:

$$\int_0^1 x^2\,dx = \frac{1}{3}$$

which represents the area under the curve $y = x^2$ from $x = 0$ to $x = 1$.

Double Integrals

Double integrals extend the concept of integration to two variables and are widely used in physics and engineering for computing areas, volumes, and mass distributions. The general form of a double integral is:

$$\int_a^b \int_c^d f(x, y)\,dy\,dx$$

where the inner integral integrates over y, and the outer integral integrates over x. This type of integration is useful in computing volumes of three-dimensional regions.

For example, the volume under a surface $f(x, y) = x^2 + y^2$ over a rectangular region can be computed as:

$$\int_0^1 \int_0^2 (x^2 + y^2)\,dy\,dx$$

which evaluates the total accumulated "height" over the given domain.

Triple Integrals

Triple integrals are used to compute volumes in three-dimensional space and are fundamental in physics for applications such as mass density calculations and fluid flow analysis. The general form of a triple integral is:

$$\int_a^b \int_c^d \int_e^f f(x, y, z)\, dz\, dy\, dx$$

where integration is performed successively over three variables. These integrals are commonly used in mechanics and electromagnetism to compute quantities such as total mass given a density function $\rho(x, y, z)$:

$$M = \int_V \rho(x, y, z)\, dV$$

where dV represents the volume element.

Notation and Best Practices in LaTeX

When using summations and integrals in LaTeX, consider the following formatting best practices:

- In inline mode, limits appear beside the symbols:

$$\textstyle\sum_{i=1}^n x_i.$$

- In display mode, limits appear directly above and below:

$$\sum_{i=1}^n x_i, \quad \int_a^b f(x)\, dx$$

This ensures clarity, especially when working with large equations. The `align` environment in LaTeX is particularly useful for structuring multiline expressions, keeping integrals and summations properly aligned.

3.3 Fractions, Binomials, Roots, and Powers

Mathematical expressions often involve fractions, binomial coefficients, roots, and exponents. These elements appear frequently in algebra, calculus, and advanced mathematical fields. LaTeX provides an elegant and efficient way to typeset such expressions, ensuring clarity and consistency in mathematical writing. This section explores how to properly format fractions, binomial coefficients, roots, and powers using LaTeX while also discussing best practices for structuring equations.

3.3.1 Fractions in LaTeX

Fractions are one of the most fundamental mathematical notations, used extensively in arithmetic, algebra, and calculus. LaTeX provides the `\frac` command to format fractions properly, ensuring they are displayed with the numerator above and the denominator below the fraction bar.

For instance, the fraction representing $\frac{a}{b}$ can be written as:

$$\frac{a}{b}$$

This is achieved using the command:

```
\frac{a}{b}
```

When used within inline text, LaTeX scales the fraction appropriately, ensuring it fits well within the sentence. However, in display mode, fractions appear larger and more centered:

$$\frac{x^2 + y^2}{x + y}$$

For complex expressions, especially when working with long numerators or denominators, enclosing the entire fraction within display math mode (`\[ ...\]`) is recommended for better readability.

Fraction

LaTeX Code:

```
The fraction
$\frac{a}{b}$
represents the
division of $a$
by $b$.
```

Output:

The fraction $\frac{a}{b}$ represents the division of a by b.

You can use fractions both in *inline math mode* and *display math mode*. In display mode, fractions are centered and appear larger:

```
\[
\frac{a}{b}.
\]
```

This displays the fraction on its own line, centered:

$$\frac{a}{b}.$$

3.3.2 Binomial Coefficients

Binomial coefficients, commonly seen in combinatorics and probability theory, represent the number of ways to choose k elements from a set of n elements. These coefficients are expressed mathematically as:

$$\binom{n}{k} = \frac{n!}{k!(n-k)!}$$

In LaTeX, the `\binom` command is used to write binomial coefficients:

```
\binom{n}{k}.
```

This notation is particularly useful in combinatorial proofs, the binomial theorem, and Pascal's triangle. Since binomial coefficients tend to be larger expressions, using them in display mode often improves clarity, particularly when writing expanded equations such as:

$$(a+b)^n = \sum_{k=0}^{n} \binom{n}{k} a^{n-k} b^k$$

Binomial

LaTeX Code:

```
The binomial
$\binom{n}{k}$
represents the
selection of
$k$ out of $n$.
```

Output:

The binomial $\binom{n}{k}$ represents the selection of k out of n.

3.3.3 Square Roots and Higher-Order Roots

Radical notation is an essential part of algebra and calculus, particularly in dealing with square roots, cube roots, and higher-order roots. LaTeX provides the `\sqrt` command to typeset square roots. For instance, the square root of x is written as:

$$\sqrt{x}$$

using the command:

```
\sqrt{x}.
```

For roots of higher order, an optional argument can be used to specify the degree of the root. The general syntax is:

$$\sqrt[n]{x}$$

where n represents the order of the root. This is written in LaTeX as:

```
\sqrt[n]{x}.
```

For example, the cube root of a variable y is represented as:

$$\sqrt[3]{y}.$$

This notation extends to fourth and higher-order roots, commonly encountered in solving polynomial equations and in certain areas of physics and engineering.

3.3.4 Powers and Exponents

Exponents, also known as superscripts, are a key feature of mathematical notation, used to denote repeated multiplication, growth rates, and higher-degree polynomials. In LaTeX, superscripts are created using the caret (^) symbol. The expression x^2 is written as:

```
x^2.
```

This produces:

$$x^2.$$

If the exponent consists of multiple characters, curly braces are required to group them correctly. For instance, the expression x^{n+1} must be written as:

```
x^{n+1}.
```

This results in:

$$x^{n+1}.$$

When exponents involve fractions, radicals, or other complex expressions, enclosing them in braces ensures proper formatting. Consider the exponential function:

$$e^{\frac{x^2}{2}}$$

which is written as:

```
e^{\frac{x^2}{2}}.
```

3.3.5 Combining Fractions, Roots, and Exponents in Expressions

Mathematical notation often requires combining fractions, exponents, and roots into a single expression. A common example is the quadratic formula:

$$x = \frac{-b \pm \sqrt{b^2 - 4ac}}{2a}$$

which is written in LaTeX as:

```
x = \frac{-b \pm \sqrt{b^2 - 4ac}}{2a}.
```

In expressions involving nested exponents or multiple mathematical operations, LaTeX handles precedence correctly, but proper bracketing ensures clarity. For example, the general exponential function:

$$y = e^{\sqrt{x^2+1}}$$

is formatted using:

```
y = e^{\sqrt{x^2 + 1}}.
```

This equation appears frequently in fields like differential equations and physics.

Below, we list some common Mathematica structures (Table 3.5).

Structure	**Command**	**Example input**	**Example output**
Subscript	`_{}`	`x_{10}`	x_{10}
Superscript	`^{}`	`3^{20}`	3^{20}
Fraction	`\frac{}{}`	`\frac{a+b}{x+y}`	$\frac{a+b}{x+y}$
Binomial	`\binom{}{}`	`\binom{m+k}{k}`	$\binom{m+k}{k}$
Square root	`\sqrt{}`	`\sqrt{x+y}`	$\sqrt{x+y}$
nth root	`\sqrt[n]{}`	`\sqrt[3]{x+y}`	$\sqrt[3]{x+y}$
Sum	`\sum_{}^{}`	`\sum_{i=1}^{10} i^2`	$\sum_{i=1}^{10} i^2$
Product	`\prod_{}^{}`	`\prod_{i=1}^{10} i^2`	$\prod_{i=1}^{10} i^2$
Integral	`\int_{}^{}`	`\int_{0}^{\infty}xdx`	$\int_{0}^{\infty} x\,dx$

Table 3.5: Mathematical structures and their LaTeX commands

3.4 Matrices, Arrays, and Tables in Mathematics

Matrices, arrays, and tables are essential tools in mathematics, often used to organize data or represent systems of equations. LaTeX provides specialized environments to create these structures in a clean and professional format. In this section, we will explore how to create matrices, arrays, and tables in mathematical expressions.

3.4.1 Matrices

Matrices play a crucial role in linear algebra, computer science, and engineering, serving as a structured representation of numerical or symbolic data. They are used in solving systems of equations, performing transformations, and representing networks or datasets. In LaTeX, matrices are conveniently typeset using dedicated matrix environments, ensuring a clean and professional layout.

A matrix is typically written in a structured grid format, where rows and columns align clearly. LaTeX provides different matrix environments that allow for various styles of enclosures, such as parentheses, brackets, or vertical bars, depending on the context of use.

Basic Matrix Representation

A fundamental matrix without enclosing brackets can be written using the `matrix` environment. This structure is useful when the matrix does not require specific delimiters. Each row of the matrix is separated by double backslashes (\\), and elements within a row are separated by ampersands (`&`).

Basic Matrix

LaTeX Code:

```
\[
\begin{matrix}
1 & 2 & 3 \\
4 & 5 & 6 \\
7 & 8 & 9
\end{matrix}
\]
```

Output:

$$\begin{matrix} 1 & 2 & 3 \\ 4 & 5 & 6 \\ 7 & 8 & 9 \end{matrix}$$

This representation is often used in informal settings where additional structure is unnecessary. However, in most cases, enclosing brackets or parentheses provide a more formal appearance.

Parenthesized Matrices

In mathematical writing, matrices are frequently enclosed within parentheses to indicate their structured nature. LaTeX provides the `pmatrix` environment to achieve this:

Parenthesized Matrix

LaTeX Code:

```
\[
\begin{pmatrix}
1 & 2 & 3 \\
4 & 5 & 6 \\
7 & 8 & 9
\end{pmatrix}
\]
```

Output:

$$\begin{pmatrix} 1 & 2 & 3 \\ 4 & 5 & 6 \\ 7 & 8 & 9 \end{pmatrix}$$

This notation is commonly used in linear algebra to indicate matrices explicitly, especially in determinant calculations or matrix multiplication.

Square-Bracketed Matrices

For matrices that are part of vector representations or systems of equations, square brackets often provide a more appropriate notation. The `bmatrix` environment allows for square-bracketed matrices in LaTeX:

Braced Matrix

LaTeX Code:

```
\[
\begin{bmatrix}
1 & 2 & 3 \\
4 & 5 & 6 \\
7 & 8 & 9
\end{bmatrix}
\]
```

Output:

$$\begin{bmatrix} 1 & 2 & 3 \\ 4 & 5 & 6 \\ 7 & 8 & 9 \end{bmatrix}$$

This notation is frequently seen in engineering applications, such as control systems and circuit analysis.

Determinants and Vertical-Bar Matrices

For determinant calculations, matrices are commonly enclosed by vertical bars. LaTeX allows this representation using the `vmatrix` environment:

Determinant Matrix

LaTeX Code:

```
\[
\begin{vmatrix}
1 & 2 & 3 \\
4 & 5 & 6 \\
7 & 8 & 9
\end{vmatrix}
\]
```

Output:

$$\begin{vmatrix} 1 & 2 & 3 \\ 4 & 5 & 6 \\ 7 & 8 & 9 \end{vmatrix}$$

This notation is crucial in linear algebra when computing determinants, which help analyze matrix invertibility and eigenvalues.

Curly-Braced Matrices

For special cases, such as defining systems of equations or structured vector spaces, curly braces are sometimes used. The `Bmatrix` environment generates this style:

Curly-Braced Matrix

LaTeX Code:

```
\[
\begin{Bmatrix}
1 & 2 & 3 \\
4 & 5 & 6 \\
7 & 8 & 9
\end{Bmatrix}
\]
```

Output:

$$\begin{Bmatrix} 1 & 2 & 3 \\ 4 & 5 & 6 \\ 7 & 8 & 9 \end{Bmatrix}$$

3.4.2 Expanding Matrices to Higher Dimensions

While 2D matrices are the most common, LaTeX also supports higher-dimensional matrices, including column vectors and tensors. Column vectors can be represented using a single-column matrix:

$$\begin{bmatrix} 1 \\ 2 \\ 3 \end{bmatrix}$$

while three-dimensional tensors require more advanced formatting, which can be achieved using the `array` environment or TikZ for visual representation.

3.4.3 Arrays

In mathematical typesetting, arrays offer a flexible way to structure tabular data within mathematical environments. Unlike the `matrix` environment, which is mainly used for matrices with uniform spacing, the `array` environment allows greater customization in column alignment and spacing, making it particularly useful for displaying structured data in equations.

Basic Structure of Arrays

The `array` environment operates similarly to the `tabular` environment but is designed specifically for mathematical expressions. Each row within the array is separated by double backslashes (\\), and elements within a row are separated by ampersands (`&`). Unlike `matrix` environments, which default to centered column alignment, the `array` environment allows explicit specification of column alignments.

To create an array, the column alignment is defined within curly brackets \{\} following `\begin{array}`. The possible alignment options are:

- `l`: Left-aligned columns
- `c`: Centered columns
- `r`: Right-aligned columns

For example, consider a 3×3 array where all columns are centered:

Centered Array

LaTeX Code:

```
\[
\begin{array}{ccc}
a & b & c \\
d & e & f \\
g & h & i
\end{array}
\]
```

Output:

$$\begin{array}{ccc}
a & b & c \\
d & e & f \\
g & h & i
\end{array}$$

In this example, the column specification {`ccc`} ensures that all three columns are centered.

Customizing Column Alignment

Unlike `matrix` environments, the `array` environment enables fine-grained control over the alignment of individual columns. Suppose we want the first column left-aligned, the second centered, and the third right-aligned:

Custom Column Alignment in Arrays

LaTeX Code:

```
\[
\begin{array}{lcr}
1 & 2 & 3 \\
4 & 5 & 6 \\
7 & 8 & 9
\end{array}
\]
```

Output:

$$\begin{array}{lcr} 1 & 2 & 3 \\ 4 & 5 & 6 \\ 7 & 8 & 9 \end{array}$$

Here, the alignment settings are as follows: `l` for left alignment in the first column, `c` for center alignment in the second column, and `r` for right alignment in the third column.

Using Arrays in Equations

Arrays are especially useful when working with structured mathematical expressions, such as solving systems of equations. Suppose we want to represent a system of equations neatly.

System of Equations in Arrays

LaTeX Code:

```
\[
\left\{
\begin{array}{rcl}
x + y & = & 5 \\
2x - y & = & 3
\end{array}
\right.
\]
```

Output:

$$\left\{ \begin{array}{rcl} x + y & = & 5 \\ 2x - y & = & 3 \end{array} \right.$$

In this system of equations, the `{rcl}` alignment ensures that the variables (`r`), equal signs (`c`), and constants (`l`) are neatly arranged. The `\left{` and `\right.` commands generate the enclosing curly braces.

Expanding Arrays for Advanced Formatting

The `array` environment allows for even more structured formatting, such as defining augmented matrices, piecewise functions, or organizing step-by-step calculations.

For example, consider an augmented matrix used in solving systems of equations:

Augmented Matrix

LaTeX Code:

```
\[
\left[
\begin{array}{ccc|c}
1 & 2 & -1 & 4 \\
3 & -1 & 2 & 6 \\
0 & 5 & -3 & 1
\end{array}
\right]
\]
```

Output:

$$\left[\begin{array}{ccc|c} 1 & 2 & -1 & 4 \\ 3 & -1 & 2 & 6 \\ 0 & 5 & -3 & 1 \end{array}\right]$$

Here, the vertical bar (`|`) within the column specification indicates a partition between the coefficient matrix and the constants.

3.4.4 Tables in Mathematics

Tables serve as an essential tool in mathematical documents, allowing for the structured representation of numerical data, algebraic expressions, or relationships between variables. LaTeX provides the `tabular` environment, which is widely used for arranging data in rows and columns. While primarily designed for text-based tabular formatting, it is also highly effective in mathematical writing, particularly in organizing formulas, function values, probability distributions, and more.

Basic Structure of Tables

A table in LaTeX is constructed using the `tabular` environment, where columns are defined by alignment specifiers enclosed within curly braces. The most common column alignments are `l`—left-aligned column, `c`—center-aligned column, and `r`—right-aligned column.

Vertical bars (`|`) can be used to add separating lines between columns, and the command `\hline` inserts horizontal lines between rows.

A simple example of a three-column table containing numerical data is shown below (Table 3.6).

Basic Mathematical Table

LaTeX Code:

```
\begin{table}[h]
\centering
\begin{tabular}{|c|c|c|}
\hline
$x$ & $y$ & $z$ \\
\hline
1 & 2 & 3 \\
4 & 5 & 6 \\
7 & 8 & 9 \\
\hline
\end{tabular}
\caption{A basic table
representing numerical
values}
\end{table}
```

Output:

x	y	z
1	2	3
4	5	6
7	8	9

Table 3.6: A basic table representing numerical values

Enhancing Tables with Formatting

To improve readability and structure, tables can be formatted using spacing commands, bold text, and different alignments. The following example demonstrates how to customize table entries using `\textbf` (bold text) and align numerical values properly (Table 3.7).

Formatted Table with Bold Headers

LaTeX Code:

```
\begin{table}[h]
\centering
\begin{tabular}{|c|r|l|}
\hline
\textbf{Variable} & \textbf{Value}
& \textbf{Description} \\
\hline
$x_1$ & 2.35 & First variable \\
$x_2$ & 5.71 & Second variable \\
$x_3$ & 8.92 & Third variable \\
\hline
\end{tabular}
\caption{A formatted table with aligned
values and descriptions}
\end{table}
```

Output:

Variable	**Value**	**Description**
x_1	2.35	First variable
x_2	5.71	Second variable
x_3	8.92	Third variable

Table 3.7: A formatted table with aligned values and descriptions

Here, the first column is centered, the second column is right-aligned, and the third column is left-aligned, ensuring better organization of numbers and text.

Mathematical Tables for Functions and Equations

Tables can also be used to represent functions and their corresponding values at specific points. For example, a table displaying function values for $f(x) = x^2$ at different points can be created as follows (Table 3.8):

Function Table

LaTeX Code:

```
\begin{table}[h]
\centering
\begin{tabular}{|c|c|}
\hline
$x$ & $f(x) = x^2$ \\
\hline
$-2$ & $4$ \\
$-1$ & $1$ \\
$0$ & $0$ \\
$1$ & $1$ \\
$2$ & $4$ \\
\hline
\end{tabular}
\caption{Function
values of $f(x) = x^2$}
\end{table}
```

Output:

x	$f(x) = x^2$
-2	4
-1	1
0	0
1	1
2	4

Table 3.8: Function values of $f(x) = x^2$

This structured table allows for a quick visualization of how the function behaves at different points.

Tables with Spanning Columns and Rows

LaTeX also allows merging of cells using the `\multicolumn` and `\multirow` commands. These features are particularly useful when working with more complex mathematical tables.

For example, a probability distribution table with a spanning header is created as follows (Table 3.9):

Table with Merged Cells

LaTeX Code:

```
\begin{table}[h]
\centering
\begin{tabular}{|c|c|c|}
\hline
\multicolumn{3}{|c|}
{Probability Distribution}
\\
\hline
$x$ &$P(X=x)$&Cumulative Probability \\
\hline
0 & 0.1 & 0.1 \\
1 & 0.3 & 0.4 \\
2 & 0.4 & 0.8 \\
3 & 0.2 & 1.0 \\
\hline
\end{tabular}
\caption{Example of a probability table
with merged headers}
\end{table}
```

Output:

Probability distribution		
x	$P(X = x)$	Cumu. probability
0	0.1	0.1
1	0.3	0.4
2	0.4	0.8
3	0.2	1.0

Table 3.9: Example of a probability table with merged headers

3.5 Advanced Math: Theorems, Proofs, and Equations

In mathematical writing, presenting theorems, proofs, and equations clearly is essential. LaTeX provides powerful tools to structure these components in a formal, elegant, and consistent way. In this section, we will explore how to format theorems, write proofs, and handle complex equations in LaTeX.

3.5.1 Theorems

Mathematical writing often involves the presentation of theorems, lemmas, corollaries, and propositions, which help structure logical arguments and proofs. In LaTeX, theorem environments provide a standardized way to format such statements, ensuring clarity and consistency. The `amsthm` package from the American Mathematical Society (AMS) is widely used for defining and customizing theorem environments.

Loading the `amsthm` Package

To work with theorem-like environments in LaTeX, the first step is to include the `amsthm` package in the preamble:

```
\usepackage{amsthm}
```

This package provides the `\newtheorem` command, which allows defining custom theorem styles and numbering schemes.

Defining a Basic Theorem Environment

The simplest way to define a theorem environment is by using the `\newtheorem` command. The syntax for defining a theorem is:

```
\newtheorem{theorem}{Theorem}
```

This creates a theorem environment named `theorem`, which can then be used to state mathematical results. The numbering of theorems is automatically handled by LaTeX.

Basic Theorem Environment

LaTeX Code:

```
\documentclass{article}
\usepackage{amsthm}
\newtheorem{theorem}{Theorem}
\begin{document}

\begin{theorem}
  Let $a$ and $b$ be  real numbers.
  If $a > b$, then $a^2 > b^2$.
\end{theorem}

\end{document}
```

Output:

Theorem 1. *Let a and b be real numbers. If $a > b$, then $a^2 > b^2$.*

Customizing Theorem Numbering

By default, theorems are numbered independently. However, for more structured documents, it is often useful to number theorems within sections. This can be achieved by modifying the numbering scheme in `\newtheorem`:

```
\newtheorem{theorem}{Theorem}[section]
```

With this setup, theorem numbering resets within each section. A theorem in Section 2 would be labeled as "Theorem 2.1," "Theorem 2.2," and so on.

Theorem Numbering by Section

LaTeX Code:

```
\documentclass{article}
\usepackage{amsthm}

\newtheorem{theorem}
{Theorem}[section]

\begin{document}

\section{Introduction}
\begin{theorem}
  The sum of two even
  numbers is even.
\end{theorem}

\section{Algebra}
\begin{theorem}
  If $a > b$, then
  $a^2 > b^2$.
\end{theorem}

\end{document}
```

Output:

Section 1: Introduction
Theorem 1.1. The sum of two even numbers is even.
Section 2: Algebra
Theorem 2.1. If $a > b$, then $a^2 > b^2$.

Defining Lemmas, Corollaries, and Propositions

Mathematical proofs often involve lemmas (supporting results), corollaries (immediate consequences), and propositions (statements that require proof). These can be defined using `\newtheorem` in a similar manner.

```
\newtheorem{lemma}{Lemma}
\newtheorem{corollary}{Corollary}
\newtheorem{proposition}{Proposition}
```

Below is an example showing different theorem-like environments:

Lemmas Corollaries and Propositions

LaTeX Code:

```
\documentclass{article}
\usepackage{amsthm}
\newtheorem{theorem}{Theorem}
\newtheorem{lemma}{Lemma}
\newtheorem{corollary}
{Corollary}
\newtheorem{proposition}
{Proposition}
\begin{document}
\begin{lemma}
  If $n$ is even, then $n^2$ is even.
\end{lemma}
\begin{theorem}
  Every even number greater than 2 can
  be written as the sum of two primes.
\end{theorem}
\begin{corollary}
There are infinitely many prime numbers.
\end{corollary}
\begin{proposition}
  If $x$ is rational, then
  $x^2$ is also rational.
\end{proposition}
\end{document}
```

Output:

Lemma 1. If n is even, then n^2 is even.
Theorem 1. Every even number greater than 2 can be written as the sum of two primes.
Corollary 1. There are infinitely many prime numbers.

Proposition 1. *If x is rational, then x^2 is also rational.*

3.5.2 Proofs

Mathematical proofs serve as the foundation for establishing the validity of statements and theorems. A well-structured proof is essential in mathematical writing, and LaTeX provides a dedicated environment, called the `proof` environment, for presenting proofs in a formal and professional manner.

Using the Proof Environment

The `proof` environment automatically formats the word "Proof" in boldface at the beginning of the proof and appends a Q.E.D. symbol (denoted by a small square □) at the end to indicate its completion. This is a convention widely followed in academic papers, textbooks, and research documents.

To use the `proof` environment, it is necessary to include the **`amsthm`** package in the preamble:

```
\usepackage{amsthm}
```

Once the package is included, a proof can be written as follows:

Basic Proof Environment

LaTeX Code:

```
\documentclass{article}
\usepackage{amsthm}

\begin{document}

\begin{proof}
```

```
Let $a$ and $b$ be real numbers such
that $a > b$. By the properties of real
numbers, squaring both sides preserves
the inequality, so $a^2 > b^2$.
Hence, the theorem is proved.
\end{proof}

\end{document}
```

Output:

Proof. Let a and b be real numbers such that $a > b$. By the properties of real numbers, squaring both sides preserves the inequality, so $a^2 > b^2$. Hence, the theorem is proved. □

The Q.E.D. symbol (□) is automatically appended to indicate the completion of the proof. However, if you prefer a different symbol or wish to remove it, you can override it using:

```
\renewcommand{\qedsymbol}{\blacksquare}
```

This replaces the default □ with a filled square ■.

Numbering Theorems and Proofs

In most mathematical documents, proofs are associated with theorems, lemmas, or propositions. Numbering theorems makes it easier to reference them later. To ensure consistency, LaTeX allows theorem numbering and linking proofs to specific statements.

```
\newtheorem{theorem}{Theorem}

\begin{theorem}
```

```
If $x > 0$, then $x^2 > 0$.
\end{theorem}

\begin{proof}
Since $x$ is positive, we have
$x \cdot x > 0$, so $x^2 > 0$.
\end{proof}
```

Proof for a Theorem

LaTeX Code:

```
\documentclass{article}
\usepackage{amsthm}

\newtheorem
{theorem}{Theorem}

\begin{document}

\begin{theorem}
If $x > 0$,
then $x^2 > 0$.
\end{theorem}

\begin{proof}
Since $x$ is positive,
we have $x \cdot x > 0$,
so $x^2 > 0$.
\end{proof}
\end{document}
```

Output:

Theorem 1. *If $x > 0$, then $x^2 > 0$.*

Proof. Since x is positive, we have $x \cdot x > 0$, so $x^2 > 0$. □

Using Structured Proofs

Some proofs require multiple steps, case distinctions, or specific logical structures. In such cases, you may use enumerated proofs or cases.

Proof by Cases If a proof requires dividing the problem into separate cases, you can structure it as follows:

Proof by Cases

LaTeX Code:

```
\begin{proof}
We consider two cases:

\textbf{Case 1:} If
$x = 0$,then $x^2 = 0$.

\textbf{Case 2:} If
$x > 0$, then $x^2 > 0$
follows from basic
algebra. Thus, in both
cases, $x^2 \geq 0$.
\end{proof}
```

Output:

Proof. We consider two cases: **Case 1:** If $x = 0$, then $x^2 = 0$. **Case 2:** If $x > 0$, then $x^2 > 0$ follows from basic algebra. Thus, in both cases, $x^2 \geq 0$. □

Proofs Without Q.E.D.

For informal mathematical writing, or if you do not want to use the Q.E.D. symbol, you can remove it by redefining it as empty:

```
\renewcommand{\qedsymbol}{}
```

Alternatively, you can manually insert a Q.E.D. symbol at a desired location using:

```
\begin{proof}
  Proof content goes here. \qed
\end{proof}
```

3.5.3 Complex Equations

LaTeX excels at formatting mathematical equations, providing multiple environments and tools to ensure that even the most complicated expressions are clear and well-organized. In this section, we will explore several key ways to handle single-line equations, multiline equations, alignment, and numbering.

Single-Line Equations

In mathematical writing, it is often necessary to display equations separately from the surrounding text, especially when they convey fundamental relationships or need to be referenced later. LaTeX provides a dedicated environment for such equations, ensuring that they are properly formatted and numbered for easy reference.

A commonly used method for displaying standalone equations is the `equation` environment. This environment places the equation on its own line and automatically numbers it.

Equation Environment

LaTeX Code:

```
\begin{equation}
  E = mc^2
\end{equation}
```

Output:

$$E = mc^2 \tag{1}$$

This example demonstrates the famous equation from Einstein's theory of relativity, where energy (E) is related to mass (m) and the speed of light (c). The equation is centered on the page, and the equation number is placed to its right.

Referencing Equations In longer documents, it is often necessary to refer back to previously stated equations. LaTeX allows equations to be labeled and referenced dynamically, which ensures consistency throughout the document. This is achieved using the `\label` and `\ref` commands.

To label an equation, include a unique identifier inside the `\label` command within the equation environment. Later, the `\ref` command can be used to refer to the equation number.

Referencing Equations

LaTeX Code:

```
\begin{equation}
  F = ma.\label{eq:n}
\end{equation}
According to equation
\ref{eq:n}, force is
equal to mass times
acceleration.
```

Output:

$$F = ma. \quad (2)$$

According to equation (2), force is equal to mass times acceleration.

In this example, the Newtonian equation of motion $F = ma$ is labeled using `\label{eq:n}`. Later, the equation number is recalled using `\ref{eq:n}`, ensuring that the reference updates automatically if equation numbering changes.

Suppressing Equation Numbers In some cases, numbered equations may not be necessary, such as when displaying equations in quick explanations or derivations. The equation number can be suppressed by using the `equation*` environment, which is available in the `amsmath` package.

Equation Without Number

LaTeX Code:

```
\begin{equation*}
  a^2 + b^2 = c^2
\end{equation*}
```

Output:

$$a^2 + b^2 = c^2$$

By using the `equation*` environment, the equation is displayed in the same way as before but without an equation number.

Aligning Equations

In mathematical writing, it is often necessary to present multiple equations in a structured manner, particularly when performing step-by-step derivations or when dealing with equations that share common terms. LaTeX provides the `align` and `aligned` environments to facilitate this, ensuring that related equations are neatly arranged for improved readability.

The primary difference between these two environments is that `aligned` is used within a broader equation structure (such as `equation` or `gather`), while `align` can function independently and provides automatic numbering for each equation.

Basic Equation Alignment When dealing with multiple equations, aligning them at a common symbol (such as the equal sign) enhances clarity. The `aligned` environment uses the ampersand (&) to specify alignment points, ensuring that similar elements of each equation are lined up vertically.

Basic Aligned Equations

LaTeX Code:

```
\[ \begin{aligned}
   a + b &= c \\
   d + e &= f + g.
\end{aligned} \]
```

Output:

$$\begin{aligned} a + b &= c \\ d + e &= f + g. \end{aligned}$$

In this example, the equations are aligned at the equals sign, which makes the relationships between the terms easier to follow. The use of the `aligned` environment ensures that each equation remains within the same mathematical block without being assigned individual equation numbers.

Aligning and Numbering Equations If numbering is required for each equation, the `align` environment should be used instead of `aligned`. The `align` environment functions similarly but automatically assigns numbers to each equation. It also allows users to selectively disable numbering on specific lines using the `\nonumber` or `\notag` command.

Numbered Equations Using align

LaTeX Code:

```
\begin{align}
a + b &= c\nonumber\\
d + e &= f + g.
\end{align}
```

Output:

$$\begin{aligned} a + b &= c \\ d + e &= f + g. \qquad (3.3) \end{aligned}$$

In this example, the first equation is displayed without a number due to the `\nonumber` command, while the second equation is assigned a number automatically.

Mixing Text and Aligned Equations In many cases, mathematical derivations require explanatory text alongside equations. The `aligned` environment can be embedded within the `equation` environment to integrate text and mathematical expressions smoothly.

Text and Aligned Equations

LaTeX Code:

```
\begin{equation}
\begin{aligned}
F &= ma, \quad \text{by Newton's
Second Law}, \\
v &= u + at, \quad \text{by kinematics}.
\end{aligned}
\end{equation}
```

Output:

$$\begin{aligned} F &= ma, \quad \text{by Newton's Second Law}, \\ v &= u + at, \quad \text{by kinematics}. \end{aligned} \tag{3.4}$$

Here, explanatory text is included within the alignment, ensuring that both equations and their contextual explanations remain neatly formatted.

Multiline Equations with Alignment

Mathematical expressions often span multiple lines, especially when dealing with derivations, equations that require step-by-step simplification, or long algebraic manipulations. LaTeX provides several environments to handle multiline equations effectively while maintaining a structured and readable format. The most commonly used environments for this purpose are `aligned`, `align`, and `eqnarray`. Each of these offers different formatting options depending on the needs of the document.

Using the `aligned` Environment The `aligned` environment is useful when embedding a multiline equation inside another mathematical construct. It is particularly helpful when equations need to be grouped together without introducing additional numbering.

Multiline Equations Using aligned

LaTeX Code:

```
\[
\begin{aligned}
f(x)
&= 3x^2 + 2x + 1 \\
&= (x + 1)(3x + 1) \\
&= 3x^2 + x + 3x + 1.
\end{aligned}
\]
```

Output:

$$\begin{aligned} f(x) &= 3x^2 + 2x + 1 \\ &= (x+1)(3x+1) \\ &= 3x^2 + x + 3x + 1. \end{aligned}$$

In this example, the three-step simplification of $f(x)$ is neatly aligned at the equal sign, ensuring that each step is visually clear. The `aligned` environment does not provide equation numbering by itself, but it can be used inside the `equation` environment if numbering is required.

Using the `eqnarray` Environment Another approach to writing multiline equations in LaTeX is the `eqnarray` environment, which aligns expressions in three columns—two mathematical expressions separated by a relational operator (such as =). The alignment is specified using the ampersand (&) symbol.

Multiline Equations Using eqnarray

LaTeX Code:

```
\begin{eqnarray}
  f(x) &=& 3x^2 + 2x + 1 \\
       &=& (x + 1)(3x + 1) \\
       &=& 3x^2 + x + 3x + 1.
\end{eqnarray}
```

Output:

$$
\begin{eqnarray}
f(x) &=& 3x^2 + 2x + 1 \qquad (3.5)\\
&=& (x+1)(3x+1) \qquad (3.6)\\
&=& 3x^2 + x + 3x + 1. \qquad (3.7)
\end{eqnarray}
$$

Each equation in the eqnarray environment is automatically numbered. If numbering is not needed, the eqnarray* environment can be used instead.

Eqnarray Without Numbering

LaTeX Code:

```
\begin{eqnarray*}
f(x)
&=&3x^2 + 2x + 1 \\
&=&(x + 1)(3x + 1) \\
&=&3x^2 + x + 3x + 1.
\end{eqnarray*}
```

Output:

$$
\begin{eqnarray*}
f(x) &=& 3x^2 + 2x + 1\\
&=& (x+1)(3x+1)\\
&=& 3x^2 + x + 3x + 1
\end{eqnarray*}
$$

Using the `align` Environment The `align` environment is the preferred modern method for aligning equations, offering flexibility and automatic numbering. Unlike `eqnarray`, `align` provides better spacing and alignment.

Multiline Equations Using align

LaTeX Code:

```
\begin{align}
  f(x) &= 3x^2 + 2x + 1 \\
       &= (x + 1)(3x + 1) \\
       &= 3x^2 + x + 3x + 1.
\end{align}
```

Output:

$$f(x) = 3x^2 + 2x + 1 \qquad (3.8)$$
$$= (x + 1)(3x + 1) \qquad (3.9)$$
$$= 3x^2 + x + 3x + 1. \qquad (3.10)$$

The `align` environment automatically numbers equations, and if numbering is not needed, the `align*` environment can be used instead.

Gathered Equations

In mathematical writing, there are situations where multiple equations need to be presented together but do not require alignment. When equations are independent of each other and do not share alignment points, the `gather` environment in LaTeX is the most appropriate choice. This environment ensures that each equation appears centered on its own line, providing a clear and structured layout without enforcing unnecessary alignment.

Unlike the `align` or `eqnarray` environments, which align equations at specific symbols (such as the equals sign), the `gather` environment simply stacks the equations vertically, centering them on the page.

Basic Usage of the gather Environment The `gather` environment is particularly useful when writing independent mathematical statements that do not share common variables or formatting structures. The syntax for using `gather` is straightforward:

Gathered Equations

LaTeX Code:

```
\begin{gather}
  x + y = z \\
  a^2 + b^2 = c^2
\end{gather}
```

Output:

$$x + y = z \quad (3.11)$$
$$a^2 + b^2 = c^2 \quad (3.12)$$

In this example, both equations are displayed on separate lines and are centered. Unlike the `align` environment, no alignment symbols are required, since `gather` is designed to center independent equations rather than align related expressions.

Suppressing Equation Numbering By default, equations in the `gather` environment are numbered. If numbering is not needed, the `gather*` environment can be used instead. This variant prevents LaTeX from assigning numbers to each equation while preserving the centered layout.

Gathered Equations Without Numbering

LaTeX Code:

```
\begin{gather*}
\sin x + \cos y = 1 \\
e^x + e^y = e^z
\end{gather*}
```

Output:

$$\sin x + \cos y = 1$$
$$e^x + e^y = e^z$$

Using `gather*` ensures that the equations remain neatly formatted without including numbers, which is often useful in derivations where the focus is on displaying relationships rather than referencing specific equation numbers.

Combining the gather Environment with Labels Although `gather` does not align equations, it still allows referencing individual equations by using the `\label` and `\ref` commands. If equation numbering is enabled, each equation can be labeled separately for later citation in the text.

Referencing Gathered Equations

LaTeX Code:

```
\begin{gather}
a + b = c \label{eq:first} \\
x^2 + y^2 = r^2 \label{eq:second}
\end{gather}
Equation \eqref{eq:first} represents a
simple sum, while equation
\eqref{eq:second} is the equation of a
circle.
```

Output:

$$a + b = c \tag{1}$$
$$x^2 + y^2 = r^2 \tag{2}$$

Equation (1) represents a simple sum, while equation (2) is the equation of a circle.

Splitting Long Equations

In mathematical documents, some equations are too long to fit on a single line, requiring them to be broken into multiple lines for better readability. LaTeX provides several ways to handle long equations while ensuring clarity and proper alignment. The most commonly used methods for splitting long equations include the `split`, `eqnarray`, and `align` environments.

Using the Split Environment The `split` environment is particularly useful when an equation needs to be broken across multiple lines but should still be treated as a single entity with a single equation number. The environment is placed inside an `equation` block to ensure proper formatting.

Splitting Equations with split

LaTeX Code:

```
\begin{equation}
\begin{split}
f(x)
&= 3x^2 + 2x + 1 \\
&\quad + 4x^3 + 7x + 5.
\end{split}
\end{equation}
```

Output:

$$\begin{split} f(x) &= 3x^2 + 2x + 1 \\ &\quad + 4x^3 + 7x + 5. \end{split} \tag{3.13}$$

The \quad command introduces horizontal spacing, ensuring that the second part of the equation is aligned neatly after the equal sign. This improves readability by keeping the terms visually distinct.

Using the Eqnarray Environment The eqnarray environment provides another way to split long equations. This environment allows multiple lines, each consisting of three parts separated by &: the left-hand expression, a relation symbol (such as =), and the right-hand expression.

Splitting Equations with Eqnarray

LaTeX Code:

```
\begin{eqnarray}
f(x) &=& 3x^2 + 2x + 1 \\
     &&+ 4x^3 + 7x + 5.
\end{eqnarray}
```

Output:

$$\begin{array}{rcl} f(x) & = & 3x^2 + 2x + 1 \\ & & +4x^3 + 7x + 5. \end{array} \tag{3.14}$$

By placing the relation symbol (e.g., =) in the second column, all equal signs are aligned, creating a structured presentation.

Using the Align Environment The `align` environment also provides a way to break long equations across multiple lines while maintaining proper alignment.

Splitting Equations with align

LaTeX Code:

```
\begin{align}
f(x)
=& 3x^2 + 2x + 1
 \nonumber\\
 &+ 4x^3 + 7x + 5.
\end{align}
```

Output:

$$f(x) = 3x^2 + 2x + 1$$
$$+ 4x^3 + 7x + 5. \quad (3.15)$$

The & symbol is used to align each equation at the desired position, ensuring a clear presentation of long expressions.

Systems of Equations

A system of equations consists of multiple mathematical expressions that need to be grouped together in a structured format. LaTeX provides the `cases` environment to display piecewise functions and related structures where different conditions apply.

Using the Cases Environment The `cases` environment is useful for defining piecewise functions, where the function value depends on different conditions.

Cases Environment for Systems of Equations

LaTeX Code:

```
\[
f(x) =
\begin{cases}
0 & \text{if } x = 0\\
1 & \text{if } x > 0\\
-1 & \text{if } x < 0.
\end{cases}
\]
```

Output:

$$f(x) = \begin{cases} 0 & \text{if } x = 0 \\ 1 & \text{if } x > 0 \\ -1 & \text{if } x < 0. \end{cases}$$

The vertical brace groups the conditions together, making it visually clear that $f(x)$ is defined by different expressions depending on the value of x.

Using Align for Systems of Equations The `align` environment can also be used for structured systems of equations.

Using align for Systems of Equations

LaTeX Code:

```
\begin{align}
   x + y &= 5 \\
   2x - y &= 3.
\end{align}
```

Output:

$$x + y = 5 \quad (3.16)$$
$$2x - y = 3. \quad (3.17)$$

This format ensures that equations remain properly aligned, improving readability in more complex systems.

Advanced Customization of Equation Numbering

By default, LaTeX automatically numbers all equations sequentially. However, sometimes you need more control over how equations are numbered.

Custom Equation Tags You can customize equation numbers using the `\tag{}` command.

Custom Equation Tag

LaTeX Code:

```
\begin{equation}
E = mc^2 \tag{Einstein}
\end{equation}
```

Output:

$$E = mc^2 \quad \text{(Einstein)}$$

Instead of the default numbering, the equation is labeled as (Einstein).

Grouping Equations Under One Number In mathematical writing, it is common to encounter multiple equations that are part of the same derivation or closely related to each other. Instead of numbering them separately, LaTeX allows these equations to be grouped under a single equation number with distinct sub-labels. This approach improves readability and keeps related equations organized.

LaTeX provides the `subequations` environment to achieve this. When using this environment, all enclosed equations share a common number, with individual equations distinguished by an alphabetical sub-number.

The following example illustrates how two related equations can be grouped under a single main equation number:

Subequation Environment

LaTeX Code:

```
\begin{equation}
\begin{subequations}
\begin{align}
  x + y &= z \\
  x - y &= w
\end{align}
\end{subequations}
\end{equation}
```

Output:

$$x + y = z \quad (3a)$$

$$x - y = w \quad (3b)$$

Here, both equations share the main number (3), while each equation is distinguished by the sub-labels (a) and (b). This notation is particularly useful in cases where equations describe different aspects of the same mathematical relationship, such as components of a vector equation or conditions for a system of inequalities.

Another way to use the `subequations` environment is to enclose an entire system of equations within it:

System of Equations Using subequations

LaTeX Code:

```
\begin{subequations}
\begin{align}
  Ax + By &= C \\
  Dx + Ey &= F
\end{align}
\end{subequations}
```

Output:

$$Ax + By = C \quad (4a)$$

$$Dx + Ey = F \quad (4b)$$

This method ensures that the equations are visually grouped together while still allowing individual references to each equation when necessary. For example, you can refer to equation (4a) separately from (4b), or you can refer to the entire system as equation (4).

Matrices in Equations

When working with linear algebra, you will often need to include matrices in your equations. LaTeX provides the `pmatrix`, `bmatrix`, and `vmatrix` environments for this purpose.

Matrices in Equation

LaTeX Code:

```
\begin{equation}
A =
\begin{pmatrix}
  a & b \\
  c & d
\end{pmatrix}
\end{equation}
```

Output:

$$A = \begin{pmatrix} a & b \\ c & d \end{pmatrix}$$

Matrices can be integrated directly into equations, allowing for complex linear algebraic expressions.

3.5.4 Placing Symbols Above or Below Expressions

In mathematical notation, it is often necessary to place symbols, labels, or modifications above or below certain expressions to indicate relationships, structures, or emphasis. LaTeX provides several built-in commands for achieving this, such as overlining, underlining, braces, accents, and stacking symbols. This section explores these commands in detail, with practical examples.

Overlining and Underlining

To emphasize a mathematical expression by placing a horizontal line above or below it, LaTeX provides the commands `\overline` and `\underline`. The former places a line above the expression, while the latter places it below.

Overlining and Underlining

LaTeX Code:

```
\[
\overline{x+1}
\]
\[
\underline
{\text{Name of}}
\]
```

Output:

$$\overline{x+1}$$

$$\underline{\text{Name of}}$$

Overlining is commonly used to denote complex conjugates (e.g., $\overline{z}$) or to highlight a particular section of an expression. Underlining, on the other hand, is used less frequently in mathematical notation but can be useful in emphasizing text or distinguishing parts of an equation.

Braces Above and Below Expressions

In some cases, you may need to group terms together visually using braces while providing additional labels. LaTeX provides the `\overbrace` and `\underbrace` commands to achieve this.

Braces Over and Under

LaTeX Code:

```
\[
\overbrace{a + b + c + d}
\]
\[
a +\underbrace{b + c}_{
\text{label}} + d
\]
\[
\overbrace{a +\underbrace
{b + c}_{\text{inner}} +
d}^{\text{outer}}
\]
```

Output:

$$\overbrace{a + b + c + d}$$

$$a +\underbrace{b + c}_{\text{label}} + d$$

$$\overbrace{a +\underbrace{b + c}_{\text{inner}} + d}^{\text{outer}}$$

Braces are particularly useful for summations, series, or nested expressions, helping to indicate which parts of an equation belong together.

For example, to indicate a large sum involving 26 terms, you can write:

Nested Braces with Labels

LaTeX Code:

```
\[
\underbrace{a +
\overbrace{b + \cdots
+ y + z}^{25}}_{26}
\]
```

Output:

$$\underbrace{a + \overbrace{b + \cdots + y + z}^{25}}_{26}$$

Accents in Mathematics

In mathematical notation, accents are used to modify letters or symbols, typically in vector notation, differential calculus, or phonetic markings. LaTeX provides a variety of accent commands (Table 3.10):

Accent	Command	Accent	Command
â	\hat{a}	$\vec{a}$	\vec{a}
ā	\bar{a}	$\widehat{a}$	\widehat{a}
ȧ	\dot{a}	$\widetilde{a}$	\widetilde{a}
ä	\ddot{a}	á	\acute{a}
à	\grave{a}	ǎ	\check{a}
ã	\tilde{a}	$\breve{a}$	\breve{a}

Table 3.10: Accents and their LaTeX commands

Among the most frequently used accents in vector calculus and physics are `\veca` for vectors $\vec{a}$, `\dota` for derivatives $\dot{a}$ (first derivative), and `\ddota` for second derivatives $\ddot{a}$.

Stacking Symbols

Stacking symbols is a common practice in logic, set theory, and mathematical notation to show equivalence, definitions, or transformations. The `\stackrel` command allows you to place one symbol or label above another.

Stacking Symbols

LaTeX Code:

```
\[
A \stackrel{a}
{\rightarrow}
B \stackrel{b}
{\rightarrow} C.
\]
\[
\vec{x}
\stackrel{\text{def}}
{=} (x_1, \dots, x_n).
\]
```

Output:

$$A \stackrel{a}{\rightarrow} B \stackrel{b}{\rightarrow} C.$$

$$\vec{x} \stackrel{\text{def}}{=} (x_1, \dots, x_n).$$

The `\stackrel` command is particularly useful when defining equivalences or showing logical implications. It is often used in functional analysis, algebra, and physics.

3.5.5 Spacing in Math Mode

Spacing plays an important role in making mathematical expressions readable. In LaTeX, spacing within math mode differs from normal text mode, and specific commands are required to adjust spaces effectively.

Horizontal Spacing in Math Mode

In math mode, LaTeX automatically determines appropriate spacing between characters and symbols. However, sometimes additional spacing is needed for clarity. The following commands allow fine control over horizontal spacing (Table 3.11):

Command	Function
\,	Inserts a thin space ( )
\:	Inserts a medium space ( )
\;	Inserts a thick space ( )
\quad	Inserts a wider space ( )
\qquad	Inserts an even wider space ( )
\!	Inserts a negative thin space (removes space)

Table 3.11: Spacing commands in math mode

These spacing commands can be used within a mathematical expression as follows:

Spacing in Math Mode

LaTeX Code:

```
\[
a \, + \, b \quad x \:
+ \: y \quad c \! + \! d
\]
```

Output:

$$a \, + \, b \quad x \: + \: y \quad c \! + \! d$$

Horizontal and Vertical Spacing in Text Mode

In normal text mode, spacing adjustments can be made using the commands \hspace (horizontal spacing) and \vspace (vertical spacing).

The \hspace command inserts extra horizontal space, while the \vspace command inserts vertical space.

Spacing in Text Mode

LaTeX Code:

```
We are \hspace{1cm}
bounded by a system.

\vspace{1cm}

So, we have to help
each other.
```

Output:

We are   bounded by a system.

So, we have to help each other.

Removing Extra Spaces

LaTeX automatically adjusts spacing based on the context, but sometimes unwanted spaces appear in output. Use the \! command in math mode to remove small spaces, and avoid extra blank lines in the LaTeX source code to prevent unintended vertical spacing.

Remark 3.5.1 *Unlike normal text mode, where spaces are inserted naturally, math mode requires explicit commands for spacing adjustments. Proper use of spacing commands enhances the clarity of mathematical expressions.*

3.5.6 Changing Style in Math Mode

Below are the commands used to change style in math mode (Table 3.12):

Command	Use
`\mathit`	For italic
`\mathrm`	For roman
`\mathbf`	For boldface
`\mathsf`	For sans serif
`\mathtt`	For typewriter

`\mathcal`	For calligraphic uppercase letters only
`\mathbb`	For blackboard bold (uppercase letters and numbers only)
`\mathfrak`	For Fraktur style
`\mathscr`	For script style (uppercase letters only, requires `mathrsfs` package)

Table 3.12: Commands for changing style in math mode

Example 3.5.2 *In this example, we will see in the table how R (you can apply the same over any symbol) changes with different command (Table 3.13)*

Command	***Output***
`\mathit{R}`	R
`\mathrm{R}`	R
`\mathbf{R}`	$\mathbf{R}$
`\mathsf{R}`	R
`\mathtt{R}`	$\mathtt{R}$
`\mathcal{R}`	$\mathcal{R}$
`\mathbb{R}`	$\mathbb{R}$
`\mathfrak{R}`	$\mathfrak{R}$
`\mathscr{R}`	$\mathscr{R}$

Table 3.13: Commands for changing style of R in math mode

Exercises for Chap. 3: Working with Mathematical Content

3.1 Inline and Display Math Mode

1. *Inline vs. Display Math*: Write an equation that demonstrates the difference between inline and dis-

play math modes in LaTeX. Use the Pythagorean theorem $a^2 + b^2 = c^2$ as your example.

2. *Mixing Text and Math*: Write a LaTeX paragraph that includes an inline equation explaining that the area of a circle is $A = \pi r^2$. Then, display the same equation using display math mode.

3. *Practice Using Math Environments*: Create a document with multiple equations. Use inline math for simpler equations and display math for more complex ones. Include at least three equations in each mode.

3.2 Common Mathematical Symbols and Operators

1. *Symbols Practice*: Write a LaTeX document that demonstrates how to use at least ten common mathematical symbols, including summation (`\sum`), integral (`\int`), and infinity (`\infty`).

2. *Operators Practice*: Write a document that includes the following mathematical operators: addition (+), subtraction (-), multiplication (`\times`), division (`\div`), and exponentiation (using ^).

3. *Advanced Symbols*: Use the LaTeX commands for set notation, such as $\subseteq$, $\in$, and $\cup$, and demonstrate how to write the equation $A \subseteq B$ if $x \in A$ implies $x \in B$.

3.3 Fractions, Roots, and Powers

1. *Fractions in Math Mode*: Write a LaTeX document that demonstrates the use of fractions. Include both simple fractions like $\frac{1}{2}$ and more complex ones like $\frac{a+b}{c+d}$.

2. *Square Roots and Powers*: Write a LaTeX document that includes both square roots and powers. Use examples like $\sqrt{x}$, $\sqrt[3]{x}$, and x^2.

3. *Nested Fractions and Roots*: Create a more complex expression using nested fractions and roots. For example, write $\frac{\sqrt{a+\frac{1}{b}}}{x^2}$ in LaTeX and explain the process.

3.4 Matrices, Arrays, and Tables in Mathematics

1. *Matrix Practice*: Write a LaTeX document that includes a 2x2 matrix and a 3x3 matrix using the `bmatrix` environment. For example, create the matrix $\begin{bmatrix} 1 & 2 \\ 3 & 4 \end{bmatrix}$.

2. *Arrays in Math*: Use the `array` environment to create a mathematical array with different column alignments. Create an array with three columns, where the first column is left-aligned, the second is centered, and the third is right-aligned.

3. *Tables with Math*: Create a table that includes mathematical content (e.g., fractions, equations, or matrices). Format the table with at least three rows and three columns.

3.5 Advanced Math: Theorems, Proofs, and Equations

1. *Writing Theorems*: Define a custom LaTeX environment for a theorem using the `amsthm` package. Write a theorem in LaTeX that states: "If $x > 0$, then $x^2 > 0$."

2. *Proof Writing*: Use the `proof` environment to write a formal proof in LaTeX. For example, prove that if $a + b = c$, then $c - b = a$.

3. *Complex Equations*: Write a LaTeX document that includes a complex equation spanning multiple lines. Use the `align` environment from the `amsmath` package to display the following equation:

```
a^2 + b^2 = c^2 \quad \text{(Pythagorean
 theorem)}
```

Chapter 4

Figures, Tables, and Graphics

Contents

Md Aquib, *Fundamentals of LaTeX*, University Texts in the Mathematical Sciences,
https://doi.org/10.1007/978-981-96-9318-4_4

Abstract: Visual elements play a crucial role in enhancing the clarity and effectiveness of a document. Whether you are writing a research article, a thesis, or a presentation, the ability to include well-designed figures, organized tables, and illustrative graphics is essential for conveying complex information in a digestible format.

Keywords: LaTeX figures, LaTeX tables, LaTeX graphics, Float environments, Table formatting, Captions and labels

This chapter focuses on how to work with non-textual content in LaTeX, particularly figures, tables, and images. You will learn how to insert external graphics using the `graphicx` package, how to position and scale images, and how to create figures with captions and labels that can be cross-referenced within the document. For data presentation, this chapter introduces the `tabular` environment and various techniques for constructing both simple and complex tables with proper alignment, borders, and multicolumn layouts.

We also explore floating environments such as `figure` and `table`, which allow LaTeX to automatically manage the placement of visual content while preserving layout consistency. Additionally, advanced features such as side-by-side figures and tables, subfigures, custom positioning, and graphic manipulation techniques are covered.

By the end of this chapter, you will be able to integrate high-quality visual components into your LaTeX documents, improving both their functionality and aesthetic appeal.

4.1 Inserting Images and Figures (Formats, Placement)

In LaTeX, including images and figures is an essential part of creating professional documents. Whether you are adding diagrams, photos, or illustrations, LaTeX provides powerful commands to help you control the placement, size, and format of images. In this section, we will explore how to insert images, adjust their size, and manage their placement.

4.1.1 Image Formats

When incorporating images into a LaTeX document, it is important to understand which image formats are supported and how they impact the final output. LaTeX is primarily designed for high-quality document preparation, and the choice of image format plays a crucial role in ensuring clarity, resolution, and file compatibility.

LaTeX supports a variety of image formats, each suited to different types of content.

PNG (Portable Network Graphics)

The PNG format is widely used for images that require transparency or have simple color palettes. It is a raster image format that supports lossless compression, meaning that no quality is lost when saving or displaying the image. PNG is particularly useful for diagrams, logos, and illustrations with sharp edges.

Inserting a PNG Image

LaTeX Code:

```
\documentclass{article}
\usepackage{graphicx}
\begin{document}
\begin{figure}[h]
\centering
\includegraphics[width=0.5
\textwidth]{image.png}
\caption{n example of a
PNG image}
\label{fig:png}
\end{figure}
\end{document}
```

Output:

JPEG (Joint Photographic Experts Group)

The JPEG format is commonly used for photographs and complex images with many colors. Unlike PNG, JPEG uses lossy compression, which reduces file size but may also slightly degrade image quality. It is an excellent choice for high-resolution images where transparency is not required.

Inserting a JPEG Image

LaTeX Code:

```
\documentclass{article}
\usepackage{graphicx}
\begin{document}
\begin{figure}[h]
\centering
\includegraphics[width=0.6
\textwidth]{photo.jpg}
\caption{A sample JPEG
image}
\label{fig:jpeg}
\end{figure}
\end{document}
```

Output:

PDF (Portable Document Format)

The PDF format is highly preferred for vector-based images and graphics, as it allows for excellent scalability without any loss of quality. It is especially useful for diagrams, charts, and technical drawings created using tools such as Adobe Illustrator, Inkscape, or TikZ.

One major advantage of PDF images is that they integrate seamlessly into LaTeX documents compiled using the `pdflatex` engine. Since PDFs are vector-based, they maintain their sharpness at any zoom level, making them ideal for printed materials.

Inserting a PDF Image

LaTeX Code:

```
\documentclass{article}
\usepackage{graphicx}
\begin{document}
\begin{figure}[h]
\centering
\includegraphics[width=0.5
\textwidth]{diagram.pdf}
\caption{A vector-based
PDF image}
\label{fig:pdf}
\end{figure}
\end{document}
```

Output:

EPS (Encapsulated PostScript)

EPS is an older vector format that remains useful for documents compiled with the traditional `latex` engine, which does not support direct inclusion of PDF, PNG, or JPEG images. If you are working with EPS files, they need to be converted into PDF if you are using `pdflatex`.

Inserting an EPS Image

```
\documentclass{article}
\usepackage{graphicx}
\begin{document}
\begin{figure}[h]
    \centering
    \includegraphics[width=0.5
     \textwidth]{figure.eps}
    \caption{An example of an
    EPS image}
    \label{fig:eps}
\end{figure}
\end{document}
```

Choosing the Right Image Format

The choice of image format depends on the type of image and its intended purpose in the document:

- *PNG*: Best for transparent images, logos, and simple graphics
- *JPEG*: Best for photographs and images with rich colors
- *PDF*: Best for vector graphics, technical drawings, and scalable illustrations

- *EPS*: Useful for compatibility with older LaTeX distributions

When creating professional documents, it is advisable to use vector formats (PDF or EPS) for diagrams and mathematical illustrations, while raster formats (PNG or JPEG) should be used for photos or detailed images.

By selecting the appropriate format and ensuring correct image placement, LaTeX users can maintain a high level of clarity and quality in their documents.

4.1.2 Inserting and Placing Images in LaTeX

Figures and images are integral to many LaTeX documents, particularly in technical and academic writing. Whether used for illustrations, scientific diagrams, or data visualizations, images enhance the clarity and impact of a document. LaTeX offers robust image-handling capabilities through the `graphicx` package, allowing users to insert and customize images efficiently.

Loading the `graphicx` Package

Before inserting images, it is essential to load the `graphicx` package in the document preamble. This package provides all necessary functionalities for managing images in LaTeX.

Loading the `graphicx` Package

```
\documentclass{article}
\usepackage{graphicx}

\begin{document}

% Document content
```

```
\end{document}
```

Once the graphicx package is loaded, the \includegraphics command becomes available for inserting images.

Basic Image Insertion

To insert an image, the \includegraphics command is used. The syntax is straightforward:

Basic Image Insertion

LaTeX Code:

```
\includegraphics[width=0.5
\textwidth]{image.png}
```

Explanation:

- \includegraphics: The command that inserts an image
- [width=0.5\textwidth]: Specifies that the image should occupy 50% of the text width
- {image.png}: The file name of the image (must be in the same directory or referenced with a relative path)

This command simply places the image at the point where it is called in the document. However, this may not always be desirable, as LaTeX will insert the image in a way that may disrupt the flow of text. To handle images more effectively, the figure environment is recommended.

Using Relative and Absolute Paths

When working with multiple images, it is a good practice to store them in a dedicated folder, such as `figures/`, to keep the project organized. Images can then be inserted using relative paths.

Using Relative Paths

LaTeX Code:

```
\includegraphics[width=0.8\textwidth]
{figures/chapter1/image1.png}
```

Explanation:
This command instructs LaTeX to locate the image in the `figures/chapter1/` subdirectory.

Alternatively, an absolute path can be used when the image is located outside the working directory. However, using relative paths is generally preferable, as it ensures better portability of the document.

Best Practices for Image Management in LaTeX

To maintain a structured and efficient workflow, consider the following best practices when handling images in LaTeX:

- Organize images in a dedicated folder (e.g., `figures/`) for better document management.
- Use relative paths instead of absolute paths to ensure portability across different systems.
- Prefer vector image formats such as PDF or EPS for diagrams and graphs to maintain resolution quality.
- When including raster images (PNG, JPEG), ensure they have sufficient resolution for print quality.

- Always provide captions and labels to facilitate referencing within the document.

These guidelines help streamline the document creation process and prevent issues related to image loading and formatting.

4.1.3 Controlling Image Placement

LaTeX provides a sophisticated mechanism for handling image placement within documents. By default, LaTeX determines the most suitable location for an image based on its internal algorithms, ensuring optimal page layout and spacing. However, in many cases, authors may wish to control exactly where an image appears in relation to the surrounding text. This can be achieved using the `figure` environment along with placement specifiers.

Using the Figure Environment

The most effective way to manage image placement in LaTeX is through the `figure` environment. This environment allows you to insert an image while adding essential components such as captions, reference labels, and positioning options.

Inserting an Image with the Figure Environment

LaTeX Code:

```
\begin{figure}[h]
\centering
\includegraphics[width=0.5
\textwidth]{image.png}
\caption{An example image with a
caption}
\label{fig:example}
\end{figure}
```

Explanation:

- `\begin{figure}[h]`: Creates a floating figure environment and suggests placing the image "here" using the `h` option.
- `\centering`: Centers the image horizontally.
- `\includegraphics[width=0.5\textwidth]{image.png}`: Inserts an image and scales it to 50% of the text width.
- `\caption{}`: Provides a descriptive caption below the image.
- `\label{}`: Assigns a label to the image, enabling cross-referencing within the document.

The `\label` command allows authors to reference figures dynamically without manually specifying numbers. When an image is referenced elsewhere in the text, the figure number updates automatically.

Referencing Figures

LaTeX Code:

```
See Figure
\ref{fig:example}
for an example image.
```

Output:

See Figure (1) for an example image.

Using the `\ref` command ensures that the correct figure number is referenced, even if figures are added or reordered in the document.

Placement Options for Figures

LaTeX offers several placement specifiers that guide where the figure should appear in the document. While LaTeX makes automatic decisions about placement, these options provide additional control.

The placement specifiers include:

- `h` (Here)—Places the figure at the exact location where it is defined in the source code, if possible.
- `t` (Top)—Positions the figure at the top of the current or next page.
- `b` (Bottom)—Moves the figure to the bottom of the page.
- `p` (Page of floats)—Places the figure on a separate page dedicated to floats (figures and tables).

These placement specifiers can be combined to allow LaTeX to choose the best position from multiple options. For example:

Combining Placement Options

LaTeX Code:

```
\begin{figure}[htbp]
\centering
\includegraphics[width=0.6\textwidth]
{example.png}
\caption{A figure with multiple
placement options}
\end{figure}
```

Explanation:

- h – Try placing the figure "here" in the document.
- t – If not possible, place it at the top of the page.
- b – If neither option works, place it at the bottom of the page.
- p – As a last resort, move it to a dedicated page for figures.

Forcing Image Placement

Sometimes, even with placement specifiers, LaTeX may still move an image due to space constraints. In such cases, the optional argument ! (force) can be used to influence LaTeX's decision-making.

Forcing Image Placement

LaTeX Code:

```
\begin{figure}[!h]
\centering
\includegraphics[width=0.6\textwidth]
{example.png}
\caption{Forcing the figure to appear
at a specific position}
\end{figure}
```

Explanation:
The `!` symbol forces LaTeX to place the figure in the specified location, even if it slightly disrupts the text flow.

Using the Float Package for More Control

The default behavior of LaTeX's floating figures may sometimes result in images not appearing exactly where intended. The `float` package provides an additional specifier, `H`, which forces figures to be placed exactly where they appear in the document.

To use the `float` package, add the following line in the document preamble:

Loading the Float Package

```
\usepackage{float}
```

After loading the package, use the `H` specifier:

Using H to Fix Image Placement

```
\begin{figure}[H]
\centering
\includegraphics[width=0.5\textwidth]
{fixed_image.png}
\caption{A figure forced to remain in place}
\end{figure}
```

The `H` specifier forces the figure to stay at the defined position, overriding LaTeX's default floating behavior.

Understanding image placement in LaTeX ensures that figures are positioned effectively, improving document readability and presentation.

Best Practices for Image Handling

When working with images in a LaTeX document, adhering to a few best practices can significantly improve both the quality and efficiency of the final output. To begin with, it is advisable to use vector graphics formats such as PDF, EPS, or SVG for diagrams and plots, as these formats scale without loss of resolution and maintain visual clarity in printed or zoomed views. If raster images like PNG or JPEG are used, one should ensure that they are of sufficiently high resolution to avoid pixelation, while also being cautious not to include overly large or heavily compressed images that may introduce artifacts or bloat the document size.

For organizational clarity and project maintenance, image files should be placed in logically named subdirectories, such as `figures/chapter1/` or `images/appendices/`, making it easier to manage assets and update them when needed. The use of the `clip` and `trim` options in the `\includegraphics` command can help remove unwanted whitespace or borders around images, which contributes to a more polished appearance.

Proper placement control is also important. LaTeX provides placement specifiers (like `h`, `t`, `b`, and `p`) to influence where figures appear. Using these judiciously ensures that figures are positioned logically in relation to the surrounding text without disrupting the reading flow.

Finally, authors should be mindful of compilation performance. Large or uncompressed image files can slow down the document build process, especially in long projects. In such cases, pre-optimizing images using external tools (such as image compressors or converters) can enhance efficiency without compromising quality.

By observing these practices, LaTeX users can ensure that their images are not only visually appealing and professionally presented but also well-managed within the document's structure.

4.1.4 Adjusting Image Size

Properly resizing images is an essential aspect of document preparation in LaTeX, ensuring that figures fit seamlessly within the text without disrupting the layout. The `graphicx` package provides several options to control image dimensions precisely, allowing for width and height adjustments as well as proportional scaling.

Depending on the document structure and formatting requirements, images can be resized in different ways:

1. Adjusting image width relative to the text width
2. Specifying a fixed height while maintaining proportions
3. Scaling the image proportionally to a percentage of its original size

4. Defining both width and height explicitly

Each of these methods offers flexibility in controlling image placement, ensuring they remain visually appealing without disrupting the document's flow.

Adjusting Image Width

One of the most effective ways to resize an image while maintaining readability is by defining its width relative to the text width. This approach ensures that the image scales dynamically with the document, making it particularly useful for documents with variable page sizes.

Setting Image Width

LaTeX Code:

```
\includegraphics[width=0.75\textwidth]
{image.png}
```

Explanation:

- The `width` option scales the image to 75% of the text width.
- This ensures that the image does not overflow beyond the document margins.
- It is ideal for maintaining a proportional and balanced layout.

Adjusting Image Height

In some cases, you may need to control the height of an image while allowing LaTeX to adjust the width accordingly. This is particularly useful when dealing with figures that need to fit within a defined space, such as those appearing in tables or multicolumn layouts.

Setting Image Height

LaTeX Code:

```
\includegraphics[height=3cm]{image.png}
```

Explanation:

- The `height` option specifies the exact height of the image.
- The width is adjusted automatically to maintain the aspect ratio.
- This method prevents unwanted distortion while ensuring a uniform layout.

Scaling an Image Proportionally

If maintaining the image's original proportions is a priority, the `scale` option provides a straightforward way to resize images while preserving their aspect ratio. This is useful for reducing large images without needing to manually calculate height and width adjustments.

Scaling an Image Proportionally

LaTeX Code:

```
\includegraphics[scale=0.5]{image.png}
```

Explanation:

- The `scale` option shrinks the image to 50% of its original size.

- This preserves the proportions while reducing the overall size.
- Ideal for resizing vector-based images like PDFs without losing quality.

Setting Both Height and Width

In certain scenarios, you may need to define both the width and height of an image explicitly. This approach is useful when working with images that require specific dimensions, but caution should be taken to avoid distortion.

Setting Both Height and Width

LaTeX Code:

```
\includegraphics[width=4cm, height=5cm]
{image.png}
```

Explanation:

- Both width and height are defined explicitly.
- LaTeX does not preserve the aspect ratio, so distortion may occur.
- Best used for logos or icons where proportions are not critical.

4.1.5 Best Practices for Resizing Images

Resizing images in LaTeX is a common task, especially when preparing technical or academic documents that integrate visual content alongside text. To achieve a consistent and polished result, it is essential to follow several best practices when manipulating image dimensions.

A highly recommended approach is to scale images relative to the current text width, for instance, specifying a width such as `width=0.8\textwidth` in the `\includegraphics` command. This technique ensures that images adjust gracefully across various document layouts, whether printed on standard paper or displayed in different digital formats. Such relative scaling not only improves the adaptability of the document but also guarantees a cohesive alignment with surrounding content.

When adjusting size, it is also important to maintain the original aspect ratio of the image. This can be done by setting either the width or the height, but not both simultaneously, unless a deliberate distortion is required. Preserving proportions helps prevent images from appearing stretched or squashed, which can distract readers and diminish the overall professionalism of the document.

In terms of file optimization, large high-resolution images should be scaled down to appropriate dimensions before being included in the document. Oversized images can significantly increase the file size of the compiled PDF and slow down the compilation process. Simple preprocessing using an image editor can substantially reduce file size while maintaining acceptable visual quality.

Finally, when working with diagrams or line-based illustrations, vector formats such as PDF or EPS are preferred. These formats scale infinitely without loss of resolution, making them ideal for technical illustrations, plots, and flowcharts. Unlike raster formats like PNG or JPEG, vector graphics remain sharp regardless of how much they are resized.

Thoughtful resizing not only enhances the clarity and readability of the final document but also contributes to a well-structured and visually coherent layout. In the subsequent section, we will examine techniques for rotating and mirroring images, expanding the range of visual customization available in LaTeX.

4.1.6 Image Rotation and Cropping

In many LaTeX documents, particularly technical reports and research papers, images need to be rotated or cropped to fit within the layout properly. The `graphicx` package provides built-in commands to manipulate images easily, allowing users to control orientation and trim unnecessary portions without modifying the original image files.

This section explores:

1. Rotating images using the `angle` option.

2. Cropping images using the `trim` and `clip` options.

Rotating an Image

The `angle` option in LaTeX enables precise rotation of images, helping to adjust orientation for better alignment with the text. This is particularly useful for scanned documents, landscape-oriented figures, and rotated diagrams.

To rotate an image, the basic syntax is:

Rotating an Image

LaTeX Code:

```
\includegraphics[angle=90,width=
0.5\textwidth]{example-image.png}
```

Explanation:

- The `angle=90` command rotates the image by 90 degrees counterclockwise.

- The optional `width=0.5\textwidth` ensures the image remains within the document margins.
- Any angle can be used, including negative values to rotate clockwise.

Example: Rotating an image by 45 degrees:

Rotating by 45 Degrees

LaTeX Code:

```
\includegraphics[angle=45,width=
0.5\textwidth]{example-image.png}
```

Explanation:

- The `angle=45` option rotates the image by 45 degrees counterclockwise.
- This is useful for slight adjustments in document layout.

Cropping an Image

In some cases, images contain unnecessary margins or whitespace that need to be removed. LaTeX provides the `trim` option to crop images from specific sides while preserving the original proportions.

The `clip` command ensures that only the trimmed region is displayed. Without `clip`, LaTeX will retain the entire image even after applying `trim`.

The basic syntax for cropping an image is:

Cropping an Image

LaTeX Code:

```
\includegraphics[trim=1cm 1cm 1cm 1cm,
clip, width=0.5\textwidth]
{example-image.png}
```

Explanation:

- The `trim` option removes 1 cm from each side (left, bottom, right, and top).
- The `clip` option ensures only the trimmed portion is displayed.
- Useful for removing unnecessary margins or aligning figures within the document layout.

Syntax for Trim Option:

```
trim=left bottom right top, clip
```

Example: Cropping only from the left and top:

Asymmetric Cropping

LaTeX Code:

```
\includegraphics[trim=2cm 0cm
0cm 1cm, clip, width=0.5
\textwidth]{example-image.png}
```

Explanation:

- The image is cropped by 2 cm from the left and 1 cm from the top.
- No cropping is applied to the right and bottom.
- Helps remove unnecessary white space while preserving key details.

4.1.7 Best Practices for Image Rotation and Cropping

When incorporating rotation and cropping into image handling in LaTeX, certain guidelines help maintain both the quality of presentation and the readability of the document. Carefully managing these transformations ensures that visual elements are not only stylistically aligned with the surrounding text but also technically sound for typesetting.

One of the most important considerations is the choice of image format. Whenever possible, it is recommended to use vector-based formats such as `.pdf` or `.eps` for images that may be rotated. Unlike raster formats like `.png` or `.jpg`, vector images retain their sharpness regardless of orientation, preventing pixelation and ensuring a consistent appearance across output devices.

While rotation can be a useful design element, for instance, when displaying vertical figures or labels, it should be applied with restraint. Excessive or unnecessary rotation may interfere with the flow of reading, particularly in technical documents where diagrams and tables must be interpreted precisely. A rotated table that runs counter to the reading direction can become a visual hurdle rather than a helpful aid.

Cropping is another valuable technique that allows you to focus attention on the relevant part of an image or remove extraneous whitespace. However, when cropping, it is essential to ensure that key content is not inadvertently trimmed. Alignment should be carefully reviewed after any cropping adjustments to confirm that the image integrates seamlessly with its caption and surroundings.

Interestingly, cropping in LaTeX allows not only reduction but also expansion of an image's bounding box. This is accomplished using negative values in the `trim` option—for example, `trim=-1cm -1cm -1cm -1cm`. Such an approach is particularly helpful when recovering clipped edges or adjusting alignment beyond the image's native dimensions.

Finally, after any rotation or cropping is applied, it is important to recompile the document and inspect the output. Visual elements, especially those spanning multiple columns or floating near text, may shift unexpectedly. Regular compilation helps catch these issues early, allowing for timely refinements and ensuring that the final layout remains polished and professional.

In the following section, we will explore advanced image positioning strategies, such as wrapping text around figures, to further enhance document design and readability.

4.2 Creating Tables (Basic Tables, Multicolumn, Multirow)

Tables are a fundamental way to organize data in a structured, easy-to-read format. LaTeX provides a versatile and robust `tabular` environment that allows you to create basic tables, as well as more complex layouts with multiple columns and rows. In this section, we will explore how to create basic tables, multicolumn tables, and multirow tables in LaTeX.

4.2.1 Basic Tables in LaTeX

Tables are an essential element in structured documents, allowing data to be presented in a clear and organized format. In LaTeX, tables are created using the `tabular` environment, which provides a framework for defining rows and columns. The number of columns and their alignment are specified at the beginning of the `tabular` environment. Each column is separated by an ampersand (&) within a row, and rows are ended with a double backslash (\\). Horizontal lines can be introduced using the `\hline` command to improve readability.

The following example demonstrates a simple table with three columns, where each column is centered, and horizontal and vertical lines are used to separate the entries.

Creating a Simple Table

```
\begin{tabular}{|c|c|c|}
\hline
Header 1 & Header 2 & Header 3 \\
\hline
Row 1, Col 1 & Row 1, Col 2 & Row 1, Col 3 \\
\hline
Row 2, Col 1 & Row 2, Col 2 & Row 2, Col 3 \\
\hline
\end{tabular}
```

Rendered Output (Table 4.1):

Header 1	Header 2	Header 3
Row 1, Col 1	Row 1, Col 2	Row 1, Col 3
Row 2, Col 1	Row 2, Col 2	Row 2, Col 3

Table 4.1: A basic three-column table in LaTeX

In this example, three columns are defined, each centered within its respective cell. The specification |c|c|c| ensures that all three columns are centered and that vertical lines separate them. The `\hline` command is used to introduce horizontal lines at the beginning, between rows, and at the end of the table to create a structured appearance.

Tables in LaTeX offer great flexibility in terms of formatting and styling. Depending on the content, columns can be aligned to the left, center, or right, and rows can contain a mix of text and numerical data. For numerical tables, right-aligned columns often improve readability, whereas general content tables may use left or center alignment.

While simple tables can be created using the basic `tabular` environment, LaTeX also provides options for formatting tables further, such as merging multiple columns into a single cell, spanning rows across multiple lines, and customizing column width and spacing. These advanced techniques, discussed in subsequent sections, enhance the visual presentation and utility of tables in documents that require complex data structuring.

Understanding the basic structure of tables in LaTeX lays the foundation for creating more sophisticated table designs. Once the fundamentals are in place, it becomes easier to manipulate tables by adjusting alignments, merging cells, or incorporating external packages for further customization. These additional refinements will be explored in the following sections.

4.2.2 Column Alignment and Formatting

Proper alignment of columns in a table is crucial for clarity and readability. LaTeX provides flexible options for aligning column contents, allowing users to specify whether the text or numerical values should be aligned to the left, center, or right. The choice of alignment depends on the nature of the data. For instance, numerical values are often right-aligned to facilitate comparisons, whereas general text content may be centered or left-aligned for better readability.

In the `tabular` environment, column alignment is specified within curly braces immediately after defining the table. The three primary alignment options available in LaTeX are:

- Left alignment, denoted by `l`, ensures that all entries in the corresponding column are aligned to the left.
- Center alignment, represented by `c`, centers the content within the column width.
- Right alignment, denoted by `r`, aligns entries to the right, which is particularly useful for numerical data.

Additionally, vertical lines can be inserted between columns by using the pipe symbol (`|`) to visually separate different sections of the table.

Consider the following example, which illustrates a table with mixed alignment for its columns. The first column is left-aligned, the second column is centered, and the third column is right-aligned (Table 4.2).

Aligning Table Columns

LaTeX Code:

```
\begin{tabular}{|l|c|r|}
\hline
Left & Center & Right \\
\hline
Item 1 & Value 1 & 10.5 \\
Item 2 & Value 2 & 20.75 \\
\hline
\end{tabular}
```

Output:

Left	Center	Right
Item 1	Value 1	10.5
Item 2	Value 2	20.75

Table 4.2: Example of mixed column alignments

In this example, the first column aligns text to the left, making it more readable when dealing with long strings or descriptive labels. The second column is centered, which works well for categorical values or labels, while the third column is right-aligned, ensuring numerical values line up properly, making them easier to compare.

The alignment of columns plays a significant role in structuring tables for different purposes. For instance, tables used for financial reports often require numerical data to be right-aligned for better comparison, whereas tables displaying textual information may use left or center alignment for aesthetic balance.

While defining column alignment, it is also possible to adjust the column width and spacing between them using additional formatting options, such as `p{}` for defining fixed-width columns or using the `array` package to introduce further customization. However, for most standard applications, the built-in alignment options in LaTeX provide sufficient control over the table's layout.

Understanding how to align table columns appropriately is a fundamental aspect of table formatting in LaTeX. Once the basic alignment principles are mastered, additional refinements such as merging multiple columns or rows, adjusting table width, and incorporating captions or footnotes can further enhance the presentation of tabular data. These advanced table formatting techniques will be explored in subsequent sections.

4.2.3 Adding Multicolumn Cells

In some cases, a table requires a single cell to span across multiple columns instead of being confined to just one. This is particularly useful when creating headers that extend over multiple columns or when combining columns to group related data. In LaTeX, this can be accomplished using the `\multicolumn` command, which allows merging of adjacent columns into a single larger cell.

The `\multicolumn` command takes three arguments:

- The number of columns to be merged
- The alignment and border specification
- The text that will appear inside the merged cell

The following example demonstrates how to use the `\multicolumn` command to create a table where the header spans across three columns.

Multicolumn Cells

```
\begin{tabular}{|c|c|c|}
\hline
\multicolumn{3}{|c|}
{Header spanning three columns} \\
\hline
Row 1, Col 1 & Row 1, Col 2 & Row 1, Col 3 \\
\hline
Row 2, Col 1 & Row 2, Col 2 & Row 2, Col 3 \\
\hline
\end{tabular}
```

This will display (Table 4.3):
In this example, the first row features a header that extends across three columns, achieved by using:

Header spanning three columns		
Row 1, Col 1	Row 1, Col 2	Row 1, Col 3
Row 2, Col 1	Row 2, Col 2	Row 2, Col 3

Table 4.3: Multiple-column cell

```
\multicolumn{3}{|c|}{Header Spanning 3 Columns}
```

Here, the number `3` specifies that three columns should be merged, the `|c|` argument centers the text while preserving vertical borders, and the final argument is the text to be displayed within the merged cell.

Multicolumn formatting is particularly useful for structuring complex tables, especially when dealing with hierarchical data or headers that span multiple sections. In financial reports, for example, it is common to see headers that cover both revenue and expense categories in a single row. Similarly, scientific tables frequently merge multiple columns to organize experimental data into related groups.

Another practical use of multicolumn cells is to create subheadings within a table. The example below shows how two columns are merged under separate sections (Table 4.4).

Example of Merging Two Columns

LaTeX Code:

```
\begin{tabular}{|c|c|c|}
\hline
Category & \multicolumn{2}
{|c|}{Details} \\
\hline
Item 1 & Data 1 & Data 2 \\
\hline
Item 2 & Data 3 & Data 4 \\
```

```
\hline
\end{tabular}
```

Output:

Category	Details	
Item 1	Data 1	Data 2
Item 2	Data 3	Data 4

Table 4.4: Example of a two-column merge

In this case, the "Details" section spans two columns, making it clear that the next two columns belong to a common category.

When designing tables, care should be taken to use multicolumn formatting only when necessary. Overuse of merged columns can make the table harder to read and process. It is also advisable to ensure that merged headers or cells align properly with the data below them, maintaining consistency throughout the table.

Multicolumn cells offer a powerful way to improve the organization and readability of tables in LaTeX. By using the `\multicolumn` command, users can create visually appealing tables that effectively group and structure information. When combined with other table formatting techniques such as multirow cells, spacing adjustments, and table captions, the presentation of tabular data can be significantly enhanced. The next section explores how to span multiple rows within a table, further increasing the versatility of LaTeX tables.

4.2.4 Adding Multirow Cells

For rows that need to span multiple cells, you will need the `multirow` package, which provides the `\multirow` command. To use it, first include the `multirow` package in your preamble as:

```
\usepackage{multirow}
```

Multirow Cells

```
\usepackage{multirow}
% Load this in the preamble

\begin{tabular}{|c|c|c|}
\hline
\multirow{2}{*}{Row spanning two rows}
& Row 1, Col 2
& Row 1, Col 3 \\
\cline{2-3}
& Row 2, Col 2 & Row 2, Col 3\\
\hline
\end{tabular}
```

This will display (Table 4.5):

Row Spanning 2 Rows	Row 1, Col 2	Row 1, Col 3
	Row 2, Col 2	Row 2, Col 3

Table 4.5: Multiple-row cell

In this case:

- `\multirow{2}{*}{Row Spanning 2 Rows}`: This creates a cell that spans two rows. The `*` argument tells LaTeX to automatically calculate the width of the cell.

- \cline{2-3}: This command draws a horizontal line only between the second and third columns.

4.2.5 Adding Multirow Cells

In certain table layouts, it is useful to have a single cell span multiple rows, especially when categorizing information under a shared label. This is commonly needed in tables with hierarchical data structures or in cases where multiple rows belong to a single overarching category. LaTeX enables this functionality through the \multirow command, which is provided by the multirow package.

Before using multirow cells, ensure that the multirow package is included in the document preamble:

Loading the Multirow Package

```
\usepackage{multirow}
```

Once the package is loaded, the \multirow command can be used to merge adjacent rows into a single larger cell. The command follows the syntax:

```
\multirow{number of rows}{width}{content}
```

The first argument specifies how many rows the cell should span. The second argument defines the width of the merged cell (using an asterisk * allows automatic width calculation). The third argument contains the text or content that will appear inside the merged cell.

The following example demonstrates a table where the first column contains a multirow cell that spans two rows (Table 4.6).

Creating Multirow Cells

LaTeX Code:

```
\begin{tabular}{|c|c|c|}
\hline
\multirow{2}{*}{Category}&Item &Value\\
\cline{2-3}
& Item 1 & 10.5 \\
\hline
Category B & Item 2 & 20.75 \\
\hline
\end{tabular}
```

Output:

Category	Item	Value
	Item 1	10.5
Category B	Item 2	20.75

Table 4.6: A table with multirow cells

In this table, the first column entry "Category" spans two rows, while the second and third columns retain their individual row structure. The `\cline` command ensures that horizontal lines are applied selectively to the necessary columns, preserving the visual separation of row content.

Multirow cells are particularly useful when dealing with data sets where multiple rows belong to the same category but differ in other attributes. This technique is frequently used in statistical tables, product comparisons, and research papers where grouping data logically enhances readability.

4.2.6 Combining Multicolumn and Multirow

A more complex example involves combining multirow and multicolumn cells. Below, the "Group A" label spans two rows, while "Details" spans two columns (Table 4.7).

Combining Multirow and Multicolumn Cells

LaTeX Code:

```
\begin{tabular}{|c|c|c|}
\hline
\multirow{2}{*}{Group A} &
\multicolumn{2}{|c|}{Details} \\
\cline{2-3}
& Item 1 & Value 1 \\
\hline
Group B & Item 2 & Value 2 \\
\hline
\end{tabular}
```

Output:

Group A	Details	
	Item 1	Value 1
Group B	Item 2	Value 2

Table 4.7: Example of multirow and multicolumn combination

Here, "Group A" extends over two rows, while "Details" spans two columns in the first row. This approach is useful for clearly organizing related data while reducing redundancy in labels.

When using multirow cells, it is important to keep alignment consistent across different sections of the table to maintain readability. Excessive use of merged rows may lead to formatting inconsistencies, so it is best to use this feature only when necessary to improve clarity.

By combining multirow and multicolumn techniques, LaTeX users can construct complex, well-organized tables that effectively present hierarchical or structured data. The next section explores how to further refine tables by adjusting spacing and customizing borders.

4.2.7 Creating Tables with the `longtable` Environment

When working with extensive tabular data in LaTeX, the `longtable` environment offers a practical solution for tables that span multiple pages. Unlike the standard `tabular` environment, which confines tables to a single page, `longtable` allows tables to automatically break across pages while maintaining column formatting, headers, and footers.

Before using `longtable`, ensure that the package is included in the document preamble:

Loading the Longtable Package

```
\usepackage{longtable}
```

The `longtable` environment functions similarly to `tabular` but introduces specific commands for defining repeated headers and footers. Below is a simple example demonstrating its usage.

Creating a Multipage Table with longtable

LaTeX Code:

```
\begin{longtable}{|c|c|c|}
\hline
\textbf{Column 1} & \textbf{Column 2} &
\textbf{Column 3} \\
\hline
\endfirsthead

\hline
\textbf{Column 1} & \textbf{Column 2} &
\textbf{Column 3} \\
\hline
\endhead

\hline
\multicolumn{3}{|r|}{Continued on next page}\\
\hline
\endfoot

\hline
\endlastfoot

Row 1  & Data 1  & Value 1  \\
Row 2  & Data 2  & Value 2  \\
Row 3  & Data 3  & Value 3  \\
...    & ...     & ...      \\
Row 50 & Data 50 & Value 50 \\
\end{longtable}
```

Rendered output (Table 4.8):

Column 1	**Column 2**	**Column 3**
Row 1	Data 1	Value 1
Row 2	Data 2	Value 2
Row 3	Data 3	Value 3
...	...	...
Row 50	Data 50	Value 50

Table 4.8: A multipage table using the `longtable` environment

In this table, the `\endfirsthead`, `\endhead`, `\endfoot`, and `\endlastfoot` commands ensure that headers are repeated at the beginning of each page, while footnotes and end markers are handled correctly.

The key elements in this example are:

- `\endfirsthead`: Defines the first header, which appears only at the beginning of the table.
- `\endhead`: Specifies headers repeated on subsequent pages.
- `\endfoot`: Adds a footer at the bottom of each page, often containing "Continued on next page."
- `\endlastfoot`: Marks the final footer, appearing only on the last page.

The `longtable` environment is particularly useful in research papers, financial reports, and any document requiring multipage tables. It maintains a structured layout while ensuring readability across multiple pages.

Customization options, such as adjusting column widths, adding multirow and multicolumn cells, and incorporating captions, further enhance its usability. The next sections explore these advanced formatting techniques in greater detail.

4.2.8 Best Practices for Tables in LaTeX

Tables are essential elements in academic and technical documents, allowing structured data to be presented in a concise and readable format. When working with tables in LaTeX, certain practices can help ensure that the resulting layout is both aesthetically pleasing and easy to interpret.

To begin with, the `table` environment should be used whenever a table is intended to have a caption, label, or float behavior. This environment enables LaTeX to position tables appropriately, maintaining a logical flow in the document while supporting cross-referencing and consistent formatting. Within this environment, it is recommended to center tables using the `\centering` command. This alignment not only contributes to a balanced page design but also enhances visual consistency when multiple tables are present across the document.

Another important consideration is the visual simplicity of the table. Excessive use of borders, particularly vertical rules, can make tables appear cluttered and reduce readability. Instead, thoughtful use of horizontal lines, especially those provided by the `booktabs` package, can separate content effectively without overwhelming the reader. This minimalist approach helps highlight the data itself rather than the structure around it.

Clarity should also guide the choice of the number of columns. While LaTeX supports complex table layouts, it is advisable to avoid overly wide tables with many columns, especially if the document is intended for print. Wide tables may spill into the margins or require scaling, both of which can compromise legibility. If necessary, consider rotating the table or breaking it into smaller, logically grouped subtables.

Every table should be labeled using the `\label` command immediately after the `\caption` command. This allows the table to be referenced precisely elsewhere in the text using `\ref` or `\autoref`, aiding the reader in locating supplementary information.

By following these practices, authors can produce tables that are not only functional but also harmonious with the typographic style of the document. Well-formatted tables improve both the aesthetic and communicative quality of a LaTeX document, ensuring that data presentation aligns with the standards of academic and professional writing.

4.3 Floating Figures and Tables

In LaTeX, figures and tables often need to be positioned dynamically to maintain an organized and visually appealing layout. Instead of placing them exactly where they appear in the code, LaTeX uses floating environments such as the `figure` and `table` environments, which allow the document to adjust their placement automatically. These floating environments help maintain readability by preventing large blank spaces and ensuring tables and figures do not break across pages unnecessarily.

4.3.1 Floating Figures

Figures play an essential role in mathematical and scientific writing, helping to visualize data, illustrate concepts, and provide supporting diagrams. In LaTeX, figures are inserted using the `figure` environment, which ensures they are positioned optimally.

A basic floating figure in LaTeX can be created as follows:

Floating Figure Example

LaTeX Code:

```
\begin{figure}[htbp]
```

```
    \centering
    \includegraphics[width=0.5\textwidth]
    {example-image.png}
    \caption{A floating figure example}
    \label{fig:floating_example}
\end{figure}
```

Rendered Output (Fig. 4.1):

Figure 4.1: A floating figure example

The floating behavior of figures is controlled using optional placement specifiers inside square brackets `[htbp]`. These placement specifiers suggest to LaTeX where to place the figure, though LaTeX may override these suggestions based on the document layout:

- *h* (here) – Suggests placing the figure exactly where it appears in the document.
- *t* (top) – Positions the figure at the top of the current or next page.
- *b* (bottom) – Places the figure at the bottom of the current or next page.
- *p* (page of floats) – Moves the figure to a separate page exclusively for figures and tables.

The `\centering` command ensures the image is centered within the figure environment. The `\includegraphics` command loads the specified image file (`example-image.png`) and resizes it to 50% of the text width. Below the image, `\caption{}` provides a description, while `\label{}` assigns a reference label, allowing the figure to be cited elsewhere using `\ref{fig:floating_example}`.

4.3.2 Floating Tables

Like figures, tables in LaTeX can also be floated using the `table` environment. This allows the document to adjust the positioning of tables dynamically while maintaining a structured layout.

A basic floating table can be created using the following LaTeX code:

Floating Table Example

LaTeX Code:

```
\begin{table}[htbp]
\centering
\begin{tabular}{|c|c|c|}
\hline
Column 1 & Column 2 & Column 3 \\
\hline
Row 1, Col 1 & Row 1, Col 2 & Row 1, Col 3 \\
\hline
Row 2, Col 1 & Row 2, Col 2 & Row 2, Col 3 \\
\hline
\end{tabular}
\caption{A floating table example}
\label{tab:floating_example}
\end{table}
```

Rendered Output (Table 4.9):

Column 1	Column 2	Column 3
Row 1, Col 1	Row 1, Col 2	Row 1, Col 3
Row 2, Col 1	Row 2, Col 2	Row 2, Col 3

Table 4.9: A floating table example

The table environment functions similarly to the `figure` environment, using `[htbp]` as placement specifiers to control its position. The table content itself is defined using the `tabular` environment, where vertical and horizontal rules (| and `\hline`) help format the table neatly.

The `\centering` command centers the table on the page, while the `\caption{}` command provides a descriptive label for the table. The `\label{}` command assigns a reference, which allows the table to be cited elsewhere in the document using `\ref{tab:floating_example}`.

4.3.3 Best Practices for Floating Figures and Tables

In LaTeX, figures and tables are typically handled as floating environments. This design allows LaTeX to determine optimal placement based on page layout, white space, and typographic balance. While this automation contributes to a clean and professional appearance, authors can significantly enhance the effectiveness of their figures and tables by following a set of well-established practices.

A crucial component of floating environments is the inclusion of captions. Each figure or table should be accompanied by a descriptive caption introduced with the `\caption{}` command. Captions provide context and explanation for the visual content, ensuring that readers can understand the figure or table independently of the surrounding text. A well-written caption enhances the accessibility and instructional value of the document.

Equally important is the use of the `\label{}` command. Labels allow for internal cross-referencing, enabling the author to refer to figures and tables using commands such as `\ref{}` or `\autoref{}`. This feature improves navigation and readability, especially in longer or more technical documents where readers may need to reference diagrams, charts, or data sets from various sections.

Although LaTeX manages float placement intelligently, it is advisable to guide the engine with placement specifiers. The combination `[htbp]`, which stands for "here," "top," "bottom," and "page," offers LaTeX the flexibility to place figures and tables where they fit best. However, the author can indicate a preference for placement near the reference point in the text by placing `[h]` at the beginning of the specifier.

It is also beneficial to position floats near the content that references them. This proximity maintains a coherent flow between the narrative and the associated visual or tabular information, reducing the cognitive load on the reader. Excessive separation between a float and its descriptive passage can cause confusion or diminish the impact of the illustration.

For documents requiring precise control over float behavior, especially in complex layouts, the `float` package can be employed. This package introduces the `[H]` specifier, which overrides LaTeX's standard float placement logic and forces the figure or table to appear precisely where it is declared. While this feature should be used judiciously, it can be particularly useful for side-by-side figures and tables, or when a float must remain on the same page as a specific paragraph.

Ultimately, by balancing LaTeX's automatic float handling with deliberate authorial input, through captions, labels, placement specifiers, and layout packages, figures and tables can significantly enhance both the clarity and aesthetics of a document. In the subsequent sections, we will delve into advanced techniques that build on these principles, including fine-tuning float spacing, customizing caption styles, and combining visual and tabular data within unified environments.

4.3.4 Controlling Placement with the Float Package

By default, LaTeX determines the optimal placement of figures and tables to maintain a well-structured document layout. While this automated approach works in most cases, there are times when authors need stricter control over where a figure or table appears. This is particularly useful when a figure should appear exactly at a certain location, rather than being moved to the top or bottom of a page.

To achieve this level of control, LaTeX provides the `float` package. This package introduces the `[H]` placement specifier, which overrides LaTeX's default floating behavior and ensures that the figure or table appears precisely at the specified location in the document.

Before using the `[H]` specifier, the `float` package must be included in the document preamble:

Loading the `float` Package

LaTeX Code:

```
\usepackage{float}
```

Once the package is loaded, the `[H]` specifier can be used inside a `figure` or `table` environment. The following example demonstrates how to insert a figure and force it to appear exactly where it is declared in the document.

Forcing LaTeX to Insert a Figure at a Specific Location

LaTeX Code:

```
\begin{figure}[H]
    \centering
    \includegraphics[width=0.5\textwidth]
    {example-image.png}
    \caption{A figure placed exactly here}
    \label{fig:exact_placement}
\end{figure}
```

In this example, the figure is forced to appear at the specified location using the `[H]` specifier. Unlike other placement options such as `[htbp]`, which allow LaTeX to move figures dynamically, the `[H]` specifier ensures strict placement control. This is useful in cases where an image must appear immediately after its reference in the text, such as in educational material or research papers where images and explanations need to be tightly coupled.

Similarly, tables can also be placed precisely using the `[H]` option. The following example demonstrates how to force a table to appear at an exact location in the document:

Forcing LaTeX to Insert a Table at a Specific Location

LaTeX Code:

```
\begin{table}[H]
    \centering
    \begin{tabular}{|c|c|c|}
        \hline
        Column 1 & Column 2 & Column 3 \\
        \hline
```

```
        A & B & C \\
        \hline
        D & E & F \\
        \hline
    \end{tabular}
    \caption{A table placed exactly here}
    \label{tab:exact_placement}
\end{table}
```

Rendered Output (Table 4.10):

Column 1	Column 2	Column 3
A	B	C
D	E	F

Table 4.10: A table placed exactly here

4.3.5 Best Practices for Using the [H] Specifier

The [H] placement specifier, introduced by the float package, is a powerful tool that allows authors to place figures and tables exactly at the point in the document where they are declared. Unlike LaTeX's standard float positioning, which optimizes the placement for overall visual appeal and spacing, the [H] option overrides this behavior, locking the float in place. While this can be useful in specific cases, it must be applied with careful consideration.

Absolute placement is most appropriate when a figure or table must appear immediately adjacent to a specific piece of content, such as when visual context is essential for comprehension or when preparing instructional material where figure placement is tightly synchronized with textual explanations. However, if flexibility in placement is permissible, it is generally preferable to use the `[htbp]` specifier instead. This combination grants LaTeX the freedom to optimize layout while still honoring the author's intent.

Overusing the `[H]` specifier can result in unintended formatting issues, such as large areas of blank space, awkward page breaks, or visual clutter when multiple fixed-position floats accumulate on a single page. Such issues not only disrupt the reading experience but also detract from the professional appearance of the document. It is important, therefore, to allow LaTeX's float management to function where possible, intervening only when necessary.

In all cases, whether using `[H]` or other placement options, authors should provide meaningful captions using the `\caption{}` command and assign unique `\label{}` identifiers to facilitate accurate cross-referencing. This ensures that even if floats shift position during typesetting, their narrative and navigational context within the document remains intact.

When multiple figures or tables must appear together in a controlled layout, a better alternative than forcing individual placement with `[H]` is to group them using environments such as `subfigure` or `subtable`. These packages allow for tightly integrated, visually coherent layouts without sacrificing LaTeX's ability to manage overall document flow.

4.3.6 Adding Captions and Labels

Figures and tables in LaTeX documents often require captions and labels to be referenced within the text. Captions provide descriptions that help readers understand the content of figures and tables, while labels allow authors to create numbered references throughout the document.

LaTeX offers two essential commands for this purpose:

- The `\caption` command, which adds a description beneath figures and tables
- The `\label` command, which assigns a reference label that can be recalled later using the `\ref` command

By integrating captions and labels, authors ensure that figures and tables are clearly documented and easily referenced within the text.

Using Captions in Tables

The `\caption` command is typically placed inside the `table` or `figure` environment, right after the content. The following example illustrates how to add a caption to a table:

Adding a Caption to a Table

LaTeX Code:

```
\begin{table}[H]
    \centering
    \begin{tabular}{|c|c|}
        \hline
        Name & Score \\
        \hline
        Alice & 90 \\
        Bob & 85 \\
        \hline
    \end{tabular}
    \caption{Scores of students}
\end{table}
```

Rendered Output (Table 4.11):

Name	Score
Alice	90
Bob	85

Table 4.11: Scores of students

In this example, the caption appears below the table and describes its contents, ensuring clarity for readers.

Assigning Labels and Referencing Tables

To reference a table within the text, the `\label` command is added immediately after the caption. This label is later recalled using the `\ref` command, which automatically inserts the correct table number.

The following example demonstrates how to add a label to a table:

Assigning a Label to a Table

LaTeX Code:

```
\begin{table}[H]
    \centering
    \begin{tabular}{|c|c|}
        \hline
        Name & Score \\
        \hline
        Alice & 90 \\
        Bob & 85 \\
        \hline
    \end{tabular}
    \caption{Scores of students}
    \label{tab:scores}
\end{table}
```

Rendered Output:

Name	Score
Alice	90
Bob	85

Table 4.12: Scores of students

With this label, the table can now be referenced anywhere in the document. For example, to refer to this table in a paragraph, one would write:

Referencing a Table

LaTeX Code:

```
See Table \ref{tab:scores} for student scores.
```

Rendered Output:
See Table 4.12 for student scores.

Adding Captions and Labels to Figures

The same approach applies to figures. The `\caption` and `\label` commands are used inside the `figure` environment to describe and reference images.

Adding Captions and Labels to a Figure

LaTeX Code:

```
\begin{figure}[H]
    \centering
    \includegraphics[width=0.5\textwidth]
    {example-image.png}
    \caption{An example image}
    \label{fig:image_example}
\end{figure}
```

Rendered Output:

Figure 4.2: An example image

Once a figure has a label, it can be referenced in the text using:

Referencing a Figure

LaTeX Code:

```
As shown in Figure \ref{fig:image_example},
the image demonstrates...
```

Rendered Output:

As shown in Figure 4.2, the image demonstrates...

Best Practices for Captions and Labels

In any well-structured LaTeX document, captions and labels play a vital role in organizing visual content such as figures and tables. They not only aid in the interpretation of visual elements but also enable precise cross-referencing, which is especially important in academic, technical, and scientific writing.

To begin with, every figure or table should be accompanied by a caption that clearly and concisely describes its content. A well-crafted caption improves the reader's comprehension and allows visual material to be understood independently of the surrounding text. While brevity is important, the caption should still convey enough information to make the purpose of the figure or table apparent. If more in-depth explanation is required, it is often better to include this discussion in the main body of the text rather than within the caption itself.

Labels are equally important, as they enable references to figures and tables from elsewhere in the document. For cross-referencing to work reliably, the `\label` command should always be placed after the corresponding `\caption`. This ensures that the reference will point to the correct figure or table number assigned by LaTeX.

Naming conventions for labels should be both consistent and descriptive. For instance, a label like `tab:experimental_results` immediately suggests a table containing results, while `fig:network_diagram` clearly refers to a figure. This practice not only makes the LaTeX source code easier to navigate but also reduces the likelihood of duplication or confusion when working on large or collaborative documents.

Authors should also ensure that all visual elements referenced in the text actually appear in the compiled document. Omitting a figure that has been cited disrupts the narrative flow and can confuse the reader. For longer documents with many figures and tables, it is advisable to review all references as part of the proofreading process to confirm their accuracy and presence.

By adopting these best practices for captions and labels, authors can significantly improve the clarity, navigability, and professional quality of their LaTeX documents. The next section will explore techniques for grouping figures and tables together within the same floating environment, a useful strategy for presenting related content in a coherent and visually unified manner.

4.3.7 Floating Figures and Tables Together

In some instances, a figure and a table may be conceptually related and should be presented together in the document. Rather than letting LaTeX position them separately, both elements can be placed within the same floating environment. This ensures that they remain together, maintaining logical flow and coherence in the document layout.

A common approach is to enclose both the `figure` and `table` within a single floating environment, such as `figure`. By doing so, LaTeX treats them as a single entity, ensuring they appear together while still allowing flexible placement within the document.

The example below illustrates this concept:

Combining a Figure and Table in One Floating Environment

LaTeX Code:

```
\begin{figure}[htbp]
    \centering
    \includegraphics[width=0.4\textwidth]
    {example-image.png}
    \caption{A floating figure}
    \label{fig:combined_figure}

    \vspace{1cm} % Adds some vertical space
    between the figure and table

\begin{tabular}{|c|c|}
        \hline
```

```
        A & B \\
        \hline
        C & D \\
        \hline
\end{tabular}
 \caption{A floating table below the figure}
    \label{tab:combined_table}
\end{figure}
```

Rendered Output (Figs. 4.3 and 4.4):

Figure 4.3: A floating figure

A	B
C	D

Figure 4.4: A floating table below the figure

Explanation and Best Practices

In this example, both the image and table are enclosed within the same `figure` environment, ensuring they are placed together rather than being separated by LaTeX's float management system. The `\vspace{1cm}` command is used to insert vertical space between the figure and the table, preventing them from appearing too close together.

This technique is particularly useful in situations where a figure and a table represent related data and should be interpreted together. For example, a figure might present a graphical representation of data, while the accompanying table provides numerical details. Keeping them together prevents readers from searching through the document to connect the two.

Alternative Approaches

While enclosing both elements in a single floating environment is effective, another option is to use the `subfigure` or `subfloat` package, which provides finer control over positioning. These packages allow multiple elements, including figures and tables, to be placed side by side or stacked while maintaining individual numbering and references.

For instance, using the `subfigure` package, we can create a side-by-side arrangement of a figure and a table:

Alternative Approach Using Subfigure Package

LaTeX Code:

```
\usepackage{subcaption}
% Include in the preamble

\begin{figure}[htbp]
centering
\begin{subfigure}{0.4\textwidth}
\centering
        \includegraphics[width=\textwidth]
        {example-image.png}
        \caption{A subfigure}
        \label{fig:sub_figure}
\end{subfigure}
    \hspace{1cm} % Horizontal space between
```

```
    figure and table
\begin{subfigure}{0.4\textwidth}
    \centering
    \begin{tabular}{|c|c|}
            \hline
            A & B \\
            \hline
            C & D \\
            \hline
    \end{tabular}
    \caption{A subtable}
    \label{tab:sub_table}
\end{subfigure}
\caption{A figure and table placed
side by side}
\label{fig:side_by_side}
\end{figure}
```

Rendered Output (Fig. 4.5):

a: A subfigure.

A	B
C	D

b: A subtable.

Figure 4.5: A figure and table placed side by side.

Choosing the Right Method

The choice of method depends on how the figure and table should be presented:

- If they should be stacked, placing them inside a single `figure` environment with `\vspace` is recommended.

- If they should be positioned side by side, using the `subfigure` package provides more flexibility.
- If LaTeX is moving the float undesirably, the `float` package's `[H]` option can enforce placement.

By carefully selecting the right floating method, figures and tables can be arranged in a way that enhances clarity and comprehension in the document.

The next section will explore advanced floating techniques, ensuring proper placement even in complex layouts.

4.4 Creating Diagrams in the `picture` Environment

The `picture` environment in LaTeX provides a way to create simple diagrams, shapes, and line drawings directly within your document. While it lacks the advanced capabilities of packages like `TikZ`, the `picture` environment is lightweight and can be used to illustrate basic concepts or create straightforward diagrams without the need for additional packages. This section covers the syntax and examples of various elements that can be created using the `picture` environment.

4.4.1 Setting up the `picture` Environment

The `picture` environment in LaTeX is a simple yet effective tool for creating basic diagrams, structured illustrations, and simple graphical elements. Unlike advanced graphics packages such as `TikZ`, the `picture` environment is lightweight and requires no external dependencies. It is particularly useful for quick sketches or structured representations where complex graphical features are unnecessary.

To create a diagram, the `picture` environment must be defined with a specific width and height. The basic syntax follows this structure:

Basic Syntax of the `picture` Environment

LaTeX Code:

```
\begin{picture}(100, 50)
    % Content of the picture environment
\end{picture}
```

This creates a rectangular drawing area where the first number represents the width, and the second represents the height. By default, measurements are in points (pt), but they can be adjusted according to document settings.

Adjusting the Origin in the `picture` Environment

By default, the lower-left corner of the picture frame is considered the origin, assigned the coordinate (0,0). However, LaTeX allows for flexibility in shifting the coordinate system. The origin can be redefined by specifying additional coordinates:

Shifting the Origin in the `picture` Environment

LaTeX Code:

```
\begin{picture}(100, 50)(-20, -10)
    % Content of the picture environment
\end{picture}
```

In this case, the origin is shifted to (-20, -10), meaning the new bottom-left corner is positioned accordingly, affecting how elements are placed within the environment.

Example: Defining a Basic Drawing Area

To illustrate the difference between the default and adjusted origin, the following example presents two empty drawing areas: one using the standard origin placement and the other with a shifted origin.

Example: Default vs. Adjusted Origin

LaTeX Code:

```
\documentclass{article}
\begin{document}

\setlength{\unitlength}{1pt}
% Defines unit length

\textbf{Default Origin (0,0):}
\begin{picture}(80, 40)
    \put(0, 0){\framebox(80,40){Default}}
\end{picture}

\bigskip

\textbf{Adjusted Origin (-20,-10):}
\begin{picture}(80, 40)(-20,-10)
    \put(-20, -10){\framebox(80,40)
    {Shifted Origin}}
\end{picture}

\end{document}
```

The output demonstrates how changing the origin modifies the placement of elements within the picture frame.

Rendered Output:

Default

Default Origin (0,0):

Shifted Origin

Adjusted Origin (-20,-10):

Choosing the Appropriate Origin Placement

Keeping the default origin at (0,0) works well when all elements are positioned relative to a fixed reference point. However, shifting the origin simplifies placement when dealing with multiple components in different locations. By carefully adjusting the coordinate system, one can streamline the layout of diagrams and improve element alignment.

This foundation prepares us for more advanced operations within the `picture` environment, including text placement, line drawing, and structured grid arrangements, which will be explored in the following sections.

4.4.2 Positioning Elements with \put

The `\put` command is essential for placing elements at specific coordinates within the `picture` environment. The syntax is:

```
\put(x, y){content}
```

where `x` and `y` define the position relative to the lower-left corner of the `picture` environment, and `content` represents the text, shapes, or other graphical elements.

4.4.3 Placing Ordinary Text and Creating Boxes

The simplest use of the \put command is inserting text at a defined position within the picture environment. The reference point for the text aligns to its bottom-left by default.

Placing Text in Picture Environment

LaTeX Code:

```
\begin{picture}(20,10)
\put(5,5){An ordinary
text}
\end{picture}
```

Output:

An ordinary text

To highlight text with a border, the framebox command creates a framed box with specified width and height. The text is centered by default within the box.

Creating Framed Box

```
\begin{picture}(20,20)
\put(3, 6){\framebox(4, 2){Boxed}}
\end{picture}
```

By default, text inside a framebox is centered, but optional positioning arguments can align it differently. These include left (l), right (r), top (t), bottom (b), and bottom-right (br).

Creating Box with Text Alignment Optional

```
\begin{picture}(20,10)
\put(6,-4){\framebox(4,3)[t]{LATEX}}
\put(10,7){\framebox(7,5)[br]{LATEX}}
\end{picture}
```

4.4.4 Creating Boxes Without Borders

If a border is unnecessary, the `makebox` command functions like `framebox` but without drawing a visible frame.

Using Makebox to Position Text

```
\begin{picture}(20,10)
\put(5,5){\makebox(0,0){Text Without Borders}}
\end{picture}
```

The command `makebox(0,0)` is useful for precise text positioning since it prevents additional spacing beyond the text content.

4.4.5 Creating Dashed Boxes

The `dashbox` command functions like `framebox` but produces a dashed-line border instead of a solid one. An additional argument determines the width of each dash.

Creating a Dashed Box

```
\begin{picture}(20,10)
\put(5,4.5){\dashbox{0.5}(5,4){Dashed Box}}
\end{picture}
```

Unlike the `framebox` command, `dashbox` requires an initial argument specifying the width of each dash in the border.

4.4.6 Drawing Lines and Vectors

The `picture` environment in LaTeX allows for the creation of simple line-based diagrams. Two essential commands, `\line` and `\vector`, help in drawing lines and arrows. The `\line` command is used to create straight lines, while `\vector` functions similarly but adds an arrowhead at the endpoint.

A line is drawn by specifying a coordinate pair that defines its direction, followed by a length parameter. The slope of the line is given by an integer pair `(a, b)`, while the length determines how far the line extends. The `\vector` command follows the same structure but includes an arrow.

The following example demonstrates how to create horizontal and vertical lines along with a diagonal arrow:

Creating Lines and Arrows

LaTeX Code:

```
\begin{picture}(100,100)
\put(10,10){\line(1,0){80}}
% Horizontal line
\put(10,10){\line(0,1){80}}
% Vertical line
\put(10,10){\vector(1,1){60}}
% Diagonal arrow
\end{picture}
```

Output:

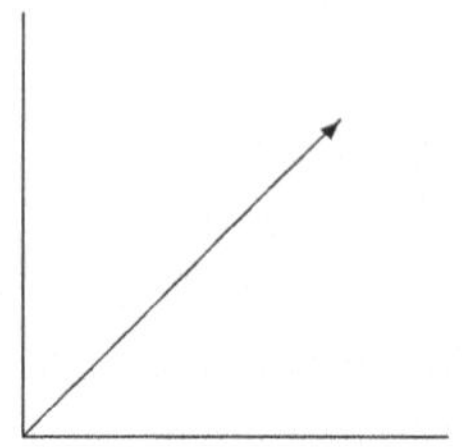

This example creates a horizontal line extending 80 points to the right, a vertical line of equal length, and a diagonal arrow from the starting point at (10,10) moving in the (1,1) direction with a length of 60 points.

When specifying the slope `(a, b)`, certain constraints must be considered. The values for `a` and `b` must be integers that do not have divisors other than 1. In the case of the `\line` command, these integers must range between −6 and +6, whereas for `\vector`, they should be between −4 and +4.

4.4.7 Drawing Geometric Shapes

By combining multiple lines, it is possible to construct various geometric figures such as triangles and squares. A triangle is formed by connecting three points using the `\line` command, ensuring that the segments meet at their endpoints.

The following code generates a right triangle, where the base lies horizontally, the right side extends vertically, and the hypotenuse connects the two:

Drawing a Triangle

LaTeX Code:

```
\begin{picture}(200,100)
\put(25, 10)
{\line(1,0){75}}
% Base
\put(100, 10)
{\line(0,1){75}}
% Right side
\put(100, 85)
{\line(-1,-1){75}}
% Hypotenuse
\end{picture}
```

Output:

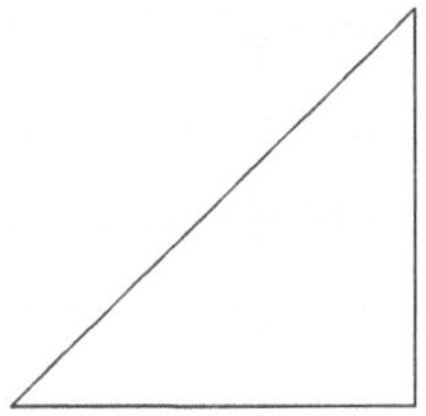

Each segment of the triangle is drawn using a separate `\line` command. The base starts from (25,10) and extends horizontally for 75 points. From the endpoint, a vertical line rises by 75 points. Finally, the hypotenuse is drawn diagonally, connecting the top of the vertical segment back to the starting point of the base.

A square follows a similar construction, except that all four sides have equal lengths. The process involves sequentially drawing four line segments, each meeting at a right angle. The example below illustrates this:

Drawing a Square

LaTeX Code:

```
\begin{picture}(200,100)
\put(25, 10){\line(1,0){75}}
% Bottom edge
\put(100, 10){\line(0,1){75}}
% Right edge
```

```
\put(100, 85){\line(-1,0){75}}
% Top edge
\put(25, 85){\line(0,-1){75}}
% Left edge
\end{picture}
```

Output:

To construct the square, the bottom edge is first drawn from (25,10) extending rightward for 75 points. The right edge rises vertically from its endpoint. The top edge follows the same length in the opposite direction, and the left edge completes the shape by connecting the top-left corner back to the bottom-left.

4.4.8 Drawing Shapes: Circles and Ovals

The `picture` environment in LaTeX allows for drawing simple geometric shapes, including circles and ovals, using built-in commands. The `\circle` command is used to draw a circle, while the `\oval` command is employed to create ovals with different orientations.

A circle is defined by specifying its diameter, ensuring that it is centered at the given coordinates. Ovals, on the other hand, require width and height parameters to determine their proportions. Additionally, ovals can be modified with an optional argument to indicate specific orientations, such as right, left, top, or bottom. When two such orientation arguments are provided, the resulting oval takes a quarter shape.

To illustrate these concepts, consider the following example, where a standard circle is drawn alongside two ovals, one of which is rotated using an optional argument:

Creating a Circle and Ovals

LaTeX Code:

```
\begin{picture}(150,100)
    \put(30,30){\circle{40}}
% Circle with diameter 40
    \put(80,30){\oval(40,20)}
% Oval with width 40 and height 20
    \put(130,30){\oval(40,20)[r]}
% Right-oriented half oval
\end{picture}
```

Output:

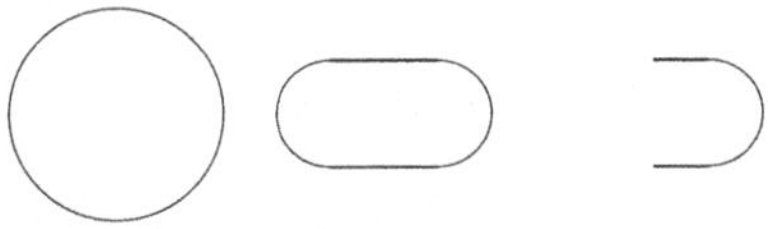

In this example, the first shape is a circle with a diameter of 40 units, centered at (30,30). The second shape is an oval with a width of 40 and height of 20, positioned at (80,30). The third shape, placed at (130,30), is a right-oriented half-oval, achieved by adding the optional argument `[r]`.

4.4.9 Drawing a Solid Disc

In addition to circles, LaTeX allows for the creation of filled circular shapes, known as discs, using the `\circle*` command. Unlike a regular circle, this command produces a solid-filled shape instead of a hollow outline.

The following example demonstrates how to draw a filled disc with a specified diameter:

Drawing a Solid Disc

LaTeX Code:

```
\begin{picture}(100,50)
\put(50,25){\circle*{15}}
% Solid disc with
diameter 15
\end{picture}
```

Output:

The command `\circle*` functions in the same way as `\circle`, except that the interior of the shape is filled. The example above places a solid disc at coordinates (50,25) with a diameter of 15 units.

4.4.10 Stacks and Grids

Stacks

The `picture` environment includes a useful feature for stacking multiple lines of text in a single position. The command `\shortstack` allows text to be stacked vertically within an invisible box. The reference point for this box is positioned at the lower-left corner by default. Each new row within the stack is separated using the `\\` command.

To demonstrate, consider the following example, where the words "LaTeX" and "HTML" are stacked on top of each other within a `picture` environment:

Creating a Stack of Text

LaTeX Code:

```
\begin{picture}(50,40)
\put(2, 5){
\shortstack{LaTeX\\HTML}}
\end{picture}
```

Output:

LaTeX
HTML

By default, the text is center-aligned. However, alignment can be modified using an optional argument. Specifying `[l]` aligns the text to the left, while `[r]` aligns it to the right. The following example illustrates these alignments:

Aligning a Shortstack

LaTeX Code:

```
\begin{picture}(50,40)
\put(5, 8){\shortstack[l]
{LaTeX\\HTML}}
\end{picture}

\begin{picture}(50,40)
\put(7, 9){\shortstack[r]
{LaTeX\\HTML}}
\end{picture}
```

Output:

LaTeX
HTML

LaTeX
HTML

Grids

The `picture` environment also allows users to create grids, which are useful for positioning elements precisely. This is achieved using the `\graphpaper` command, which generates a grid with a specified starting position, width, and height.

The example below demonstrates how to create a grid spanning 200 units in width and 100 units in height, starting from a lower-left corner offset of (-75,0):

Creating a Grid in the Picture Environment

LaTeX Code:

```
\begin{picture}
(250,100)
\graphpaper
(-75, 0)(200,100)
\end{picture}
```

Output:

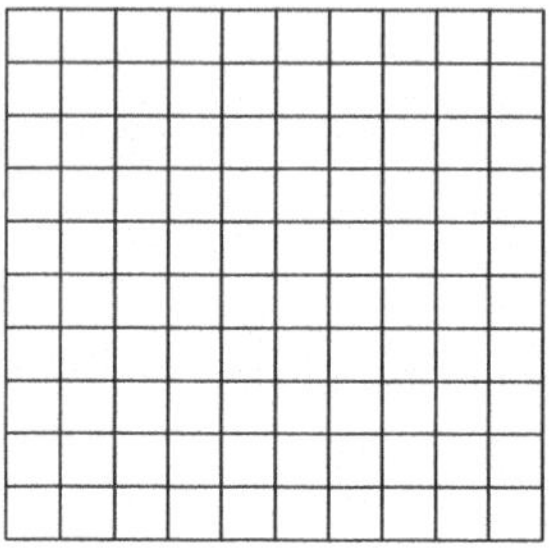

4.4.11 A Complete Example of a Diagram

To illustrate how various elements within the `picture` environment can be combined, consider the following example. It features a coordinate system with labeled axes, a grid, a labeled circle, a rectangular shape, and an arrow connecting these elements.

Creating a Simple Diagram

LaTeX Code:

```
\begin{picture}(150, 150)
    % Axes
\put(10,10){\vector(1,0){130}}
% x-axis
\put(10,10){\vector(0,1){130}}
% y-axis
\put(140,5){\makebox(0,0){$x$}}
```

```
%x-axis label
\put(5,140){\makebox(0,0){$y$}}
% y-axis label

    % Grid lines
    \multiput(20,10)(10,0){12}
    {\line(0,1){130}}
    \multiput(10,20)(0,10){12}
    {\line(1,0){130}}

    % Circle and Label
    \put(50,50){\circle{20}}
% Circle
    \put(50,50){\makebox(0,0){A}}
% Label at the center

    % Rectangular Shape
    \put(70,70){\line(1,0){40}}
    \put(70,90){\line(1,0){40}}
    \put(70,70){\line(0,1){20}}
    \put(110,70){\line(0,1){20}}
    \put(90,80){\makebox(0,0)
    {Rectangle}}

    % Diagonal Arrow
    \put(50,50){\vector(1,1){40}}
% Arrow from circle to rectangle
\end{picture}
```

Output:

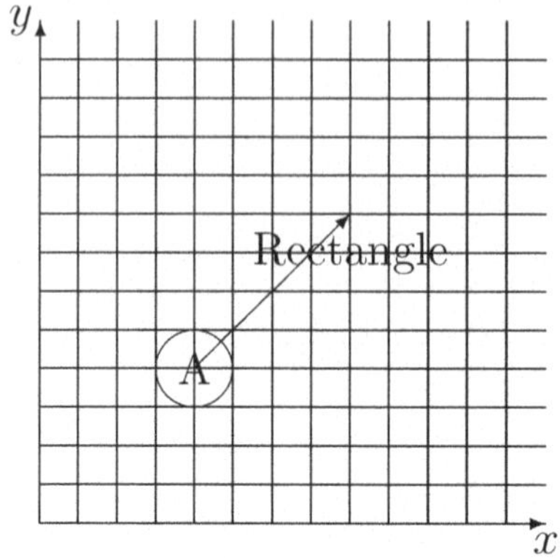

This example combines various elements to create a structured diagram. It defines a coordinate system with labeled x and y axes, generates a grid for precise positioning, places a labeled circle at a specific location, draws a rectangular shape, and connects the elements using a diagonal arrow.

4.4.12 Summary of Key Commands in the `picture` Environment

Here is a quick reference of key commands for creating diagrams with the `picture` environment:

- `\put(x, y){content}`: Place content at coordinates `(x, y)`.
- `\line(a, b){length}`: Draw a line with slope `(a, b)`.
- `\vector(a, b){length}`: Draw a vector (arrow) with slope `(a, b)`.
- `\circle{diameter}`: Draw a circle with a given diameter.

- `\oval(width, height)[orientation]`: Draw an oval with a specified width, height, and optional orientation.
- `\makebox(0,0){text}`: Place text at specified coordinates.
- `\multiput(x, y)(dx, dy){count}{content}`: Repeatedly place `content` with offsets.

While the `picture` environment is limited compared to modern graphics packages, it is useful for creating basic diagrams in a simple and efficient manner. For more complex diagrams, packages such as `TikZ` or `PGFPlots` are recommended.

Exercises for Chap. 4: Figures, Tables, and Graphics

4.1 Inserting Images and Figures (Formats, Placement)

1. *Inserting an Image*: Write a LaTeX document that inserts an image using the `\includegraphics` command. Experiment with different image formats (e.g., PNG, JPEG, PDF) and sizes. Use the `width` option to resize the image to half the width of the text block.

2. *Figure Placement*: Insert an image in a LaTeX document and try different placement options (e.g., `[h]`, `[t]`, `[b]`). Observe how the image moves around the document based on these options.

3. *Adding Captions and Labels*: Create a figure with a caption and a label. Reference the figure in the body of the text using the `\ref` command.

4.2 Creating Tables (Basic Tables, Multicolumn, Multirow)

1. *Basic Table*: Write a LaTeX document that includes a basic table with three rows and three columns. Add a caption and label to the table for later reference in the text.

2. *Multicolumn and Multirow Tables*: Create a table that demonstrates the use of the `\multicolumn` and `\multirow` commands. For example, create a table where one cell spans multiple columns or rows.

3. *Table Borders and Alignment*: Modify a table's border and alignment settings. Experiment with different column alignments (left, right, center) and add horizontal lines using the `\hline` command.

4.3 Floating Figures and Tables

1. *Floating a Figure*: Create a LaTeX document that includes a floating figure. Experiment with different figure placement options and observe how LaTeX places the figure in different parts of the document.

2. *Floating a Table*: Write a LaTeX document that includes a floating table. Use the `\begin{table}` and `\end{table}` environments to control the table placement.

3. *Referencing Floating Figures and Tables*: Insert a figure and a table in your document. Add captions and labels, and then reference both the figure and the table using the `\ref` command.

4.4 Creating Diagrams in the `picture` Environment

1. *Basic Diagram with* ***`picture`***: Draw a simple rectangle and circle using the `picture` environment. Label each shape and demonstrate the use of `\put` and coordinate placement.

2. *Combining Shapes*: Combine at least three different shapes (e.g., lines, vectors, and ovals) in a single diagram using the `picture` environment. Practice using scaling and positioning commands.

3. *Annotated Diagram*: Add text annotations and arrows to the diagram. Use the `\vector` and `\line` commands to indicate direction or flow within your figure.

Chapter 5

Managing References and Citations

Contents

Md Aquib, *Fundamentals of LaTeX*, University Texts in the Mathematical Sciences,
https://doi.org/10.1007/978-981-96-9318-4_5

Abstract: Accurate and consistent referencing is a cornerstone of scholarly and professional writing. Whether you are authoring a research paper, thesis, or academic book, citing sources correctly not only lends credibility to your work but also enables readers to locate the original sources for further study. LaTeX offers powerful tools for managing bibliographic data, formatting citations, and generating reference lists with precision and efficiency.

Keywords: BibTeX, BibLaTeX, LaTeX citations, Bibliography management, Citation styles, natbib package

This chapter explores how to handle references and citations in LaTeX, beginning with manual citation using the `thebibliography` environment and progressing to automated bibliography management with `BibTeX` and `biblatex`. You will learn how to insert in-text citations, create bibliographies, choose and apply citation styles (such as APA, IEEE, and Chicago), and organize bibliographic entries using a separate `.bib` file.

We will also examine how to integrate citation packages, customize bibliography formatting, and resolve common issues such as duplicate entries, sorting orders, and missing references. By mastering these techniques, you will be equipped to manage sources in a systematic, scalable, and professional manner, no matter how complex your document becomes.

5.1 Adding Citations and Bibliography Using `biblatex`

Managing references and citations is a crucial aspect of academic and scientific writing. LaTeX provides several methods to handle bibliographies, with `biblatex` being one of the most powerful and flexible options. This package allows for extensive customization, supports multiple citation styles, and integrates seamlessly with the `biber` backend. Unlike traditional methods such as `natbib`, `biblatex` offers more advanced features, including better localization support, flexible bibliography formatting, and dynamic citation commands.

This section explores how to set up and use `biblatex` efficiently in a LaTeX document. It covers loading the package, configuring citation styles, linking an external bibliography file, and generating the final bibliography.

5.1.1 Installing and Loading the `biblatex` Package

To use `biblatex`, the package must first be included in the document preamble. The `backend` option determines how the bibliography is processed. The most common choice is `biber`, which provides superior sorting and encoding capabilities compared to the older `bibtex`. Additionally, the `style` and `citestyle` options define how citations appear in the text and how the bibliography is formatted.

The following example demonstrates how to load `biblatex` with `biber` as the backend, using a numeric citation style:

Loading biblatex in a LaTeX Document

LaTeX Code:

```
\documentclass{article}
\usepackage[backend=biber,style=numeric,
citestyle=numeric]{biblatex}
\addbibresource{references.bib}
% Link the bibliography file
\begin{document}
This document cites an important
source~\cite{einstein1905}.
\printbibliography
% Print the bibliography at the end
\end{document}
```

Output:

This document cites an important source [1].

References:

1 Einstein, A. (1905). Zur Elektrodynamik bewegter Körper. Annalen der Physik.

This setup ensures that citations within the document are formatted numerically in square brackets, and the corresponding bibliography is printed at the end. The `\addbibresource` command links an external `.bib` file, which contains structured reference data.

In many cases, the choice of citation style is dictated by journal guidelines or academic requirements. The `style` and `citestyle` parameters allow users to choose between different formats, such as:

- `numeric`: Citations appear as numbers in square brackets.
- `authoryear`: Citations use an author-year format, common in social sciences.

- `alphabetic`: Uses alphabetic labels based on author names.
- `apa`: Formats citations according to APA (American Psychological Association) standards.
- `ieee`: Styles citations following IEEE (Institute of Electrical and Electronics Engineers) standards.

For example, if author-year citations are preferred instead of numeric citations, the package can be loaded as:

Changing Citation Style to Author-Year

```
\usepackage[backend=biber, style=authoryear,
            citestyle=authoryear]{biblatex}
```

With this setting, a citation would appear as "(Einstein, 1905)" instead of "[1]," making it more suitable for disciplines that emphasize the year of publication.

5.1.2 Creating the .bib File

In academic and scientific writing, managing references efficiently is crucial. The `biblatex` package allows references to be stored in a separate `.bib` file, which serves as a centralized database for citations. This file follows a structured format where each reference entry is categorized by its type, such as books, journal articles, conference papers, or websites.

A `.bib` file is essentially a plain-text file containing bibliographic entries formatted in BibTeX style. Each reference is assigned a unique citation key, which is later used within the LaTeX document to cite the source. The `.bib` file structure ensures consistency in formatting and allows easy modification of references without altering the main document.

To create a `.bib` file, open a text editor and save the file with a `.bib` extension (e.g., `references.bib`). Below is an example of a simple `.bib` file containing two references, a book and a journal article.

Example: Structure of a `.bib` File

LaTeX Code:

```
@book{lamport94,
  author    = {Leslie Lamport},
  title     = {LaTeX: A Document
  Preparation System},
  publisher = {Addison-Wesley},
  year      = {1994},
  edition   = {2nd},
  address   = {Massachusetts}
}

@article{knuth84,
  author    = {Donald E. Knuth},
  title     = {Literate Programming},
  journal   = {The Computer Journal},
  year      = {1984},
  volume    = {27},
  number    = {2},
  pages     = {97--111}
}
```

These entries define the key elements of a bibliographic reference. Each reference begins with an identifier (e.g., `@book` or `@article`) that specifies the type of source. The fields within curly braces contain metadata such as the author's name, title, publication year, and other relevant information.

Understanding the Structure of a `.bib` Entry

Each entry in the `.bib` file consists of structured fields.

For books, the `@book` entry represents books and requires fields such as:

- `author`: Specifies the name(s) of the author(s)
- `title`: The title of the book
- `publisher`: The name of the publishing house
- `year`: The year of publication
- `edition`: Indicates the edition (optional)
- `address`: The location of the publisher (optional)

For journal articles, the `@article` entry is used for journal publications and typically includes:

- `author`: Lists the authors of the article
- `title`: The title of the article
- `journal`: The journal name where the article is published
- `year`: The year of publication
- `volume` and `number`: The volume and issue number of the journal

- `pages`: The page range of the article

Each entry is assigned a unique citation key (e.g., `lamport94` or `knuth84`), which is used when citing the source in the LaTeX document. The citation key should be meaningful and typically follows a convention such as the author's last name followed by the year of publication.

Additional Bibliographic Entry Types

The `.bib` format supports various other entry types, including:

- `@inproceedings`: Used for conference papers
- `@techreport`: Represents technical reports from institutions
- `@phdthesis`: For doctoral dissertations
- `@misc`: Used for sources that do not fit standard categories, such as online references

Below is an example of a conference paper and a technical report:

Example: Conference Paper and Technical Report

LaTeX Code:

```
@inproceedings{turing36,
  author    = {Alan Turing},
  title     = {On Computable Numbers,
               with an Application to
               the Entscheidungsproblem},
  booktitle = {Proceedings of the London
                Mathematical
                Society},
  year      = {1936},
  volume    = {42},
```

```
  pages       = {230--265}
}

@techreport{shannon49,
  author      = {Claude Shannon},
  title       = {Communication Theory of
                  Secrecy Systems},
  institution = {Bell Labs},
  year        = {1949}
}
```

The `@inproceedings` entry represents a paper presented at a conference and requires the `booktitle` field, which contains the name of the conference proceedings. The `@techreport` entry is used for institutional reports and includes the `institution` field specifying the organization responsible for the report.

Incorporating the `.bib` File in a LaTeX Document

Once the `.bib` file is created and saved, it must be linked to the LaTeX document using the `\addbibresource{}` command. Below is an example that includes the bibliography file and cites an entry within the text.

Example: Citing a Reference and Printing the Bibliography

LaTeX Code:

```
\documentclass{article}
\usepackage[backend=biber,
style=authoryear]{biblatex}
\addbibresource{references.bib}
% Link the .bib file
```

```
\begin{document}

Turing's foundational work in
computability~\cite{turing36} laid
the groundwork for modern
theoretical computer science.

\printbibliography
% Print the bibliography at the end

\end{document}
```

The above document cites a reference using the `\cite{}` command and automatically generates a formatted bibliography at the end.

5.1.3 Citing References in the Document

After setting up the `.bib` file and linking it to the document, the next step is to cite references appropriately. Proper citation ensures academic integrity and provides a structured way of referring to external sources.

In `biblatex`, citations are inserted using the `\cite{}` command, which fetches the relevant reference based on the citation key assigned in the `.bib` file. For instance, to cite a book by Leslie Lamport in the document, the following command is used:

Example: Citing a Reference

LaTeX Code:

```
In his book, Lamport explains how
to use LaTeX~\cite{lamport94}.
```

This will produce an in-text citation corresponding to the `lamport94` key, linking it to the complete reference in the bibliography.

The citation format depends on the bibliography style specified when loading `biblatex`. If the `numeric` style is chosen, the citation will appear as a number in brackets, e.g., `[1]`. In contrast, if an author-year style such as `authoryear` is used, the citation will appear in the format (Lamport, 1994). These styles can be modified using the `style` and `citestyle` options in `biblatex`, offering flexibility in formatting citations based on the document's requirements.

5.1.4 Printing the Bibliography

To include a list of references at the end of the document, the `\printbibliography` command is used. This command automatically generates a formatted bibliography based on the references cited throughout the document.

Below is an example demonstrating how to print the bibliography with a custom title:

Example: Printing the Bibliography

LaTeX Code:

```
\printbibliography[title={References}]
```

When this command is executed, LaTeX generates a bibliography section titled "References," listing all cited sources in the format specified by the `style` option. If the bibliography needs to be organized into different sections, filtering options can be used to separate books, journal articles, and other types of sources.

For instance, to print only books, the `keyword` option can be used:

Example: Printing Only Books in the Bibliography

LaTeX Code:

```
\printbibliography[title={Books},
keyword=book]
```

This ensures that only entries classified as books in the `.bib` file appear in the bibliography. Similar filtering can be applied to journal articles or other reference types.

5.1.5 Compilation Process with `biblatex`

When using `biblatex` with the `biber` backend, proper compilation is essential to ensure that all references are correctly processed and displayed. Unlike the traditional `bibtex` workflow, which operates in two compilation steps, `biblatex` with `biber` requires an additional processing step.

To compile a LaTeX document with citations and a bibliography, follow these steps:

1. First, run `pdflatex` (or `latex`) on the main `.tex` file. This step identifies the citations used in the document but does not yet resolve them.

2. Next, execute the `biber` command, which reads the `.bib` file, processes the references, and generates an auxiliary file with formatted citations.

3. Finally, rerun `pdflatex` (or `latex`) to incorporate the citations and generate the final bibliography.

Most modern LaTeX editors automate this process, allowing users to compile the document with a single command. However, if compiling manually, the sequence of commands in the terminal should be:

Example: Manual Compilation with biber

Terminal Commands:

```
pdflatex main.tex
biber main
pdflatex main.tex
pdflatex main.tex
```

Running `pdflatex` twice at the end ensures that all references are properly linked. If an error occurs or citations do not appear as expected, checking the `biber` log file (`main.blg`) can help diagnose the issue.

Full LaTeX Code Example

```
\documentclass{article}
\usepackage[backend=biber, style=authoryear,
citestyle=authoryear]{biblatex}
\addbibresource{references.bib}

\begin{document}

In his book, Lamport explains how to use
\LaTeX~\cite{lamport94}. Additionally,
Knuth discusses the concept of literate
programming in his article \cite{knuth74}.

\printbibliography[title={References}]

\end{document}
```

This document uses the `authoryear` citation style, which shows citations as `(Author, Year)`. Citations refer to entries in the `.bib` file, which is specified using `\addbibresource`.

5.2 In-text Citations and Bibliography Styles

One of the most important aspects of managing references in LaTeX is understanding how to format in-text citations and how to control the style of your bibliography. The `biblatex` package offers a wide variety of citation and bibliography styles that you can customize depending on your needs. Whether you prefer numeric citations (e.g., [1]) or author-year citations (e.g., (Lamport, 1994)), `biblatex` allows you to tailor the output to your preference.

In this section, we will explore different types of in-text citations and how to control the overall formatting of your bibliography.

5.2.1 In-text Citations with `biblatex`

One of the most crucial aspects of academic writing is properly citing references within the text. The `biblatex` package offers a variety of citation commands that allow for different citation styles, providing flexibility in formatting references based on specific requirements.

The basic citation command in `biblatex` is `\cite`, which automatically formats citations according to the chosen style. However, depending on the context, alternative citation commands can be used to better integrate references into the text.

For instance, when citing a source as part of the natural flow of a sentence, the `\textcite` command is preferable. This ensures that the author's name is incorporated into the sentence structure, while the publication year appears in parentheses. In contrast, `\parencite` places the entire citation in parentheses, making it useful for citations that are not directly mentioned in the sentence. If footnotes are required, `\footcite` automatically moves the citation to the bottom of the page.

The following example demonstrates different citation methods:

Example: In-text Citations Using `biblatex`

LaTeX Code:

```
\documentclass{article}
\usepackage[backend=biber,
style=authoryear]{biblatex}
\addbibresource{references.bib}

\begin{document}

Lamport \textcite{lamport94} discusses
the role of LaTeX in structured document
preparation.

In a broader sense, literate programming
has been explored extensively
(\parencite{knuth74}).

For further technical details,
see \footcite{knuth74}.

\printbibliography

\end{document}
```

The expected output of this example is (Fig. 5.1):

Expected Output: Sample Citation Formatting

Lamport (1994) discusses the role of LaTeX in structured document preparation.
In a broader sense, literate programming has been explored extensively (Knuth, 1984).
For further technical details, see Knuth (1984) in a footnote.

Figure 5.1: Different in-text citation formats in `biblatex`

This example demonstrates three common citation methods:

1. Author-Year in Sentence: The `\textcite` command places the author's name within the sentence structure, followed by the publication year in parentheses.

2. Parenthetical Citation: The `\parencite` command encloses the entire citation within parentheses, keeping it separate from the sentence.

3. Footnote Citation: The `\footcite` command moves the citation to a footnote, which is useful for less intrusive references.

Each of these citation methods serves a different purpose, depending on how the source is referenced in the text. The citation style itself is controlled by the options passed to the `biblatex` package when it is loaded. For example, the `authoryear` style generates author-year citations, while the `numeric` style formats them as numbers.

5.2.2 Customizing In-text Citations

Beyond the basic citation commands, `biblatex` allows for fine-tuned control over how citations appear. Depending on the needs of the document, additional commands can be used to modify citation formatting:

Citing Multiple References at Once: When citing multiple references together, the `\cite` command accepts multiple keys separated by commas:

```
\cite{lamport94, knuth74}
```

This groups both citations into a single reference.
Suppressing the Author's Name: Sometimes, it is useful to suppress the author's name and only show the year. The `\citeyear` command achieves this:

```
\citeyear{lamport94}
```

This outputs only the year, which is useful in contexts where the author's name has already been mentioned.
Shortening Repeated Citations: If the same reference is cited multiple times, `biblatex` automatically shortens repeated citations depending on the bibliography style. Some styles, such as `authoryear-comp`, compact consecutive references to the same source.

By utilizing these different citation commands, authors can ensure that their references integrate smoothly into the text while maintaining readability and consistency. The next section will discuss the various citation styles available in `biblatex` and how to switch between them to best fit the document's formatting needs.

5.2.3 Different Citation Styles

The choice of citation style in a document depends on the field of study and the type of publication. The `biblatex` package provides various citation styles that format in-text references differently, ensuring consistency and compliance with academic conventions. This section explores different citation styles and how they can be implemented in a LaTeX document.

A fundamental distinction in citation styles is between numeric and author-based systems. Numeric styles assign a number to each reference and cite sources using bracketed numbers. This approach is widely used in technical and scientific writing. In contrast, author-based styles display the author's name and publication year, a format commonly preferred in the humanities and social sciences.

Numeric Style

In numeric citation style, references are assigned a unique number in the order they appear in the document. The citation itself consists of a bracketed number, which corresponds to the numbered entry in the bibliography. This method keeps citations compact and easy to locate.

To use numeric style in `biblatex`, the following setup is required in the preamble:

Example: Numeric Citation Style

LaTeX Code:

```
\usepackage[style=numeric,
citestyle=numeric]{biblatex}
\addbibresource{references.bib}
```

In the body of the document, a citation appears as:

Example Citation in Numeric Style

LaTeX Code:

```
Lamport describes LaTeX as
a powerful document
preparation system \cite{lamport94}.
```

This produces an in-text citation formatted as:

Lamport describes LaTeX as a powerful document preparation system[1].

Numeric style is especially useful in fields where sources are cited frequently, such as physics, engineering, and computer science.

Author-Year Style

The author-year citation format is commonly used in academic writing across disciplines such as social sciences, humanities, and linguistics. In this style, references include the author's name and the year of publication, allowing readers to identify sources easily.

To enable author-year citations, use the following setup:

Example: Author-Year Citation Style

LaTeX Code:

```
\usepackage[style=authoryear,
citestyle=authoryear]{biblatex}
\addbibresource{references.bib}
```

Citations in the document are formatted as follows:

Example Citation in Author-Year Style

LaTeX Code:

```
\textcite{lamport94} discusses the
advantages of using LaTeX.
```

This produces:

Lamport (1994) discusses the advantages of using LaTeX.

Alternatively, citations can also be placed in parentheses:

Alternative Author-Year Citation

LaTeX Code:

```
Many researchers have studied this topic
(\parencite{lamport94}).
```

This results in:

Many researchers have studied this topic (Lamport, 1994).

Author-year citation style is widely used in research articles and dissertations, as it helps maintain clarity while keeping references informative.

Alphabetic Style

The alphabetic citation style combines elements of both numeric and author-year formats. Instead of numbers, citations are formed using a shorthand version of the author's name and publication year. This approach is particularly useful in disciplines where distinguishing between sources is crucial.

To use the alphabetic style, the document setup includes:

Example: Alphabetic Citation Style

LaTeX Code:

```
\usepackage[style=alphabetic,
citestyle=alphabetic]{biblatex}
\addbibresource{references.bib}
```

Citations appear in the following format:

Example Citation in Alphabetic Style

LaTeX Code:

```
\cite{lamport94} provides an
introduction to LaTeX.
```

This results in:

> [Lam94] provides an introduction to LaTeX.

Alphabetic citations are commonly used in mathematics and theoretical computer science.

Footnote Citation Style

Another widely used method is footnote citations, where each reference is placed in a footnote rather than inline within the text. This format is commonly used in legal writing, history, and philosophy.

To apply footnote citation style, modify the `biblatex` setup as follows:

Example: Footnote Citation Style

LaTeX Code:

```
\usepackage[style=verbose-note,
citestyle=footnote]{biblatex}
\addbibresource{references.bib}
```

To cite a source using footnotes, the following command is used:

Example Footnote Citation

LaTeX Code:

```
LaTeX is widely used in academia.
\footcite{lamport94}
```

This results in:

LaTeX is widely used in academia.[1]

where the corresponding footnote entry will include the full citation details.

5.2.4 Customizing Bibliography Styles

The bibliography style determines how references are formatted in the bibliography section of a document. In LaTeX, the `biblatex` package provides a variety of bibliography styles, allowing authors to control the order in which references appear, how they are formatted, and how different elements such as author names, years, and titles are displayed.

One of the most important aspects of bibliography customization is defining the sorting order. By default, references appear in the order they are cited in the text. However, in many academic disciplines, it is more common to sort the bibliography alphabetically by the author's last name, or by year of publication. This can be achieved using the `sorting` option in the `biblatex` package.

Standard Bibliography Formatting

The standard bibliography formatting in `biblatex` is controlled by the `style` option, which dictates how references are displayed. By default, references in a numeric bibliography are listed in the order they appear in the text. However, sorting can be modified using predefined sorting schemes.

To use a numeric bibliography without any specific sorting, the following setup is used:

Example: Numeric Bibliography (Default Sorting)

LaTeX Code:

```
\usepackage[backend=biber,style=numeric,
sorting=none]{biblatex}
\addbibresource{references.bib}
```

When using this configuration, references will be numbered in the order they are cited in the document, and the corresponding numbers will be used in in-text citations. This format is widely used in scientific and technical writing, where concise citations are preferred.

Author-Year Bibliography Style

In fields where it is important to reference sources by the author's name and publication year, the author-year bibliography style is commonly used. This style presents references in an alphabetical list by the author's last name. If an author has multiple works, they are ordered by year of publication. The format follows standard citation conventions for disciplines such as humanities, social sciences, and economics.

To apply this style, the bibliography configuration should be modified as follows:

Example: Author-Year Bibliography Style

LaTeX Code:

```
\usepackage[backend=biber, style=
authoryear, sorting=nyt]{biblatex}
\addbibresource{references.bib}
```

In this configuration, the `sorting=nyt` option ensures that entries are sorted alphabetically by the author's last name (`n`), then by publication year (`y`), and finally by title (`t`) in case of multiple works by the same author in the same year.

This formatting produces a bibliography similar to the following:

Example Output (Author-Year Bibliography)

Bibliography:

```
Knuth, Donald E. (1984). Literate Programming.
    The Computer Journal, 27(2), 97-111.

Lamport, Leslie (1994). LaTeX: A Document
Preparation System.Addison-Wesley, 2nd edition.
```

In this case, the bibliography is sorted by the authors' last names, ensuring a structured reference list that is easy to navigate.

Custom Bibliography Sorting

For specialized applications, it may be necessary to customize how references are sorted. Some researchers prefer to list references chronologically, ensuring that older works appear before newer ones. Others may require sorting by topic, journal, or another criterion.

The `biblatex` package provides several predefined sorting schemes that can be modified based on specific needs. One commonly used option is sorting by year first, followed by the author's name and then the title.

To implement this approach, the following setup is used:

Example: Custom Bibliography Sorting

LaTeX Code:

```
\usepackage[backend=biber, style=
authoryear, sorting=ynt]{biblatex}
\addbibresource{references.bib}
```

Here, the `sorting=ynt` option specifies that references should be sorted by:

1. Year (`y`): Older references appear first. 2. Name (`n`): Within each year, entries are sorted alphabetically by author. 3. Title (`t`): If multiple works have the same year and author, they are sorted alphabetically by title.

With this method, the bibliography would be structured as follows:

Example Output (Sorted by Year, Name, Title)

Bibliography:

```
Knuth, Donald E. (1974). Structured
Programming. ACM Computing Surveys,
6(4), 261-301.

Lamport, Leslie (1983). Specifying Concurrent
Systems. ACM Transactions on Programming
Languages, 5(3), 190-222.

Knuth, Donald E. (1984). Literate Programming.
    The Computer Journal, 27(2), 97-111.

Lamport, Leslie (1994). LaTeX: A Document
Preparation System.Addison-Wesley, 2nd
edition.
```

In this format, earlier research contributions are presented first, followed by more recent publications, making it easier to track the chronological development of the field.

5.2.5 Switching Between Citation and Bibliography Styles

In academic writing, different disciplines require different citation and bibliography styles. Some fields, such as physics and engineering, favor numeric citations for conciseness, while humanities and social sciences prefer author-year citations for clarity. The `biblatex` package allows users to switch between citation and bibliography styles with minimal modifications to their LaTeX document.

The citation style controls how references appear in the text, whereas the bibliography style determines the formatting of the references at the end of the document. These styles are specified in the document preamble using the `style` and `citestyle` options in the `\usepackage` command.

The most commonly used citation and bibliography styles in `biblatex` include:

- Numeric Style: References are numbered and appear in brackets, following the order in which they are cited. This style is common in technical and scientific writing.

- Author-Year Style: The citation includes the author's last name and the publication year, making it easy to track sources. This format is widely used in humanities and social sciences.

- Alphabetic Style: A combination of numeric and author-year styles, where references are labeled using the author's name and year (e.g., "[Lam94]").

- Footnote Style: Instead of appearing in the text, citations are placed in footnotes, offering a classic reference format commonly used in history and law.

The following table illustrates how each citation style appears within a document (Table 5.1):

Style	**In-text Citation**	**Bibliography Entry Format**
Numeric	`[1]`	Numbered list by citation order
Author-Year	`(Lamport, 1994)`	Sorted alphabetically by author
Alphabetic	`[Lam94]`	Sorted alphabetically by author
Footnote	Citation in a footnote	Footnotes containing references

Table 5.1: Comparison of different citation styles in `biblatex`

5.2.6 Example: Switching Between Citation and Bibliography Styles

To demonstrate how switching styles affects the appearance of citations and the bibliography, consider the following LaTeX example:

Example: Switching to Author-Year Style

LaTeX Code:

```
\documentclass{article}
\usepackage[backend=biber,
style=authoryear,
citestyle=authoryear]{biblatex}
\addbibresource{references.bib}
```

```
\begin{document}

As Lamport explains in his book,
\textcite{lamport94},\LaTeX~is a
powerful tool for document preparation.
For a more technical perspective,
Knuth's article on \parencite{knuth74}
provides deeper insights into
literate programming.

\printbibliography[title={References}]

\end{document}
```

The output of this code is displayed below:

In-text Citations:

- "As Lamport explains in his book, Lamport (1994), LaTeX is a powerful tool..."
- "For a more technical perspective, Knuth's article on (Knuth, 1984) provides insights..."

Bibliography:

```
Knuth, Donald E. (1984). Literate Programming.
    The Computer Journal, 27(2), 97-111.

Lamport, Leslie (1994). LaTeX: A Document
Preparation System. Addison-Wesley, 2nd
edition.
```

5.2.7 Modifying Citation Styles

If a different citation style is required, it is easy to modify the `biblatex` options. For instance, changing the citation style to numeric can be achieved by replacing:

Modifying Citation Style to Numeric

Modify this line in the preamble:

```
\usepackage[backend=biber, style=numeric,
citestyle=numeric]{biblatex}
```

After recompiling, citations in the text will now appear as:

In-text Citations:

- "As Lamport explains in his book [1], LaTeX is a powerful tool..."
- "For a more technical perspective, Knuth's article on [2] provides insights..."

Bibliography:

```
[1] Leslie Lamport, LaTeX: A Document
Preparation System, Addison-Wesley,
2nd edition, 1994.

[2] Donald E. Knuth, Literate Programming,
The Computer Journal, vol. 27, no. 2,
pp. 97-111, 1984.
```

5.3 Managing Multiple References

In academic writing, there are many cases where you need to cite multiple references together. Whether you are referring to several papers that discuss a similar topic or citing a range of sources that contribute to an argument, LaTeX makes it easy to manage multiple references in a clean, efficient way.

In this section, we will cover various methods for citing multiple references using `biblatex` and other LaTeX citation packages. You will learn how to combine citations, format them, and manage them effectively in your document.

5.3.1 Citing Multiple References with `biblatex`

Academic writing often requires citing multiple sources within a single reference. The `biblatex` package allows for this by simply listing multiple citation keys within a single `\cite` command, separating them with commas. This approach is particularly useful when referencing several studies that support a particular argument or concept.

For example, if multiple authors have discussed the role of LaTeX and literate programming in scientific writing, a single citation can include all relevant references, ensuring a concise yet informative citation format.

The following example demonstrates how multiple references can be cited in an author-year citation style:

Example: Citing Multiple References

LaTeX Code:

```
\documentclass{article}
```

```
\usepackage[backend=biber,
style=authoryear]{biblatex}
\addbibresource{references.bib}

\begin{document}

Several studies \cite{lamport94,knuth74}
have addressed the use of LaTeX and
literate programming.

\printbibliography
\end{document}
```

This produces the following in-text citation (Fig. 5.2):

Output:

- "Several studies (Lamport, 1994; Knuth, 1984) have addressed the use of LaTeX and literate programming."

Figure 5.2: Example output for multiple citations

The references are automatically sorted and formatted according to the selected citation style. In this case, the author-year style arranges the references in alphabetical order of the authors' last names. If the numeric citation style were used instead, the result would appear as "[1,2]," following the order of references in the bibliography.

5.3.2 Customizing the Separator Between Multiple References

By default, `biblatex` separates multiple citations with a semicolon when using author-year or alphabetic styles.

However, there may be instances where a different delimiter, such as a comma, is preferred. This customization can be achieved using the `\multicitedelim` command.

For instance, if the desired format requires references to be separated by a comma rather than a semicolon, the following command should be included in the document preamble:

Example: Changing Citation Separator

LaTeX Code:

```
\renewcommand*{\multicitedelim}
{\addcomma\space}
```

After recompiling, the citation will now appear in the modified format (Fig. 5.3):

Output (Modified Separator):

- "Several studies (Lamport, 1994, Knuth, 1984) have addressed the use of LaTeX and literate programming."

Figure 5.3: Example output with custom citation separator

This ensures that citations are formatted consistently with journal or institutional requirements.

5.3.3 Using Other Citation Commands for Multiple References

While the standard `\cite` command is widely used for in-text citations, the `biblatex` package provides additional citation commands that allow for more flexibility in how references are presented. Depending on the context, authors may prefer citations in parentheses, integrated into the text, or placed in footnotes.

A common alternative to `\cite` is `\parencite`, which ensures that multiple references appear in parentheses. This style is particularly useful when citations are placed at the end of a sentence or when multiple sources are being referenced in the same argument. Additionally, for citations that should appear in footnotes rather than in the main text, `\footcite` provides an effective solution.

Consider the following example, which demonstrates how multiple references can be included using different citation commands:

Example: Using Different Citation Commands

LaTeX Code:

```
\documentclass{article}
\usepackage[backend=biber,
style=authoryear]{biblatex}
\addbibresource{references.bib}

\begin{document}

Several approaches \parencite{lamport94,
knuth74} have been proposed for document
preparation. The detailed explanation of
literate programming can be found in
\footcite{knuth74, lamport94}.

\printbibliography
\end{document}
```

In the compiled document, the citations will appear as follows (Fig. 5.4):

Output:

- "Several approaches (Lamport, 1994; Knuth, 1984) have been proposed for document preparation. The detailed explanation of literate programming can be found in a footnote."

Figure 5.4: Example output for different citation styles

The citation generated by `\parencite` places the references in parentheses, ensuring a clear and readable format. On the other hand, `\footcite` moves the references to a footnote, reducing clutter in the main text while still maintaining proper attribution.

Another useful citation command is `\textcite`, which integrates the reference directly into the flow of a sentence. This is particularly useful when discussing the author's contributions in a narrative form. For example:

Example: Using Textcite for Integrated Citations

LaTeX Code:

```
\textcite{lamport94} describes LaTeX as
a powerful document preparation system,
emphasizing its structured approach to
typesetting.
```

This produces (Fig. 5.5):

Output:

- "Lamport (1994) describes LaTeX as a powerful document preparation system, emphasizing its structured approach to typesetting."

Figure 5.5: Example output for integrated citations

The advantage of using `\textcite` is that it naturally integrates the citation into the narrative, making the writing more fluid while still providing proper attribution.

By carefully choosing the appropriate citation command, writers can ensure that their references enhance readability and clarity. Whether using parenthetical citations for a concise reference style, footnotes for a cleaner main text, or inline citations for a more integrated narrative, `biblatex` provides the flexibility needed for various academic and technical writing scenarios.

The next section will explore how to group references into separate sections in a bibliography, allowing for further customization in how citations are organized and presented.

5.3.4 Grouping References into Bibliography Sections

If your document contains different types of references (e.g., books, articles, websites), it might be useful to split them into separate sections within the bibliography. With `biblatex`, you can use the `keyword` option to categorize references and print them in separate sections.

First, add keywords to your `.bib` file as:

```
@book{lamport94,
  author    = {Leslie Lamport},
  title     = {LaTeX: A Document Preparation
               System},
  publisher = {Addison-Wesley},
  year      = {1994},
  edition   = {2nd},
  address   = {Massachusetts},
  keywords  = {book}
}
```

```
@article{knuth74,
  author    = {Donald E. Knuth},
  title     = {Literate Programming},
  journal   = {The Computer Journal},
  year      = {1984},
  volume    = {27},
  number    = {2},
  pages     = {97--111},
  keywords  = {article}
}
```

Next, print the bibliography in sections as:

```
\printbibliography[heading=subbibliography,
title={Books}, keyword=book]
\printbibliography[heading=subbibliography,
title={Articles}, keyword=article]
```

This will generate separate bibliography sections, one for books and one for articles.

5.3.5 Grouping References into Bibliography Sections

In academic and technical writing, it is often necessary to distinguish between different types of sources, such as books, journal articles, conference papers, and online sources. Organizing the bibliography into separate sections can improve clarity and readability, allowing readers to quickly locate references relevant to specific categories.

With `biblatex`, references can be categorized using the `keyword` field within the `.bib` file. This enables the creation of sub-bibliographies where entries are grouped under distinct headings based on their type.

To illustrate this approach, consider the following `.bib` file, which contains a book reference and a journal article. Each entry is assigned a keyword that reflects its type.

Example: Assigning Keywords in the `.bib` File

LaTeX Code:

```
@book{lamport94,
  author    = {Leslie Lamport},
  title     = {LaTeX: A Document
               Preparation System},
  publisher = {Addison-Wesley},
  year      = {1994},
  edition   = {2nd},
  address   = {Massachusetts},
  keywords  = {book}
}

@article{knuth74,
  author    = {Donald E. Knuth},
  title     = {Literate Programming},
  journal   = {The Computer Journal},
  year      = {1984},
  volume    = {27},
  number    = {2},
  pages     = {97--111},
  keywords  = {article}
}
```

Each reference entry includes a `keywords` field. The book by Lamport is assigned the keyword `book`, while the journal article by Knuth is labeled with `article`. These keywords serve as filters, allowing the bibliography to be divided into multiple sections.

Once the references are properly categorized, they can be printed in separate sections using the `printbibliography` command. The following example demonstrates how to generate distinct bibliography sections for books and journal articles.

Example: Printing the Bibliography in Sections

LaTeX Code:

```
\documentclass{article}
\usepackage[backend=biber,
style=authoryear]{biblatex}
\addbibresource{references.bib}

\begin{document}

This document contains references
categorized into books and journal
articles.

\printbibliography[heading
=subbibliography,
title={Books}, keyword=book]
\printbibliography[heading
=subbibliography,
title={Articles}, keyword=article]

\end{document}
```

The output of the above LaTeX code will appear as follows:

Output:

- **Books**
  - Lamport, Leslie (1994). *LaTeX: A Document Preparation System.* Addison-Wesley.

- **Articles**
  - Knuth, Donald E. (1984). "Literate Programming". *The Computer Journal*, 27(2), 97-111.

In this example, the bibliography is organized into two sections, each with its own title. The `heading=subbibliography` option ensures that each section is visually distinct, making it easier for readers to locate specific references.

Grouping references into categories is particularly useful when working with large bibliographies, as it enhances organization and readability. This technique is commonly employed in academic dissertations, review papers, and technical reports where multiple types of sources are used. It is also beneficial for interdisciplinary research, where literature from different fields needs to be clearly delineated.

Beyond simply categorizing references into books and articles, this method can be extended to include conference papers, websites, reports, and even personal communications by adding appropriate keywords in the `.bib` file. This ensures a well-structured bibliography that aligns with best practices in scholarly writing.

5.3.6 Ordering and Sorting Multiple References

In academic writing, the way references are ordered in citations and bibliographies plays a crucial role in maintaining clarity and consistency. The `biblatex` package automatically manages the sorting of references based on the chosen citation style. For example, in a numeric citation style, references appear in the order they are cited within the text, whereas in an author-year style, citations are sorted by the author's last name followed by the year of publication.

For those who require greater control over sorting, `biblatex` provides the `sorting` option, allowing customization of how references are ordered in the bibliography. The following example demonstrates how to sort the bibliography by year first, then by author name, and finally by the title.

Example: Sorting References by Year Author and Title

LaTeX Code:

```
\documentclass{article}
\usepackage[backend=biber,
style=authoryear, sorting=ynt]{biblatex}
\addbibresource{references.bib}

\begin{document}

Several works have discussed document
preparation systems
\cite{lamport94, knuth74, goossens93}.

\printbibliography[title={References}]

\end{document}
```

The `sorting=ynt` option ensures that entries in the bibliography are ordered first by year, then by author name, and finally by title in cases where the year and author match (Fig. 5.6).

Output:

- Knuth, Donald E. (1984). "Literate Programming". *The Computer Journal*, 27(2), 97–111.
- Lamport, Leslie (1994). *LaTeX: A Document Preparation System.* Addison-Wesley.
- Goossens, Michel (1997). *The LaTeX Companion.* Addison-Wesley.

Figure 5.6: Example output for sorted bibliography

As shown in the output, the bibliography is now sorted chronologically, ensuring that older works appear first, followed by newer references. Within each year, entries are arranged alphabetically by author, and when authors share the same year, their works are ordered by title.

5.3.7 Controlling Citation Order Within a Document

While bibliography sorting affects how references are displayed at the end of the document, `biblatex` also controls how multiple citations appear in the text. By default, citations are automatically sorted according to the chosen citation style. However, in cases where references need to appear in a specific order (e.g., following a logical progression in the discussion), manual citation sequencing can be enforced by listing citation keys in the desired order.

The following example demonstrates how multiple references can be grouped into a single citation while ensuring correct ordering:

Example: Manually Controlling Citation Order

LaTeX Code:

```
\documentclass{article}
\usepackage[backend=biber,
style=authoryear]{biblatex}
\addbibresource{references.bib}

\begin{document}

The development of document formatting
systems has been widely discussed
\cite{goossens93, knuth74, lamport94}.

\printbibliography[title={References}]

\end{document}
```

In this example, even though the default sorting would typically place Knuth (1984) first, followed by Lamport (1994), and then Goossens (1997), the order in the citation follows the sequence specified within the `\cite` command: Goossens, Knuth, Lamport (Fig. 5.7).

Output:

- (Goossens, 1997; Knuth, 1984; Lamport, 1994)

Figure 5.7: Example output for manually ordered citations

5.3.8 Using Citation Sorting Options

For those requiring different types of citation ordering, `biblatex` offers the `sortcites` option. This setting ensures that references in the same citation command are sorted automatically.

Example: Enforcing Automatic Citation Sorting

LaTeX Code:

```
\usepackage[backend=biber,
style=authoryear,
sortcites=true]{biblatex}
```

With `sortcites=true`, the order of references inside a single citation block will always be alphabetized according to the citation style, overriding any manually specified order.

The next section will explore advanced features such as grouping citations, using sub-bibliographies for different types of references, and customizing citation styles for specific disciplines.

5.4 Cross-Referencing Sections, Equations, and Figures

In any structured document, it is often necessary to refer to different parts of the text dynamically. Instead of manually entering numbers, LaTeX provides a robust system for cross-referencing sections, equations, figures, and tables using automatic numbering. This feature ensures that all references remain accurate even when the document undergoes changes.

The mechanism behind cross-referencing in LaTeX is based on two fundamental commands: `\label` and `\ref`. The `\label` command assigns a unique identifier to an element (such as a section or figure), and `\ref` retrieves the automatically assigned number when referring to it later in the text.

5.4.1 Cross-Referencing Sections and Subsections

In structured writing, sections and subsections often need to be referenced to maintain coherence and allow readers to navigate easily. LaTeX enables cross-referencing sections by assigning a label immediately after the section definition.

Labeling and Referencing a Section

To reference a section dynamically, a label should be placed inside or immediately after the `\section` command. Later in the document, the section number can be retrieved using the `\ref` command.

Example: Labeling and Referencing a Section

LaTeX Code:

```
\section{Introduction}
\label{sec:intro}

As discussed in Section~\ref{sec:intro},
cross-referencing ensures numbering
updates automatically.
```

The corresponding output is (Fig. 5.8):

Output:

- **Section 1 Introduction**
- As discussed in **Section 1**, cross-referencing ensures numbering updates automatically.

Figure 5.8: Example output for section referencing

In this example, the label `sec:intro` is assigned to the "Introduction" section. The `\ref` command dynamically retrieves the section number, ensuring that if the section number changes due to document modifications, the reference updates automatically.

Referencing a Subsection

The same approach applies to subsections. By labeling a subsection, it becomes possible to reference it later without manually entering numbers.

Example: Labeling and Referencing a Subsection

LaTeX Code:

```
\subsection{Motivation}
\label{subsec:motivation}

As discussed in Subsection~\ref{subsec:
motivation}, we explore the motivation
behind using LaTeX.
```

The output for this code will display (Fig. 5.9):

Output:

- **Subsection 1.1 Motivation**
- As discussed in **Subsection 1.1**, we explore the motivation behind using LaTeX.

Figure 5.9: Example output for subsection referencing

This example follows the same principle, ensuring that numbering remains dynamic and accurate.

5.4.2 Referencing Equations in LaTeX

Mathematical writing often requires references to equations, ensuring that the reader can follow derivations or related discussions easily. The `\label` command should be placed inside the `equation` environment to assign a reference, and the equation number can be retrieved using `\ref`.

Example: Labeling and Referencing an Equation

LaTeX Code:

```
\begin{equation}
    E = mc^2
    \label{eq:einstein}
    \end{equation}}\endalttext

As shown in Equation~\ref{eq:einstein},
energy and mass are directly related.
```

The resulting output is (Fig. 5.10):

Output:

$$E = mc^2 \tag{5.1}$$

As shown in **Equation (5.1)**, energy and mass are directly related.

Figure 5.10: Example output for equation referencing

Here, Equation (5.1) dynamically references the numbered equation.

5.4.3 Cross-Referencing Figures

Figures are another crucial component of scientific and technical writing. Labeling and referencing figures in LaTeX follows the same pattern as sections and equations.

The `\label` command should be placed inside the `figure` environment, usually below the `\caption` command.

Example: Labeling and Referencing a Figure

LaTeX Code:

```
\begin{figure}[H]
\centering
\includegraphics[width=0.5\textwidth]
{example-image}
\caption{An example figure}
\label{fig:example}
\end{figure}

Figure~\ref{fig:example} illustrates how
to reference figures in LaTeX.
```

Output:

This ensures that even if figure numbering changes, the references remain accurate.

5.4.4 Cross-Referencing Tables

In structured documents, tables often contain critical data that must be referenced throughout the text. Rather than manually typing table numbers, LaTeX provides an automated cross-referencing system that ensures table numbers remain correct even if tables are added, removed, or rearranged.

The mechanism for referencing tables in LaTeX is similar to referencing figures and equations. A label is assigned to the table using the `\label` command, and later in the text, the `\ref` command retrieves the corresponding table number.

Labeling and Referencing a Table

To reference a table dynamically, the `\label` command should be placed inside the `table` environment, typically after the `\caption` command. This ensures that LaTeX correctly associates the label with the table number.

The following example illustrates how to create and reference a table:

Example: Labeling and Referencing a Table

LaTeX Code:

```
\begin{table}[htbp]
    \centering
    \begin{tabular}{|c|c|}
        \hline
        Item & Value \\
        \hline
        A    & 100   \\
        B    & 200   \\
        \hline
    \end{tabular}
    \caption{Sample data table}
    \label{tab:sample}
\end{table}
```

```
Table~\ref{tab:sample} presents sample
values for items A and B.
```

In this example, the label `tab:sample` is assigned to the table containing sample values. The `\ref` command dynamically retrieves the table number, ensuring that if the numbering changes due to modifications in the document, all references remain accurate.

Referencing Tables in Different Sections

When working with long documents such as research papers or theses, it is useful to reference tables from different sections. The `\ref` command works seamlessly across sections, ensuring consistency in table numbering.

For example:

Example: Cross-referencing Tables Across Sections

LaTeX Code:

```
\section{Results}
\label{sec:results}

Table~\ref{tab:sample} in Section
~\ref{sec:tables} illustrates sample
values.

\section{Tables}
\label{sec:tables}

\begin{table}[htbp]
    \centering
    \begin{tabular}{|c|c|}
        \hline
```

```
        Item & Value \\
        \hline
        A    & 100   \\
        B    & 200   \\
        \hline
    \end{tabular}
    \caption{Sample data table}
    \label{tab:sample}
\end{table}
```

The resulting output dynamically links the reference in the "Results" section to the correct table in the "Tables" section.

5.4.5 Hyperlinks for Cross-References

Cross-referencing is a powerful feature in LaTeX that allows for seamless navigation within a document. By default, references to sections, figures, tables, and equations appear as plain text. However, to enhance readability and accessibility in the resulting PDF, LaTeX offers the `hyperref` package, which automatically converts these references into clickable hyperlinks. This functionality ensures that users can jump directly to the referenced element with a single click, making navigation intuitive in large documents such as research papers, dissertations, and books.

Enabling Hyperlinks in LaTeX

To enable hyperlinks in your LaTeX document, the `hyperref` package must be loaded in the preamble:

Example: Enabling Hyperlinks

LaTeX Code:

```
\documentclass{article}
\usepackage{hyperref}

\begin{document}

\section{Introduction}
\label{sec:intro}

As mentioned in Section~\ref{sec:intro},
cross-referencing is an essential
feature in structured documents.

\end{document}
```

In this example, loading the `hyperref` package ensures that when compiled, the reference to `Section~\ref{sec:intro}` appears as a clickable link in the PDF. Readers can navigate directly to the labeled section without manually scrolling through the document.

Hyperlinking Figures, Equations, and Tables

Beyond sections, the `hyperref` package also enables clickable references for figures, equations, and tables, ensuring that each numbered reference remains interactive. The following example demonstrates how hyperlinks work with different elements:

Example: Hyperlinked Cross-references for Figures Equations and Tables

LaTeX Code:

```
\documentclass{article}
\usepackage{hyperref}
\usepackage{graphicx}
\begin{document}
\section{Introduction}
\label{sec:intro}
Cross-referencing figures, equations,
and tables helps maintain coherence
in structured documents.
\begin{figure}[htbp]
 \centering
 \includegraphics[width=0.5\textwidth]
 {example-image.png}
 \caption{An example image}
 \label{fig:example}
\end{figure}
As illustrated in
Figure~\ref{fig:example}, a sample
image is included for demonstration.
{\begin{equation}
    E = mc^2
    \label{eq:einstein}
\end{equation}}\endalttext
Einstein's famous equation is given in
Equation~\ref{eq:einstein}.
\begin{table}[htbp]
    \centering
    \begin{tabular}{|c|c|}
        \hline
        Item & Value \\
```

```
        \hline
        A     & 100     \\
        B     & 200     \\
        \hline
    \end{tabular}
    \caption{Sample data table}
    \label{tab:sample}
\end{table}
The values presented in
Table~\ref{tab:sample} provide
an overview of
the recorded data.
\end{document}
```

The output of this code dynamically links the references in the text to the corresponding figure, equation, and table, ensuring a seamless reading experience (Fig. 5.11).

Output:

- As illustrated in Figure **??**, a sample image is included for demonstration.
- Einstein's famous equation is given in Equation **??**.
- The values presented in Table **??** provide an overview of the recorded data.

Figure 5.11: Example output for hyperlinked references

Here, ref{} will show the figure, equation, and table numbering when referred correctly.

Customizing Hyperlink Colors and Behavior

By default, LaTeX generates hyperlinks in a color determined by the PDF viewer, often blue or red. To customize hyperlink colors, additional options can be passed to the `hyperref` package, allowing greater control over link appearance and behavior:

Example: Customizing Hyperlink Colors

LaTeX Code:

```
\usepackage[colorlinks=true,
linkcolor=blue, urlcolor=red,
citecolor=green]{hyperref}
```

This command modifies hyperlink settings as follows:

- `colorlinks=true`: Enables colored hyperlinks instead of default boxed links.
- `linkcolor=blue`: Changes internal document links (e.g., sections, figures, equations) to blue.
- `urlcolor=red`: Changes hyperlinks to external URLs to red.
- `citecolor=green`: Changes citation links to green.

Applying this customization ensures that hyperlinks integrate well with the document's formatting style, maintaining clarity while preserving accessibility.

Exercises for Chap. 5: Managing References and Citations

5.1 Adding Citations and Bibliography Using biblatex

1. **Setting Up a Bibliography**: Write a LaTeX document that includes a bibliography using the `biblatex` package. Create a separate `.bib` file with at least three references (books or articles) and include it in your document.

2. **Using Different Backends**: Modify your LaTeX document to compile using both `biber` and `bibtex`. Observe any differences in the output and explain when you might prefer one backend over the other.

3. **Basic Citation**: Add citations to your document using `\cite{}` and `\fullcite{}`. Ensure that each reference from your `.bib` file appears correctly in the final bibliography.

5.2 In-text Citations and Bibliography Styles

1. **Using Different Citation Styles**: Modify your LaTeX document to experiment with different citation styles provided by `biblatex` (e.g., numeric, author-year, alphabetic). Compile the document using each style and observe the changes in both in-text citations and the bibliography format.

2. **Creating a Custom Citation Style**: Customize a citation style using options from `biblatex`. For example, change the delimiter between multiple author names or modify the appearance of the in-text citations.

3. **Citation Placement**: Add multiple in-text citations to different sections of your document. Place citations at the end of sentences, within sentences, and as part of the text. Explain when and why you might use each type of placement.

5.3 Managing Multiple References

1. **Citing Multiple Sources**: Write a LaTeX document where you cite multiple sources at once. Use the `\cite{}` command to reference two or more sources in the same citation.

2. **Sorting References**: Modify the order in which references are displayed when you cite multiple sources. For example, ensure that citations are sorted numerically or alphabetically based on author name.

3. **Grouping Citations**: Write a LaTeX document that groups related citations together in a meaningful way. For example, group citations from the same author or year.

5.4 Cross-Referencing Sections, Equations, Figures

1. **Cross-referencing Sections**: Write a LaTeX document that includes at least three sections. Use the `\label` and `\ref` commands to reference the sections from within the text. For example, reference Section 2 from Section 1.

2. **Cross-referencing Equations**: Include a mathematical equation in your document and label it. Reference the equation from other parts of the document using the `\ref` command.

3. **Cross-referencing Figures and Tables**: Insert a figure and a table in your document, add captions and labels to each, and reference them using `\ref`. Ensure the references automatically update if you move or renumber the figures and tables.

Chapter 6

Customizing Layouts

Contents

Md Aquib, *Fundamentals of LaTeX*, University Texts in the Mathematical Sciences,
https://doi.org/10.1007/978-981-96-9318-4_6

Abstract: One of the key strengths of LaTeX lies in its ability to produce documents with clean, consistent, and professional layouts. While the default settings are often sufficient for many documents, there are numerous situations, such as preparing a thesis, article, report, or poster, where customizing the layout is necessary to meet institutional guidelines, publisher requirements, or personal preferences.

Keywords: Page layout, Headers and footers, Geometry package, Table of contents, Title page, Multicolumn formatting

This chapter provides a comprehensive guide to customizing the layout of a LaTeX document. We begin by exploring how to adjust margins, line spacing, and page dimensions to achieve precise control over the document's appearance. We then delve into the customization of headers and footers using packages such as `fancyhdr` and `scrlayer-scrpage`, enabling you to add running titles, page numbers, and institutional logos.

You will also learn how to modify section heading styles, change font sizes and families globally or locally, and define custom environments for structured formatting. Advanced techniques such as altering float placement for figures and tables, modifying list indentation, and redefining structural elements will also be discussed.

By the end of this chapter, you will be equipped with the tools and techniques needed to create layouts that are both visually appealing and functionally appropriate for any type of document.

6.1 Page Layout, Margins, and Spacing

Customizing the layout of a LaTeX document involves controlling the page dimensions, margins, and spacing. By default, LaTeX follows typographical standards, which means that its default margins and layouts are designed for high-quality typesetting. However, in certain cases, such as academic papers, technical reports, or presentations, you might need to adjust these settings to fit specific requirements. In this section, we will cover how to adjust page layout, margins, and spacing in LaTeX.

6.1.1 Controlling Page Layout with the `geometry` Package

The layout of a document in LaTeX is determined by various factors, including page size, margins, text width, and positioning of elements such as headers and footers. By default, LaTeX adheres to typographical standards designed for readability and high-quality typesetting. However, in some cases, such as academic theses, technical reports, or conference papers, customizing the page layout is necessary to meet specific formatting requirements.

The most efficient way to control page dimensions in LaTeX is through the `geometry` package. This package provides an intuitive method for defining page size, setting margins, and adjusting text positioning with minimal effort.

Loading the Geometry Package

To begin using the `geometry` package, it must be loaded in the document preamble. The following example demonstrates a basic configuration:

Example: Setting Page Size and Margins

LaTeX Code:

```
\documentclass{article}
\usepackage[a4paper, margin=1in]
{geometry}
\begin{document}

This document uses A4 paper with 1-inch
margins on all sides.

\end{document}
```

This configuration achieves two primary layout adjustments: The document is set to A4 paper size, which measures 210 × 297 mm, and the margins are uniformly set to 1 inch on all sides.

Specifying Custom Margins

Instead of using the general `margin` option, individual margins can be customized separately using parameters such as `top`, `bottom`, `left`, and `right`. This allows for precise control over page spacing.

For example, to set a document with 1.5-inch left margin, 1-inch right margin, 1.2-inch top margin, and 1-inch bottom margin, the following configuration is used:

Example: Customizing Individual Margins

LaTeX Code:

```
\usepackage[a4paper, left=1.5in,
right=1in, top=1.2in,bottom=1in]{geometry}
```

This approach is particularly useful when adhering to specific document formatting guidelines, such as university dissertation templates or official report standards.

Adjusting Page Width and Height

In some cases, documents require fine-tuned control over text width and page height. The `geometry` package allows for direct specification of these dimensions. The following example demonstrates how to set a text width of 6 inches and a text height of 9 inches while keeping centered margins:

Example: Customizing Text Width and Height

LaTeX Code:

```
\usepackage[a4paper, textwidth=6in,
textheight=9in]{geometry}
```

By default, LaTeX places the text block in a well-balanced position on the page. However, if more vertical space is required, adjustments to `top` and `bottom` margins should be made accordingly.

Page Orientation: Portrait vs. Landscape

The default orientation for LaTeX documents is portrait. However, for posters, diagrams, or presentation slides, switching to landscape mode may be necessary. The `geometry` package provides a simple way to accomplish this by adding the `landscape` option:

Example: Setting Landscape Orientation

LaTeX Code:

```
\usepackage[a4paper, landscape,
margin=1in]{geometry}
```

This setting rotates the entire page layout by 90 degrees, making it useful for documents that require wide tables or panoramic content.

Using Predefined Paper Sizes

Apart from A4, other standard paper sizes can be specified, such as: letterpaper: 8.5×11 inches (common in North America), legalpaper: 8.5×14 inches, and executivepaper: 7.25×10.5 inches.

To set a document to letter size with 1-inch margins, use:

Example: Setting a Letter-Sized Page

LaTeX Code:

```
\usepackage[letterpaper, margin=1in]
{geometry}
```

Similarly, for legal-sized paper with 1.5-inch margins:

Example: Setting a Legal-Sized Page

LaTeX Code:

```
\usepackage[legalpaper, margin=1.5in]
{geometry}
```

Fine-Tuning Margins for Binding

For printed books and documents that require binding, an additional inner margin is necessary to prevent content from being obscured. This can be achieved with the `bindingoffset` option. For example, to create a binding offset of 0.5 inches, use:

Example: Adding Binding Offset for Book Printing

LaTeX Code:

```
\usepackage[a4paper, margin=1in,
bindingoffset=0.5in]{geometry}
```

This setting shifts the inner margin, ensuring that printed pages have sufficient space for binding without cutting off text.

6.1.2 Customizing Margins

The margins of a document play a significant role in its readability, aesthetics, and compliance with publishing standards. By default, LaTeX sets margins that optimize readability based on traditional typesetting practices. However, specific requirements for research papers, technical reports, and books often necessitate precise control over margin settings. The `geometry` package provides a convenient and flexible way to define custom margins, allowing users to modify individual margins for the left, right, top, and bottom of a page.

To apply customized margins, the `geometry` package should be included in the preamble with explicit margin values. Consider the following example, which sets different margins for each side of the document:

Example: Setting Custom Margins

LaTeX Code:

```
\documentclass{article}
\usepackage[
  a4paper,
  left=1.5in,
  right=1in,
  top=1in,
  bottom=1.5in
]{geometry}
\begin{document}

This document demonstrates custom
margin settings.

\end{document}
```

In this configuration: The left margin is set to *1.5 inches*, providing extra space for binding in printed documents, the right margin is set to *1 inch*, ensuring proper alignment and balance, the top margin is *1 inch*, maintaining a clean layout, and the bottom margin is *1.5 inches*, which can be useful for annotations or page numbers.

Adjusting Margins Dynamically

In some cases, adjusting margins within the document itself is necessary, especially when dealing with title pages, appendices, or special sections that require distinct formatting. The `geometry` package provides the `\newgeometry` and `\restoregeometry` commands to modify margins at specific points in the document.

For example, to temporarily change the margins for a section while maintaining the default settings for the rest of the document:

Example: Changing Margins for Specific Sections

LaTeX Code:

```
\documentclass{article}
\usepackage[a4paper, margin=1in]
{geometry}

\begin{document}

\section{Regular Section}
This section follows the standard margin
settings.

\newgeometry{left=2in, right=1in,
top=1.5in, bottom=2in}

\section{Special Section}
This section has different margins to
accommodate larger figures or tables.

\restoregeometry

\section{Returning to Normal}
The document now follows the original
1-inch margin settings.

\end{document}
```

Here, `\newgeometry` modifies the margin settings for the "Special Section," while `\restoregeometry` reverts them to the original values.

Considering Layout Balance and Readability

While it is tempting to minimize margins to fit more content onto a page, overly narrow margins can compromise readability and make the document appear cluttered. Conversely, excessively wide margins might waste space, reducing the efficiency of printed documents. A well-balanced layout often considers the following factors:

1. *Printed vs. Digital Documents*: Printed materials benefit from slightly wider margins to accommodate binding and allow for easier reading.

2. *Column Layouts*: Documents with multiple columns, such as scientific papers, often require narrower margins to maximize text width.

3. *Academic and Publishing Standards*: Some institutions and publishers provide specific margin guidelines that should be adhered to.

By leveraging the `geometry` package effectively, it is possible to create well-structured documents that balance aesthetics and functionality while meeting specific formatting requirements.

6.1.3 Page Size and Orientation

By default, LaTeX uses standard page dimensions that align with professional typesetting norms. However, depending on the document type and intended audience, you may need to customize the page size or change the orientation. The `geometry` package provides an intuitive way to adjust these settings, ensuring that the document adheres to required specifications without manual formatting efforts.

The most commonly used paper sizes in LaTeX are *A4 (210mm × 297mm)* and *US Letter (8.5in × 11in)*. While

A4 is widely used in academic and professional settings worldwide, US Letter is the standard in North America. You can explicitly define the paper size by loading the `geometry` package in the document preamble as follows:

Example: Setting Page Size

LaTeX Code:

```
\documentclass{article}
\usepackage[a4paper, margin=1in]
{geometry}

\begin{document}

This document uses A4 paper with
1-inch margins.

\end{document}
```

Here, the `a4paper` option explicitly sets the page size to A4, while the `margin=1in` command ensures uniform 1-inch margins on all sides.

Switching to Landscape Mode

Certain types of documents, such as *posters, wide tables, or presentation-style reports*, benefit from a landscape orientation rather than the default portrait mode. Landscape mode rotates the page by 90 degrees, making it wider than it is tall. This can be useful when displaying large datasets, long equations, or detailed schematics.

To enable landscape orientation, modify the `geometry` package options as follows:

Example: Landscape Mode

LaTeX Code:

```
\documentclass{article}
\usepackage[letterpaper, landscape,
margin=1in]{geometry}

\begin{document}

This page is in landscape orientation,
making it suitable for wide content
such as tables and diagrams.

\end{document}
```

Here, `letterpaper` sets the paper size to US Letter, while `landscape` rotates the page. The margin remains set at 1 inch to maintain consistency.

Custom Page Sizes for Special Documents

Beyond A4 and US Letter, LaTeX supports a wide range of paper sizes, including *executive*, *legal*, and *custom-defined sizes.* If a specific page dimension is required, you can specify exact width and height measurements using the `geometry` package. For example, a document with a *7-inch by 10-inch* custom page size can be defined as:

Example: Custom Page Size

LaTeX Code:

```
\documentclass{article}
\usepackage[paperwidth=7in, paperheight=
10in, margin=0.75in]{geometry}
```

```
\begin{document}

This document is formatted with a
custom page size.

\end{document}
```

This setup ensures that the document adheres to specific printing or publishing standards without requiring external resizing.

Considerations for Digital and Print Documents

When choosing a page size, it is essential to consider whether the document is intended for *digital viewing or physical printing*. Digital formats, such as PDF documents meant for screen reading, often use wider margins for better readability on different devices. On the other hand, print documents need sufficient margin space for binding or trimming.

For digital-first documents, a slightly modified layout with more generous outer margins can improve on-screen legibility. Meanwhile, print-oriented documents may require *mirror margins*, ensuring that left-hand and right-hand pages align correctly in a bookbinding format.

Combining Page Layout Settings

The flexibility of the `geometry` package allows combining multiple settings in a single command. For instance, the following configuration creates an *A4 document in landscape mode with custom margins*:

Example: Combining Page Layout Settings

LaTeX Code:

```
\documentclass{article}
\usepackage[a4paper, landscape, left=1in,
right=0.75in, top=1.5in, bottom=1in]
{geometry}

\begin{document}

This A4 document is in landscape mode
with asymmetric margins.

\end{document}
```

This configuration ensures optimal space usage while maintaining an aesthetic layout that meets the document's specific needs.

By leveraging the capabilities of the `geometry` package, LaTeX users can *fine-tune page layout settings* to produce documents that are both visually appealing and functionally appropriate for different presentation contexts.

6.1.4 Controlling Spacing with setspace

Line spacing plays a crucial role in document formatting, ensuring that text remains readable and properly structured. While LaTeX provides *single spacing* by default, some document types—such as theses, reports, and manuscripts—may require *one-and-a-half* or *double spacing.* The most efficient way to modify line spacing in LaTeX is by using the `setspace` package.

Loading the `setspace` Package

To enable flexible spacing adjustments, the `setspace` package must first be included in the document's preamble:

Enabling the `setspace` Package

LaTeX Code:

```
\documentclass{article}
\usepackage{setspace}
\begin{document}
```

Once the package is loaded, spacing can be adjusted either *globally* for the entire document or *locally* within specific sections.

Setting Global Line Spacing

If the entire document requires uniform spacing, a predefined spacing command can be placed at the start of the document:

Example: Global Line Spacing

LaTeX Code:

```
\documentclass{article}
\usepackage{setspace}

\begin{document}
\onehalfspacing
% Applies 1.5 spacing to the entire
document.

This entire document will use
one-and-a-half spacing.
```

```
\end{document}
```

Available global spacing options:

1. `\singlespacing` → Default LaTeX single spacing.
2. `\onehalfspacing` → Sets 1.5-line spacing (commonly used in academic papers).
3. `\doublespacing` → Enables double spacing (standard in theses and dissertations).

Adjusting Spacing for Specific Sections

Instead of applying a global setting, *local spacing adjustments* can be applied to individual sections or paragraphs. This is useful for *quotations, captions, or appendices* that may need different spacing than the main text.

Example: Localized Double Spacing

LaTeX Code:

```
This paragraph is in single spacing.

\begin{doublespace}
This section will use double spacing.
\end{doublespace}

This paragraph returns to the
document's default spacing.
```

Fine-Tuning Spacing with \setstretch

For cases where predefined options are not sufficient, spacing can be *customized* using the `\setstretch` command. This allows users to set custom line spacing ratios.

Example: Custom Spacing Factor

LaTeX Code:

```
\usepackage{setspace}
\renewcommand{\baselinestretch}{1.3}
% Custom spacing factor.
```

In this case, *1.3 spacing* is applied, allowing a fine-tuned adjustment between *single* and *one-and-a-half* spacing.

Spacing in Footnotes and Captions

In formal documents, *footnotes* and *captions* often require tighter spacing. The `\renewcommand` function allows for such modifications.

Example: Adjusting Footnote Spacing

LaTeX Code:

```
\renewcommand{\footnotesize}
{\setstretch{1.2}\small}
```

This ensures that footnotes remain *readable*, while preventing excessive spacing.

6.1.5 Fine-Tuning Paragraph Spacing

Proper paragraph spacing improves document readability and ensures a visually appealing layout. In LaTeX, paragraph spacing is controlled using two key parameters:

the vertical space between paragraphs and the indentation of the first line of each paragraph. These can be adjusted using the `\parskip` and `\parindent` commands.

Adjusting Space Between Paragraphs

By default, LaTeX does not insert additional vertical space between paragraphs. Instead, it relies on indentation to visually separate paragraphs. However, in some document styles, such as reports, presentations, or modern typographic layouts, it is preferable to increase the spacing between paragraphs rather than relying on indentation.

The spacing between paragraphs can be controlled using the `\parskip` command, which defines the amount of vertical space inserted before each new paragraph.

Example: Modifying Paragraph Spacing

LaTeX Code:

```
\documentclass{article}
\usepackage{setspace}

\setlength{\parskip}{0.5em}
% Adds extra space between paragraphs

\begin{document}

This is the first paragraph. Notice the
extra space before the next paragraph.

This is the second paragraph, now
clearly separated by vertical spacing.

\end{document}
```

In this example, the command:

```
\setlength{\parskip}{0.5em}
```

adds 0.5em of space between paragraphs. The unit `em` is relative to the font size, ensuring consistent spacing across different document styles.

Controlling Paragraph Indentation

Traditional documents, especially those in academic writing and book publishing, use indented paragraphs rather than additional spacing. By default, LaTeX indents the first line of every paragraph. The size of this indentation can be adjusted using the `\parindent` command.

Example: Adjusting Paragraph Indentation

LaTeX Code:

```
\documentclass{article}

\setlength{\parindent}{2em}
% Indents paragraphs by 2em

\begin{document}

This paragraph is indented by 2em.

This is another paragraph, continuing
the indentation style.

\end{document}
```

The command:

```
\setlength{\parindent}{2em}
```

sets the paragraph indentation to 2em, where 1em is approximately the width of a lowercase letter "m" in the current font.

Combining Paragraph Spacing and Indentation

In some document styles, especially those used in academic research papers, both paragraph indentation and spacing are combined. This ensures clarity while maintaining a professional layout.

For example, to define both paragraph indentation and spacing, use:

Example: Combining Indentation and Spacing

LaTeX Code:

```
\documentclass{article}

\setlength{\parindent}{2em}
% Indent paragraphs
\setlength{\parskip}{1em}
%Add vertical spacing between paragraphs

\begin{document}

This document uses both indentation and
additional paragraph spacing.

This ensures clear paragraph separation
while maintaining traditional indentation.

\end{document}
```

With these settings, each paragraph is indented by 2em while also having 1em of vertical spacing between consecutive paragraphs.

Removing Indentation for a Modern Look

For a modern document style (such as web-friendly PDFs or reports), indentation can be completely removed while increasing paragraph spacing. This is useful for documents where a clean, minimalist look is preferred.

To remove indentation, set:

```
\setlength{\parindent}{0pt}
```

This will result in paragraphs that are separated only by spacing, without indentation.

6.1.6 Adjusting Header and Footer Margins

The placement of headers and footers plays a crucial role in document readability and overall aesthetics. In LaTeX, the space between the main text and the headers or footers can be adjusted using the `geometry` package. This flexibility is especially useful in documents that require well-structured formatting, such as research papers, books, and dissertations.

By default, LaTeX provides a well-balanced header and footer spacing. However, if a document requires custom positioning of headers and footers, the `geometry` package allows fine control over their placement. The most relevant parameters for these adjustments include:

- `headheight`—Defines the height allocated for the header.
- `headsep`—Controls the vertical distance between the header and the main text.
- `footskip`—Determines the space between the footer and the body text.

For example, the following LaTeX code customizes these values to achieve a distinct separation between the header, footer, and the body content:

Adjusting Header and Footer Margins

```
\usepackage[
headheight=15pt,
% Increases the height of the header
headsep=20pt,
% Adds vertical space between header and text
footskip=30pt
% Adjusts the gap between the footer and
main text
]{geometry}
```

In this configuration, the header is given a height of 15 points, ensuring it accommodates larger section titles or custom header content. The `headsep` parameter increases the vertical spacing between the header and the document body, providing a cleaner visual distinction. The `footskip` setting ensures that the footer is placed at an appropriate distance from the main text.

Example: A Complete LaTeX Document with Custom Margins and Spacing

To illustrate how these settings affect the overall document layout, consider the following example. This example defines a document with specific margin configurations, custom header and footer spacing, and controlled line spacing:

```
\documentclass{article}
\usepackage[
    a4paper,
    left=1in, right=1in, top=1in, bottom=1in,
```

```
    headheight=15pt, headsep=20pt, footskip=30pt
]{geometry}
\usepackage{setspace}
\begin{document}
\title{Customizing Page Layout in LaTeX}
\author{Author Name}
\date{\today}
\maketitle
\section{Introduction}
The layout of a document plays an essential role
in enhancing readability and aesthetics. LaTeX
provides powerful tools to customize page
margins, headers, footers, and line spacing.
Using the \texttt{geometry}  package, one can
define precise margin settings, while the
\texttt{setspace} package enables
control over line spacing.

\section{Configuring Margins and Headers}

Margins define the blank space around the text
body, which helps with readability and provides
room for annotations. The \texttt{geometry}
package allows flexible adjustments.
In this document, we set 1-inch
margins on all sides, ensuring a uniform layout.
The header height is set to 15 points, providing
sufficient space for titles or running headers.
Additionally, a 30-point \texttt{footskip}
ensures that the footer does not appear too
close to the main text.

\section{Controlling Line Spacing}
Line spacing directly influences document
readability. LaTeX's \texttt{setspace} package
provides predefined spacing modes:
```

```
\begin{itemize}
    \item `\singlespacing` -- Standard
    single-line spacing
    \item `\onehalfspacing` -- One-and-a-half
     spacing, often used in academic documents
    \item `\doublespacing` -- Double spacing,
     commonly required for theses and formal
     reports
\end{itemize}

For instance, this paragraph is formatted using
`\onehalfspacing`, providing improved
readability. The following paragraph reverts to
single-line spacing:

\onehalfspacing
This paragraph uses one-and-a-half line spacing,
making it easier to read in longer documents
where excessive whitespace may not be desirable.

\singlespacing
This paragraph returns to the default single-line
spacing, which is more compact and efficient for
space-saving layouts.
\end{document}
```

This example demonstrates how LaTeX's layout customization tools allow precise adjustments to headers, footers, and text spacing. Whether formatting a research paper, a technical report, or a book, these commands ensure a polished and professional document structure.

6.2 Creating Custom Headers and Footers

Customizing the headers and footers in LaTeX allows you to add personalized information at the top and bottom of each page, such as chapter titles, section titles, page numbers, author names, and more. LaTeX makes it easy to design custom headers and footers using the `fancyhdr` package. In this section, we will explore how to use this package to create custom headers and footers in your document.

6.2.1 Using the `fancyhdr` Package

In professional documents such as books, reports, and research papers, the appearance of headers and footers plays an important role in organization and readability. LaTeX provides the `fancyhdr` package, which allows users to create custom headers and footers with greater flexibility than the default options.

To begin using this package, it must be included in the document preamble:

Loading the fancyhdr Package

```
\usepackage{fancyhdr}
```

Once the package is loaded, the page style must be set to `fancy`, which enables custom headers and footers. By default, LaTeX's predefined page styles include `plain`, `empty`, and `headings`, but none of these allow the level of customization provided by `fancyhdr`. The following setup clears existing headers and footers and defines new ones:

Basic Header and Footer Customization

```
\pagestyle{fancy}
\fancyhf{}
% Clear existing headers and footers
\fancyhead[L]{Left Header}
% Left-aligned header content
\fancyhead[C]{Center Header}
% Center-aligned header content
\fancyhead[R]{Right Header}
% Right-aligned header content
\fancyfoot[C]{\thepage}
% Page number centered in the footer
```

In this example, the command `\fancyhf{}` first clears any existing header and footer settings, ensuring a clean starting point for customization. The `\fancyhead` commands define the left, center, and right portions of the header, where any text, symbols, or section titles can be inserted. Similarly, the footer is customized using `\fancyfoot`, with the page number (`\thepage`) placed in the center.

Example: Custom Header and Footer Layout

To illustrate how these commands affect the layout, consider the following full document example, where the headers contain section titles and page numbers:

Full LaTeX Example with Custom Headers and Footers

```
\documentclass{article}
\usepackage{fancyhdr}
\usepackage{lipsum} % For placeholder text

\pagestyle{fancy}
```

```
\fancyhf{}
% Clear previous headers and footers
\fancyhead[L]{\leftmark}
% Displays the current section title on
the left
\fancyhead[R]{\thepage}
% Displays the page number on the right
\fancyfoot[C]{Document Title}
% Adds a footer with the document title

\begin{document}

\section{Introduction}
\lipsum[1-3] % Generates placeholder text

\section{Background}
\lipsum[4-6]

\section{Conclusion}
\lipsum[7-9]

\end{document}
```

In this example, the command `\leftmark` is used in the left header to automatically display the title of the current section. This ensures that every page dynamically updates the header based on the section title, making navigation easier for the reader. Meanwhile, the page number appears in the right header, and a footer with the document title is centered at the bottom.

Customization Possibilities

The `fancyhdr` package supports extensive modifications beyond this basic setup. Users can further refine their headers and footers by adjusting text alignment, adding decorative elements such as horizontal lines, or including additional information like author names, institutional affiliations, or document classifications.

By utilizing the `fancyhdr` package, LaTeX users can create highly customized headers and footers that enhance the professionalism and usability of their documents.

6.2.2 Customizing Headers for Different Pages

In professional documents such as books and reports, it is often necessary to have different headers for odd and even pages. This is a common formatting convention, where the chapter title appears on odd-numbered (right-hand) pages, and the section title appears on even-numbered (left-hand) pages. LaTeX provides an elegant way to handle this customization using the `fancyhdr` package.

To enable custom headers, the `fancyhdr` package must first be included in the document preamble:

```
\usepackage{fancyhdr}
\pagestyle{fancy}
```

Once activated, the headers for odd and even pages can be defined separately using the following commands:

```
\fancyhf{}
% Clear existing header and footer settings
\fancyhead[LO]{\leftmark}
% Chapter title on left header of odd pages
\fancyhead[RE]{\rightmark}
% Section title on right header of even pages
\fancyfoot[C]{\thepage}
% Page number centered in the footer
```

The commands used here ensure that: The left header on odd pages (`LO`) displays the chapter title, the right header on even pages (`RE`) displays the section title, and the footer contains the page number, centered at the bottom.

By default, `\leftmark` holds the chapter title, while `\rightmark` holds the section title. This ensures that the headers automatically update as the document progresses.

Example: Custom Headers in a Book

The following example demonstrates how to apply these custom headers in a book document:

Implementing Custom Headers

```
\documentclass{book}
\usepackage{fancyhdr}
\usepackage{lipsum}
% Generates placeholder text

\pagestyle{fancy}
\fancyhf{}
% Clears default header and footer settings
\fancyhead[LO]{\leftmark}
% Chapter title on left header of odd pages
\fancyhead[RE]{\rightmark}
% Section title on right header of even pages
\fancyfoot[C]{\thepage}
% Page number centered in footer

\begin{document}

\chapter{Introduction}
\section{Background}
\lipsum[1-3] % Placeholder text
```

```
\section{Scope}
\lipsum[4-6]

\chapter{Advanced Topics}
\section{New Methods}
\lipsum[7-9]

\end{document}
```

Expected Output

When compiled, this document applies the following formatting: The odd-numbered pages display the chapter title in the left-aligned header. The even-numbered pages display the section title in the right-aligned header. The page number appears centered in the footer.

This layout is particularly useful for books, where alternating headers help readers navigate the content effectively.

6.2.3 Customizing Footers

In many professional documents, such as books, reports, and dissertations, it is often necessary to customize the footer to include specific details like the author's name, the document title, or the page number. LaTeX provides a convenient way to achieve this using the `fancyhdr` package. Custom footers can be configured to display different content on odd and even pages, ensuring a consistent and well-organized layout throughout the document.

To begin customizing the footer, the `fancyhdr` package must first be loaded and activated. This can be done by including the following lines in the document preamble:

Loading the fancyhdr Package

```
\usepackage{fancyhdr}
\pagestyle{fancy}
```

Once the package is enabled, the footer can be customized by assigning specific content to different positions. The `fancyfoot` command is used to define footers for odd and even pages, as well as for different sections of the page (left, center, or right). Below is an example of a footer layout where the author's name appears on odd pages, the document title appears on even pages, and the page number is centered:

Customizing the Footer

```
\fancyhf{}
% Clears existing header and footer settings
\fancyfoot[LO]{Author Name}
% Left-aligned footer on odd pages
\fancyfoot[RE]{Document Title}
% Right-aligned footer on even pages
\fancyfoot[C]{\thepage}
% Center-aligned footer with page number
```

In this configuration: The author's name is displayed in the footer on odd-numbered pages, which are typically right-hand pages in a book layout. The document title is displayed in the footer on even-numbered pages, which are typically left-hand pages. The page number is placed at the center of the footer on every page.

This structure is particularly useful for books and multi-chapter documents where alternating footers enhance readability and navigation. Below is a full example demonstrating how these settings are applied in a LaTeX document.

Full LaTeX Example with Custom Footers

```
\documentclass{book}
\usepackage{fancyhdr}
\usepackage{lipsum}
% Generates placeholder text
\pagestyle{fancy}
\fancyhf{}
% Clears default header and footer settings
\fancyfoot[LO]{John Doe}
% Left footer on odd pages with author name
\fancyfoot[RE]{My LaTeX Book}
% Right footer on even pages with
document title
\fancyfoot[C]{\thepage}
% Page number centered in the footer
\begin{document}
\chapter{Introduction}
\section{Background}
\lipsum[1-3] % Placeholder text
\section{Scope}
\lipsum[4-6]
\chapter{Advanced Topics}
\section{New Methods}
\lipsum[7-9]
\end{document}
```

When this document is compiled, the footers are formatted as follows: The author's name appears in the footer on odd-numbered pages. The document title appears in the footer on even-numbered pages. The page number is displayed at the bottom center of each page.

This approach ensures a polished and professional appearance, particularly for books and reports where distinguishing between odd and even pages helps maintain clarity. Additionally, footers can be further customized to include other elements such as chapter titles, section numbers, or even decorative elements.

If additional footer variations are needed for different sections of the document, the `fancyhdr` package allows for even greater flexibility. For instance, separate footer settings can be applied to the title page or index. By utilizing these features, LaTeX users can create a well-structured and aesthetically pleasing document layout.

6.2.4 Adding Horizontal Lines to Headers and Footers

In professional documents, it is often useful to visually separate the header and footer from the main text using horizontal lines. This improves readability and provides a structured appearance to the document. LaTeX offers a convenient way to implement this feature using the `fancyhdr` package. By adjusting specific commands, one can control the thickness of these lines or remove them entirely.

To define a horizontal rule above the header, the command `\renewcommand{\headrulewidth}{0.4pt}` can be used, where the value specifies the thickness of the line. Similarly, the footer rule can be added or removed using the `\footrulewidth` command.

The following example demonstrates how to apply a horizontal rule to the header while keeping the footer without a line:

Example: Adding a Horizontal Rule Above the Header

```
\documentclass{article}
\usepackage{fancyhdr}
\usepackage{lipsum}
% Generates placeholder text
\pagestyle{fancy}
\fancyhf{}
\fancyhead[L]{Document Title}
\fancyhead[C]{Chapter Name}
\fancyhead[R]{\thepage}
\renewcommand{\headrulewidth}{0.4pt}
\renewcommand{\footrulewidth}{0pt}
\begin{document}
\section{Introduction}
\lipsum[1-3]
\section{Main Content}
\lipsum[4-6]
\end{document}
```

In this example, the left section of the header contains the document title, the center section displays the chapter name, and the right section includes the page number. A horizontal line with a thickness of `0.4pt` is placed above the header to create a visual separation from the main content. The footer, however, remains without a horizontal rule since `\footrulewidth` is set to zero.

If a horizontal rule is required at the bottom of the page as well, the following modification can be applied:

Example: Adding a Horizontal Rule Below the Footer

```
\renewcommand{\footrulewidth}{0.4pt}
\fancyfoot[C]{\thepage}
```

With this addition, a thin rule is drawn below the footer, separating it from the main text. This configuration is commonly used in academic papers, reports, and books to maintain a structured appearance.

By adjusting the thickness of these lines, users can fine-tune the document's visual presentation. Setting the values to `0pt` removes the horizontal lines entirely, providing a clean layout without visual dividers. These small modifications help improve document readability and organization, making them particularly useful for professionally formatted texts.

6.2.5 Different Headers and Footers for the First Page

In many formal documents, such as academic papers, books, or reports, it is common to format the first page differently from the rest of the document. The first page of a document might not require a header or may need a different footer style to accommodate title pages or introductory sections. LaTeX allows for such customization using the `fancyhdr` package.

A distinct style for the first page can be created using the `\fancypagestyle` command. This command defines a new page style that can be applied to any page using `\thispagestyle`. For example, to remove the header on the first page while keeping the page number centered in the footer, the following setup can be used:

Example: Defining a Custom Page Style for the First Page

```
\fancypagestyle{firstpage}{
  \fancyhf{}
  % Clear default header and footer
  \fancyfoot[C]{\thepage}
  % Page number in the center of the footer
  \renewcommand{\headrulewidth}{0pt}
  % Remove header line
}
```

This configuration clears both the header and footer using `\fancyhf{}`, ensuring that no unwanted elements appear on the first page. The command `\fancyfoot[C]{323}` ensures that only the page number is displayed in the center of the footer. Additionally, the line above the header, which is often used in multipage documents, is removed by setting `\headrulewidth` to zero.

To apply this custom formatting to the first page, the `\thispagestyle` command is used immediately after the title or initial content:

Example: Applying a Different Header and Footer on the First Page

```
\documentclass{article}
\usepackage{fancyhdr}
\usepackage{lipsum}
% Generates placeholder text

\pagestyle{fancy}
```

```
% Apply fancy style to the entire document
\fancyhf{}
\fancyhead[L]{Document Title}
\fancyhead[R]{\thepage}
\fancyfoot[C]{Author Name}

\fancypagestyle{firstpage}{
  \fancyhf{}
  \fancyfoot[C]{\thepage}
  \renewcommand{\headrulewidth}{0pt}
}

\begin{document}

\title{First Page Customization in LaTeX}
\author{Author Name}
\date{\today}
\maketitle

\thispagestyle{firstpage}
% Apply custom style to the first page

\section{Introduction}
\lipsum[1-3]

\section{Main Content}
\lipsum[4-6]

\end{document}
```

In this example, the first page does not contain a header, but it includes a centered page number in the footer. From the second page onward, the default `fancy` style takes effect, displaying the document title on the left side of the header, the page number on the right, and the author's name centered in the footer.

This type of customization is particularly useful when working with structured documents that require distinct formatting for title pages, executive summaries, or chapter openings. It ensures that critical pages have a clean layout while maintaining consistency in the rest of the document. By adjusting the parameters in `\fancypagestyle`, additional refinements can be made, such as adding decorative lines, custom logos, or extra footer information.

6.2.6 Creating Headers and Footers for Special Pages

In many structured documents, such as books and theses, certain pages require distinct formatting from the rest of the document. For example, chapter title pages or sections like the table of contents often follow a different layout where headers and footers are either removed or simplified. LaTeX provides several mechanisms to accommodate these formatting needs, allowing precise control over how headers and footers appear on special pages.

A common requirement in books is that the chapter title pages should not display headers or footers, while the subsequent pages should follow the standard format. This can be achieved using the `\thispagestyle{plain}` command. By default, the `plain` page style removes the header but retains the footer, which typically contains the page number.

The following example demonstrates how to suppress headers and footers on a chapter title page while maintaining a consistent layout throughout the rest of the document.

Example: Removing Headers and Footers for a Chapter Title Page

```
\chapter{Introduction}
\thispagestyle{plain}
% Removes headers and footers from this
specific page
```

This ensures that the chapter title page appears clean, without any headers, while the following pages will continue to display the standard headers and footers set for the document.

For a more comprehensive document setup, where different page styles are applied to odd and even pages while keeping chapter title pages clean, the following LaTeX example demonstrates a structured approach:

Example: Special Formatting for Chapter Title Pages

```
\documentclass{book}
\usepackage{fancyhdr}

\pagestyle{fancy}
% Apply fancy headers and footers to most
pages
\fancyhf{}
\fancyhead[LO]{Chapter Title}
% Left header on odd pages
\fancyhead[RE]{Section Title}
% Right header on even pages
\fancyfoot[C]{\thepage}
% Page number centered in the footer

\renewcommand{\headrulewidth}{0.4pt}
```

```
% Thin line above the header
\renewcommand{\footrulewidth}{0pt}
% No line below the footer

\begin{document}

\chapter{Introduction}
\thispagestyle{plain}
% Suppresses headers for this chapter
title page

This is the first chapter of the document.
Notice that the headers and footers do not
appear on this page, but they will be
present on the following pages.

\section{Section One}
The text in this section appears on a new page,
where the headers and footers are reinstated.

\newpage

This page now includes the customized headers
and footers.

\end{document}
```

In this setup, the `\thispagestyle{plain}` command ensures that the first page of each chapter does not display headers, while the remaining pages continue with the standard layout defined by the `fancyhdr` package. The page number remains centered in the footer, ensuring that pagination is preserved throughout the document.

This approach is particularly useful in long-form documents such as books and theses, where readers expect a well-structured format that distinguishes chapter openings from regular content pages. With LaTeX's flexible page customization options, it is possible to maintain a professional and polished document layout without manual adjustments. By carefully applying different page styles, authors can enhance readability and ensure their document meets formal formatting requirements.

6.3 Title Pages, Abstracts, and Table of Contents

In LaTeX, creating a professional-looking title page, adding an abstract, and generating a table of contents are essential tasks for structuring longer documents such as books, theses, or reports. LaTeX provides simple and powerful tools to create these elements with flexibility and customization options. In this section, we will explore how to create custom title pages, add abstracts, and automatically generate a table of contents.

6.3.1 Creating a Title Page

A well-designed title page serves as the first impression of a document, providing essential information such as the title, author's name, date, and sometimes additional details like institutional affiliation or course name. In LaTeX, generating a structured and professional title page is straightforward with the `\maketitle` command. This built-in feature ensures that the title page is formatted consistently while maintaining a clean and elegant appearance.

The simplest way to create a title page is to define the title, author, and date in the preamble using the `\title`, `\author`, and `\date` commands. Once these details are specified, invoking `\maketitle` within the document body generates the title page.

Example: Basic Title Page

```
\documentclass{article}
\title{An Introduction to LaTeX}
\author{Dr. LaTeX}
\date{\today}
\begin{document}
\maketitle
\end{document}
```

When compiled, this code produces a title page with the title centered at the top, followed by the author's name and the date below it. The `\today` command automatically inserts the current date at the time of compilation.

By default, the `\maketitle` command applies a predefined style based on the document class. For instance, in the `article` class, the title is relatively compact, whereas in the `report` or `book` classes, it occupies a full page, often centered vertically. To modify the appearance of the title page, LaTeX allows for further customization using additional formatting techniques.

For documents requiring an academic or professional touch, additional elements such as an institution name, course title, or supervisor's name can be incorporated. This can be achieved by manually structuring the title page within a dedicated `titlepage` environment. The following example illustrates a more detailed title page with custom formatting:

Example: Custom Title Page

```
\documentclass{report}

\begin{document}
```

```
\begin{titlepage}
\centering
{\Huge\bfseries Advanced LaTeX Techniques\par}
\vspace{1.5cm}
{\Large Dr. LaTeX\par}
\vspace{0.5cm}
{\large University of TeX\par}
\vspace{1.5cm}
{\today\par}
\end{titlepage}
\end{document}
```

In this example, the `titlepage` environment forces the title page to appear as a separate page, ensuring proper spacing and alignment. The use of `\Huge`, `\Large`, and `\large` adjusts the font size for different elements, creating a visually appealing layout. Vertical spacing is controlled with `\vspace` to distribute elements proportionally across the page.

For more advanced customization, users can employ packages like `titling` to redefine title commands or manually position elements for complete control over the layout. This flexibility makes LaTeX a powerful tool for creating professional documents tailored to specific formatting requirements.

By understanding and utilizing these techniques, authors can craft title pages that not only convey essential information but also enhance the overall presentation of their documents.

Customizing the Title Page

For a more customized title page, you can use the `titlepage` environment to manually position elements like the title, author, and date. Here is an example of a custom title page:

```
\begin{titlepage}
    \centering
    {\Huge\bfseries My LaTeX Document \par}
    \vspace{2cm}
    {\Large\itshape Dr. LaTeX \par}
    \vfill
    {\large \today \par}
\end{titlepage}
```

Explanation:

- `\Huge`: Changes the font size to a very large size.
- `\bfseries`: Makes the text bold.
- `\itshape`: Sets the text in italics.
- `\vfill`: Vertically aligns the date at the bottom of the page.

You can further customize the layout by adding logos, spacing, and formatting as needed.

6.3.2 Adding an Abstract

An abstract serves as a concise summary of the document, offering readers a brief insight into the key points discussed in the main content. It is commonly used in research papers, reports, theses, and dissertations to provide an overview of the purpose, methodology, and conclusions of the work. In LaTeX, abstracts are conveniently formatted using the `abstract` environment, ensuring a professional presentation.

When writing an abstract in LaTeX, it is enclosed within the `abstract` environment. By default, in the article document class, the abstract appears at the beginning of the document, formatted in a centered, standalone block. In the report and book classes, however, additional customization may be needed to position the abstract appropriately. Below is an example of how to include an abstract in a LaTeX document.

Example: Adding an Abstract

```
\documentclass{article}

\begin{document}

\title{Customizing LaTeX Documents}
\author{Dr. LaTeX}
\date{\today}

\maketitle

\begin{abstract}
This document provides an overview of how to
customize LaTeX layouts, including title pages,
abstracts, and table of contents. It discusses
various formatting techniques for academic and
professional documents.
\end{abstract}

\section{Introduction}

This section introduces the main topics
covered in the document.

\end{document}
```

When compiled, this code generates a title page, followed by an abstract that appears in a distinct block, separate from the main content. The abstract is automatically formatted according to the conventions of the chosen document class.

For documents that require a more structured layout, such as reports or theses, abstracts are often placed on a separate page. In such cases, the `titlepage` environment can be used to ensure the abstract appears independently. Below is an example demonstrating this approach:

Example: Abstract on a Separate Page

```
\documentclass{report}

\begin{document}

\begin{titlepage}
    \centering
    {\LARGE Customizing LaTeX Documents\par}
    \vspace{1cm}
    {\large Dr. LaTeX\par}
    \vspace{1cm}
    {\today\par}
\end{titlepage}

\clearpage
% Ensure the abstract appears on a new page

\begin{abstract}
This document explores various methods for
formatting LaTeX documents, focusing on
title pages, abstracts, and tables of
contents. The aim is to provide a structured
guide for academic and professional writing.
\end{abstract}

\section{Introduction}
```

```
The introduction discusses the importance of
proper document structuring.

\end{document}
```

In this setup, the title page is explicitly formatted using the `titlepage` environment, and the abstract is placed on a new page using the `\clearpage` command. This approach ensures that the abstract appears distinctly before the main content begins.

For further customization, the abstract heading can be modified using the `titlesec` package, or additional formatting can be applied using manual adjustments such as changing font sizes or alignment.

By utilizing the `abstract` environment effectively, LaTeX users can ensure that their documents maintain a polished and professional appearance while adhering to academic or industry-specific formatting guidelines.

6.3.3 Generating a Table of Contents

A well-structured document benefits from a table of contents (TOC), allowing readers to navigate through sections and chapters efficiently. LaTeX provides an automatic mechanism for generating a TOC based on the document's structure, ensuring consistency and accurate pagination without requiring manual updates.

To generate a TOC, the `\tableofcontents` command is placed at the desired location in the document, typically at the beginning. This command scans the document's sectioning commands, such as `\chapter`, `\section`, and `\subsection`, and constructs an ordered list of contents with corresponding page numbers.

The following example demonstrates a basic table of contents in a LaTeX document:

Example: Basic Table of Contents

```
\documentclass{report}

\begin{document}

\tableofcontents

\chapter{Introduction}
\section{Motivation}
\subsection{Background}

\chapter{Methods}
\section{Experimental Setup}

\end{document}
```

When compiled, LaTeX generates a table of contents that includes all chapters, sections, and subsections, along with their corresponding page numbers. If the TOC does not appear correctly after the first compilation, running LaTeX multiple times ensures that the correct page numbers are reflected.

Customizing the Depth of the Table of Contents

By default, LaTeX includes all major sections and subsections in the TOC, but the level of detail can be controlled using the `tocdepth` counter. This counter determines how deep the TOC hierarchy should go. If, for example, subsubsections should be omitted while still keeping sections and subsections, the following command can be used in the document preamble:

Example: Adjusting TOC Depth

```
\setcounter{tocdepth}{2}
```

This setting ensures that:

- Chapters (if using the `book` or `report` document class) are included.
- Sections and subsections appear in the TOC.
- Subsubsections and lower levels are excluded.

Manually Adding Entries to the Table of Contents

In some cases, certain sections such as the introduction, preface, or acknowledgments may not have explicit section commands but should still appear in the TOC. LaTeX allows manual insertion of entries using the `\addcontentsline` command. The syntax specifies the TOC file (`toc`), the type of entry (e.g., `chapter`, `section`), and the desired title:

Example: Manually Adding TOC Entries

```
\addcontentsline{toc}{section}{Acknowledgments}
```

This command ensures that "Acknowledgments" appears in the TOC as a section-level entry, even if it is not formally defined in the document structure.

Creating Chapter-Specific Tables of Contents

For longer documents, such as books or theses, it is often helpful to include a mini table of contents at the beginning of each chapter. The `minitoc` package allows for such functionality, providing localized TOCs that summarize the content within individual chapters.

To use this feature, the package is loaded in the preamble, and a chapter-specific TOC is generated using the `\minitoc` command within each chapter:

Example: Mini Table of Contents

```
\documentclass{book}
\usepackage{minitoc}

\begin{document}

\tableofcontents  % Generate the main TOC
\dominitoc  % Activate mini TOCs

\chapter{Introduction}
\minitoc  % Generates a TOC for this chapter

\section{Motivation}
\subsection{Historical Background}

\end{document}
```

With this setup, each chapter includes a localized TOC summarizing its sections and subsections, improving readability and navigation.

Ensuring Proper TOC Generation

LaTeX generates the TOC dynamically based on the document's structure, meaning that if sections are added or removed, the TOC updates accordingly. However, changes to page numbers or section titles require multiple compilations for the TOC to be properly updated. If the TOC appears with incorrect page numbers or missing entries, running LaTeX twice (or using tools like Overleaf, which handle multiple passes automatically) resolves the issue.

6.3.4 Combining Title Page, Abstract, and TOC

It is common to combine the title page, abstract, and table of contents at the beginning of a document. Here is a simple layout that combines all three elements:

Example: Title Page Abstract and TOC

```
\documentclass{report}

\title{My LaTeX Document}
\author{Dr. LaTeX}
\date{\today}

\usepackage{minitoc}

\begin{document}

\maketitle

\begin{abstract}
This document provides a comprehensive
overview of creating custom layouts in
LaTeX, including title pages, abstracts,
and table of contents.
\end{abstract}

\tableofcontents

\chapter{Introduction}
This is the introduction.
```

```
\chapter{Background}
This chapter provides background information.

\end{document}
```

6.3.5 Combining Title Page, Abstract, and Table of Contents

In structured documents such as academic reports, theses, and books, it is customary to present the title page, abstract, and table of contents sequentially at the beginning. This structured layout ensures that the reader is first introduced to the document's title and author details, followed by a concise summary of the content, and finally, a navigational overview of the document through the table of contents.

Structuring the Title Page

The title page is the first element encountered in the document. It provides essential details such as the document's title, author name, and date of publication. In LaTeX, the title page can be generated using the `\maketitle` command, which compiles the title, author, and date information defined in the preamble.

To create a basic title page, define these elements in the document preamble and invoke the `\maketitle` command in the main document body:

Example: Title Page in LaTeX

```
\documentclass{report}

\title{An Introduction to LaTeX}
```

```
\author{Dr. LaTeX}
\date{\today}

\begin{document}

\maketitle

\end{document}
```

When compiled, this will produce a centered title page containing the specified title, author name, and the current date. The default layout places these elements in a standard format suitable for most academic and professional documents.

Including an Abstract

An abstract provides a concise summary of the document's content. In LaTeX, abstracts are typically included in the `abstract` environment, ensuring that they are formatted separately from the main text.

To insert an abstract after the title page, simply enclose the text within the `abstract` environment.

Example: Adding an Abstract

```
\begin{abstract}
This document provides an overview of
structuring LaTeX documents, including
the title page, abstract, and table of
contents.
\end{abstract}
```

By default, LaTeX formats the abstract separately from the main body of the document, often centering it or setting it apart from other sections. In academic papers, abstracts are typically required to summarize the document concisely.

Generating a Table of Contents

The table of contents (TOC) provides a structured outline of the document, listing chapters, sections, and subsections with corresponding page numbers. LaTeX automatically generates a TOC when the `\tableofcontents` command is used.

To ensure the TOC includes all necessary headings, place this command in the document after the abstract:

Example: Generating a Table of Contents

```
\tableofcontents
```

LaTeX processes the document structure to compile the TOC, ensuring it reflects any modifications made to the sectioning. If the TOC does not update properly after editing section headings, running LaTeX multiple times ensures accurate page numbering.

Full Example: Combining Title Page, Abstract, and TOC

By integrating all the elements discussed, we create a well-organized document that starts with a title page, followed by an abstract, and then the table of contents. The following example demonstrates this complete structure:

Example: Full Document with Title Page Abstract and TOC

```
\documentclass{report}
\title{An Introduction to LaTeX}
```

```
\author{Dr. LaTeX}
\date{\today}

\begin{document}
\maketitle

\begin{abstract}
This document provides a structured approach
to creating professional LaTeX documents,
including title pages, abstracts, and table of
contents.
\end{abstract}

\tableofcontents

\chapter{Introduction}
This chapter introduces LaTeX and its
applications.

\chapter{Document Structure}
This chapter discusses different components
of a structured LaTeX document.
\end{documont}
```

Ensuring Proper Compilation

When working with a table of contents, LaTeX requires multiple compilation runs to ensure that all references and page numbers are correctly updated. If the TOC does not appear correctly, follow this sequence:

1. Compile the document using `pdflatex` (or `latex`).
2. Recompile the document to update page numbers and TOC entries.

By following this structure, LaTeX users can generate a professionally formatted document with a clear introduction, abstract, and table of contents, enhancing readability and navigation.

6.4 Footnotes and Endnotes

Footnotes and endnotes are useful for providing additional information or references without interrupting the main flow of the text. In LaTeX, adding footnotes and endnotes is easy and flexible, allowing you to format them to fit your document's style. In this section, we will explore how to use footnotes and endnotes, customize their appearance, and manage them effectively in LaTeX.

6.4.1 Adding Footnotes in LaTeX

Footnotes are an essential part of academic and technical writing, allowing authors to provide additional explanations, citations, or clarifications without interrupting the main flow of the text. In LaTeX, footnotes are created using the `\footnote` command, which automatically numbers them and places the corresponding text at the bottom of the page.

Inserting a Basic Footnote

To include a footnote in a LaTeX document, the `\footnote` command is used within the main body of the text. LaTeX automatically generates sequential numbering for each footnote and places it at the bottom of the page where it appears.

For instance, consider the following example:

Example: Basic Footnote

```
This is a sentence with a footnote.
\footnote{This is an example footnote
in LaTeX.}
```

This code produces a footnote numbered automatically by LaTeX. The reader sees a small superscript number within the text, which corresponds to the note placed at the bottom of the page.

When compiled, the output appears as:

This is a sentence with a footnote.[1] . [1] This is an example footnote in LaTeX.

Customizing Footnote Numbering

By default, LaTeX assigns footnotes sequential numbers throughout the document. However, you can modify how footnotes are displayed using predefined commands. For example, footnotes can be formatted to use symbols or restarted at the beginning of each section.

Changing Footnote Numbering Style To use symbols instead of numbers for footnotes, the `\renewcommand` function can be used. The following example modifies the default numbering style:

Example: Using Symbols for Footnotes

```
\renewcommand{\thefootnote}{\fnsymbol
{footnote}}
```

This will replace numeric footnote indicators with symbols such as *, †, ‡, and so on.

Resetting Footnote Numbering for Each Section In longer documents such as books or reports, it may be preferable to restart footnote numbering at the beginning of each section or chapter. This can be achieved using the `chngcntr` package, which allows counters to be reset dynamically.

Example: Resetting Footnote Numbering in Each Section

```
\usepackage{chngcntr}
\counterwithin{footnote}{section}
```

With this setup, footnotes will start at 1 for every new section, ensuring a structured and organized presentation of references.

Full Example: Footnotes in LaTeX

To bring all the discussed elements together, here is a complete LaTeX example demonstrating the use of footnotes, custom numbering, and section-based resets.

Example: Implementing Footnotes in a Document

```
\documentclass{article}
\usepackage{chngcntr}
\counterwithin{footnote}{section}

\renewcommand{\thefootnote}{\fnsymbol
{footnote}}

\begin{document}

\section{Introduction}
```

```
Footnotes\footnote{This is a standard
footnote.} provide additional information
without disrupting the flow of text.

\section{Customizing Footnotes}

It is possible to customize footnote numbering
using symbols\footnote{This footnote now uses
symbols instead of numbers.} or resetting
footnotes for each section.

\end{document}
```

This example illustrates both the default and customized footnote styles. The first section contains a basic footnote, while the second demonstrates the use of symbol-based numbering.

Ensuring Proper Compilation

For footnotes to function correctly in a document, LaTeX should be compiled at least twice. This ensures that the numbering and references are properly updated across pages. If footnotes appear misplaced or incorrectly numbered, rerunning the LaTeX compiler resolves these issues.

By effectively utilizing footnotes in LaTeX, authors can create well-structured documents that provide supplementary information in an organized manner without breaking the main narrative flow.

6.4.2 Adding Endnotes in LaTeX

Endnotes function similarly to footnotes but are compiled and placed at the end of a document or chapter rather than at the bottom of each page. They are particularly useful in academic and formal writing where keeping the main text uncluttered is important. In LaTeX, endnotes can be implemented using the `endnotes` package, which provides a simple way to collect and display references at a designated location.

Setting up Endnotes in LaTeX

To enable the use of endnotes, the `endnotes` package must be loaded in the preamble. This package provides the `\endnote` command, which serves the same purpose as the `\footnote` command but places references at the end of the document.

The following example demonstrates how to incorporate endnotes:

Example: Adding Endnotes

```
\documentclass{article}
\usepackage{endnotes}

\begin{document}

This is a sentence with an endnote.
\endnote{This is an example of an endnote
in LaTeX.}

Another reference can be added later in the
document.\endnote{Second endnote example.}

\end{document}
```

In this example, the `\endnote` command is used to insert a reference. Unlike footnotes, these references are not immediately displayed but are instead collected until they are explicitly printed using the `\theendnotes` command.

Displaying Endnotes in the Document

Since endnotes do not appear automatically in the output, they must be manually placed at the appropriate location using `\theendnotes`. Typically, endnotes appear at the end of the document or a chapter in books and reports. The following example illustrates this:

Example: Printing Endnotes

```
\documentclass{article}
\usepackage{endnotes}

\begin{document}

This is an example text with an endnote.
\endnote{This note appears at the end
of the document.}

\newpage

\section*{Endnotes}
\theendnotes
% This prints all accumulated endnotes

\end{document}
```

In this setup, the `\theendnotes` command ensures that all previously defined endnotes are displayed at the end of the document under a section titled "Endnotes." The `\newpage` command forces a page break to separate the endnotes from the main text.

Using Endnotes in Books or Reports

For documents that require structured endnotes at the end of each chapter rather than at the document's conclusion, the `\chapter` command (in the `book` or `report` class) can be used to collect endnotes within each chapter. The following example demonstrates how endnotes can be formatted within a book:

Example: Endnotes in Chapters

```
\documentclass{book}
\usepackage{endnotes}

\begin{document}

\chapter{Introduction}
This is an introduction with an endnote.
\endnote{First chapter endnote.}

\chapter{Background}
More discussion is provided here.
\endnote{Endnote in the background chapter.}

\chapter*{Notes}
\theendnotes
% This prints all accumulated endnotes

\end{document}
```

In this case, each chapter can contain endnotes, and they are compiled in a separate section labeled "Notes" at the end of the book.

Differences Between Footnotes and Endnotes

While footnotes are displayed at the bottom of the page where they are referenced, endnotes are collected separately and printed later in the document. This difference allows endnotes to be used in more formal and structured documents, such as dissertations, reports, and books.

Footnotes are preferable when immediate clarification is required, whereas endnotes provide a cleaner and more concise document layout. The choice between footnotes and endnotes largely depends on the writing style and document format requirements.

Compiling Documents with Endnotes

To ensure that endnotes appear correctly in the output, the LaTeX document should be compiled at least twice. This allows LaTeX to process the `\endnote` commands and correctly place them at the specified location.

By integrating endnotes into a document, authors can maintain readability while still providing comprehensive reference details, creating a well-structured and professional layout.

6.4.3 Managing Footnotes and Endnotes

Footnotes and endnotes play a crucial role in scholarly writing, allowing authors to provide additional information, citations, or clarifications without interrupting the flow of the main text. LaTeX provides robust tools to manage both footnotes, which appear at the bottom of the page, and endnotes, which are collected at the end of the document. This section explores best practices for handling footnotes in special cases, including their use in tables, suppressing numbering, and placing multiple footnotes in the same location.

Footnotes in Tables

Unlike standard text, tables pose a challenge when inserting footnotes because LaTeX does not support direct use of the `\footnote` command inside table environments. A common solution is to separate the footnote marker from the footnote text using the `\footnotemark` and `\footnotetext` commands.

Example: Adding Footnotes in Tables

```
\begin{table}[ht]
\centering
\begin{tabular}{|c|c|}
\hline
Item & Value \\
\hline
A & 100\footnotemark[1] \\
B & 200 \\
\hline
\end{tabular}
\caption{A table with footnotes}
\label{tab:footnote}
\end{table}

\footnotetext[1]{This is a footnote for
item A.}
```

In this example, the `\footnotemark` command is placed inside the table where the footnote marker should appear. Meanwhile, the actual footnote text is specified separately using `\footnotetext`, ensuring that the footnote text appears correctly at the bottom of the page.

Suppressing Footnote Numbering

Sometimes, footnotes are used for general remarks or additional citations that should not be numbered. In such cases, the `\footnotetext` command can be used without a preceding `\footnotemark`.

Example: Adding Unnumbered Footnotes

```
This sentence contains a standard footnote.
\footnote{This is a numbered footnote.}

However, the next footnote has no number.
\footnotetext{This footnote appears without
a number.}
```

In this example, the second footnote is placed without a corresponding marker in the main text, ensuring that the footnote text is displayed at the bottom of the page without an associated number.

Using Multiple Footnotes in the Same Location

There are cases where multiple footnotes need to appear at the same location in the text. LaTeX automatically handles this scenario by numbering them sequentially.

Example: Multiple Footnotes in One Place

```
This is a sentence with two footnotes.
\footnote{First footnote.}
\footnote{Second footnote.}
```

In this case, LaTeX will number both footnotes correctly and display them in sequence at the bottom of the page.

Combining Footnotes and Endnotes

If a document requires both footnotes and endnotes, the `endnotes` package provides a way to define and manage endnotes separately from footnotes. The following example demonstrates a document that includes both:

Example: Managing Both Footnotes and Endnotes

```
\documentclass{article}
\usepackage{endnotes}
\usepackage{chngcntr}

\renewcommand{\thefootnote}{\fnsymbol
{footnote}}
% Changes footnote numbering to symbols
\counterwithin{footnote}{section}
% Resets footnote numbering in each section

\begin{document}

\section{Introduction}

This sentence has a footnote.
\footnote{This is a regular footnote.}
This one has an endnote.
\endnote{This is an endnote.}

\newpage

\section*{Endnotes}
\theendnotes  % Prints all endnotes at the
   end of the document

\end{document}
```

This example uses both footnotes, which appear at the bottom of the page, and endnotes, which are collected and displayed at the end of the document.

6.5 Multicolumn Layouts

Multicolumn layouts are a great way to organize content into multiple columns on a page, much like how a newspaper or magazine might display text. LaTeX provides several tools and packages to create multicolumn layouts for different purposes. In this section, we will explore how to create multicolumn layouts using the `multicols` package, and how to customize the column count, column breaks, and spacing.

6.5.1 Creating Multicolumn Layouts with the `multicols` Package

In some documents, it is desirable to arrange content into multiple columns to improve readability and optimize space usage. This is particularly useful for newsletters, research papers, and formatted reports. LaTeX provides an efficient way to create multicolumn layouts using the `multicols` package, which allows text to be distributed across multiple columns within a defined environment.

Basic Multicolumn Layout

To use multicolumn formatting, the `multicols` package must first be loaded in the document preamble:

Loading the `multicols` Package

```
\usepackage{multicol}
```

Once the package is included, content can be structured into multiple columns using the `multicols` environment. The number of columns is specified as an argument to this environment. The following example demonstrates a simple two-column layout:

Example: Creating a Two-Column Layout

```
\begin{multicols}{2}
This is text in the first column.
LaTeX automatically distributes
the content evenly across both columns.

Additional text continues to fill the
available space, ensuring that both
columns are balanced in length.

\columnbreak

This marks the beginning of the second column.
\end{multicols}
```

This is text in the first column. LaTeX automatically distributes the content evenly across both columns.
Additional text continues to fill the available space, ensuring that both columns are balanced in length.

This marks the beginning of the second column.

Figure 6.1: Example of a two-column layout using the `multicols` package

In this example, the text is automatically distributed between two columns. If no explicit column break is defined, LaTeX will balance the text so that both columns have approximately equal height. The `\columnbreak` command can be used if a manual column break is needed, ensuring that the remaining content moves to the next column (Fig. 6.1).

Adjusting the Number of Columns

The `multicols` package provides flexibility in determining the number of columns, allowing users to format content into three or more columns with minimal effort. For example, the following code creates a layout with three columns:

Example: Creating a Three-Column Layout

```
\begin{multicols}{3}
This text is distributed across three columns.
LaTeX automatically adjusts the content,
ensuring proper alignment and spacing.
\end{multicols}
```

This text is dis-	matically ad-	ment and spac-
tributed across	justs the con-	ing.
three columns.	tent, ensuring	
LaTeX auto-	proper align-	

Figure 6.2: Example of a three-column layout using the `multicols` package

By simply modifying the number inside the `\begin{multicols}{...}` command, any number of columns can be specified. However, it is important to consider readability when increasing the number of columns, as very narrow columns may make text harder to follow (Fig. 6.2).

Automatic Column Balancing

One of the key advantages of the `multicols` package is its ability to balance text automatically. When content does not fill all columns equally, LaTeX adjusts the spacing to maintain visual consistency. This behavior ensures a clean layout without the need for manual adjustments. However, if precise control is required, users can insert column breaks manually.

Considerations for Multicolumn Text

When using a multicolumn layout, it is important to consider how different elements, such as images, tables, and equations, will fit within the column structure. Inline elements, such as small equations or figures, may fit within a single column. However, wider elements might require spanning across all columns or breaking out of the multicolumn environment entirely. The placement of section headings should also be carefully managed to ensure a logical document flow.

By leveraging the capabilities of the `multicols` package, LaTeX users can efficiently create structured layouts that enhance readability and organization, making it an ideal solution for formatting complex documents.

6.5.2 Customizing Multicolumn Layouts

While the `multicols` package provides a straightforward method for arranging text into multiple columns, it also allows for extensive customization. Users can modify the spacing between columns to improve readability or introduce visual elements, such as vertical rules, to distinguish columns more clearly. These adjustments help enhance document aesthetics, especially when formatting articles, research papers, or magazines.

Adjusting Column Spacing

By default, LaTeX maintains a predefined amount of space between columns to ensure proper separation and readability. However, in some cases, adjusting the spacing between columns is necessary, especially when dealing with narrow or wide column configurations. This customization is achieved by modifying the `\columnsep` length.

The following example demonstrates how to increase the spacing between two columns to 1 cm:

Example: Adjusting Column Spacing

```
\documentclass{article}
\usepackage{multicol}

\setlength{\columnsep}{1cm}
% Sets column spacing to 1 cm

\begin{document}

\begin{multicols}{2}
This is text in the first column. With
increased spacing, there is more visual
separation between the columns.

\columnbreak

This is text in the second column.
\end{multicols}

\end{document}
```

This is text in the first column. With increased spacing, there is more visual separation between the columns.	This is text in the second column.

Figure 6.3: Example of increasing column spacing in a two-column layout

In this example, the `\setlength{\columnsep}{1cm}` command is used to define the space between columns. The spacing can be adjusted to larger or smaller values depending on the document's design needs (Fig. 6.3).

Adding Visual Separators Between Columns

In some document layouts, particularly in magazines, newsletters, or multicolumn reports, adding a vertical line between columns helps visually separate content. The `\columnseprule` command allows for the insertion of a thin vertical rule between columns.

The following example demonstrates how to introduce a 0.4-point thick rule between two columns:

Example: Adding a Vertical Rule Between Columns

```
\documentclass{article}
\usepackage{multicol}

\setlength{\columnseprule}{0.4pt}
% Adds a vertical rule

\begin{document}

\begin{multicols}{2}
```

```
This column is separated by a thin vertical
rule.
\columnbreak
This is the second column.
\end{multicols}

\end{document}
```

This column is separated by a thin vertical rule.	This is the second column.

Figure 6.4: Example of using a vertical rule to separate columns

In this case, the `\setlength{\columnseprule}{0.4pt}` command adds a fine dividing line between the columns. Increasing this value results in a thicker rule, while setting it to zero removes the separator entirely (Fig. 6.4).

Considerations for Column Customization

When modifying column spacing and adding visual separators, it is essential to balance aesthetics with readability. Too much spacing may cause the columns to appear disconnected, while too little space may make the text difficult to follow. Similarly, while vertical rules can enhance organization, excessive use of thick separators may make the document visually cluttered. It is recommended to experiment with different values to find an optimal layout that best suits the document's content and purpose.

Using the flexibility of the `multicols` package, LaTeX users can fine-tune the structure of their multicolumn layouts to create visually appealing and well-organized documents.

6.5.3 Handling Multicolumn Breaks

When working with multicolumn layouts in LaTeX, the text is typically distributed evenly between the columns by default. However, in some cases, you may need to control how the text flows between columns to achieve a more structured presentation. This is particularly useful when you want to manually balance the columns or place specific content in one column while ensuring the remaining text starts in the next.

To explicitly force a column break at a particular location, LaTeX provides the `\columnbreak` command. Unlike automatic balancing, which adjusts content dynamically, this command allows for precise control over how and where text transitions to the next column. Below is an example demonstrating the forced column break:

Example: Forcing a Column Break

```
\documentclass{article}
\usepackage{multicol}

\begin{document}

\begin{multicols}{2}
This is the first part of the text.
By default, LaTeX distributes the
content evenly across columns.

\columnbreak
% Forces the text to move to the next column
```

```
This text is placed in the second column,
even though the first column still has
space available.
\end{multicols}

\end{document}
```

This is the first part of the text. By default, LaTeX distributes the content evenly across columns.	This text is placed in the second column, even though the first column still has space available.

Figure 6.5: Forcing a column break to manually control text distribution

In this example, the `\columnbreak` command ensures that the second paragraph appears in the second column, rather than being placed below the first paragraph in the same column. This can be particularly useful when formatting structured documents such as newsletters or reports, where clear separation between content blocks is necessary (Fig. 6.5).

6.5.4 Combining Multicolumn Layouts with Figures and Tables

Multicolumn layouts in LaTeX are highly flexible and can be used in conjunction with various elements such as figures, tables, and lists. However, handling these elements within columns requires some adjustments to ensure proper formatting. For example, when including images, it is important to specify their width relative to the column rather than the full page, ensuring they fit appropriately within the given space.

Below is an example demonstrating how to insert an image within a two-column layout:

Example: Inserting an Image in a Multicolumn Layout

```
\documentclass{article}
\usepackage{multicol}
\usepackage{graphicx}

\begin{document}
\begin{multicols}{2}
This is the first column of text. Below,
we insert an image that fits within the
column width.
\begin{figure}[H]
    \centering
    \includegraphics[width=0.8\columnwidth]
    {example-image}
\caption{An example image within a column}
\end{figure}
This text appears below the image in the
first column.
\columnbreak
This is the second column of text. Notice
how the content is automatically adjusted
around the figure.
\end{multicols}
\end{document}
```

In this example, the width of the inserted image is set relative to the column width using `\includegraphics[width=0.8\columnwidth]`. This ensures that the image scales correctly within its column

This is the first column of text. Below, we insert an image that fits within the column width.

This text appears below the image in the first column.

This is the second column of text. Notice how the content is automatically adjusted around the figure.

Figure 6.6: Placing an image inside a multicolumn layout while maintaining proper formatting

and does not overflow into adjacent columns or beyond the page margins. The caption for the figure is also contained within the column, keeping the layout consistent (Fig. 6.6).

Considerations for Using Multicolumn Layouts

While multicolumn layouts are useful for organizing content in a structured manner, it is important to carefully manage the placement of images, tables, and other floating elements. Since LaTeX automatically adjusts content distribution within columns, inserting figures or tables may disrupt the expected text flow. Using `\columnbreak` or manually adjusting column spacing can help mitigate these issues.

By effectively combining multicolumn text with figures and tables, LaTeX users can create visually appealing and well-structured documents, making it easier for readers to navigate and interpret content.

6.5.5 Two-Column vs. Multicolumn Layouts

When structuring documents that require multiple columns, LaTeX provides two primary approaches: the global `twocolumn` document option and the more flexible `multicols` environment. The choice between these depends on whether the document requires a consistent two-column format throughout or the ability to switch between different column layouts within the same document.

The `twocolumn` option is applied at the document class level, meaning that once enabled, the entire document is formatted into two columns. This approach is commonly used in academic journals and conference proceedings, where articles are uniformly structured in a two-column format. To activate this feature, specify it as an option when defining the document class:

Example: Applying a Two-Column Layout Globally

```
\documentclass[twocolumn]{article}

\begin{document}

This is a global two-column layout for the
entire document.

\end{document}
```

While the `twocolumn` option is useful for documents that require a fixed two-column structure, it lacks flexibility. For instance, if a specific section of the document requires reverting to a single-column format, LaTeX does not provide an easy way to switch between one and two columns dynamically.

For documents that require more control over column formatting, the `multicols` package offers a more adaptable solution. Unlike `twocolumn`, which affects the entire document, `multicols` allows authors to define multicolumn layouts within specific sections while keeping other parts of the document single column. This feature is particularly useful in reports, books, and articles where certain sections, such as abstracts or large tables, need a full-width format, while the main content benefits from a multicolumn layout.

To use the `multicols` package, include it in the document preamble and wrap the desired content within the `multicols` environment. Below is an example demonstrating its usage:

Example: Using the `multicols` Package for Selective Multicolumn Formatting

```
\documentclass{article}
\usepackage{multicol}

\begin{document}

This is single-column text.

\begin{multicols}{2}
This content is split into two columns.
Unlike the global \texttt{twocolumn} option,
the \texttt{multicols} environment allows
for selective column formatting.

\columnbreak

The second column starts here. LaTeX
automatically balances content between
columns, but this behavior can be
overridden if needed.
```

```
\end{multicols}

This text returns to a single-column format.

\end{document}
```

One of the key advantages of `multicols` is its ability to accommodate dynamic column formatting. If a section requires more than two columns, simply adjust the argument passed to the environment:

Example: Creating a Three-Column Layout

```
\begin{multicols}{3}
This is a three-column format.
LaTeX distributes the text
evenly across all columns.
\end{multicols}
```

The primary differences between the `twocolumn` option and the `multicols` package can be summarized as follows:

- `twocolumn`: Applies a two-column format to the entire document, making it ideal for journals and articles that require a consistent layout.
- `multicols`: Provides flexibility to use multiple columns in specific parts of the document.

When choosing between these options, consider the document's structure and formatting needs. For a fixed layout where all content must be displayed in two columns, `twocolumn` is the simplest approach. However, for more complex formatting requirements, such as mixing single-column and multicolumn sections, the `multicols` package offers greater flexibility.

By understanding and implementing these techniques, LaTeX users can optimize the presentation of their documents, ensuring both readability and professional formatting. Whether preparing an academic paper, a technical report, or a typeset book, the ability to customize column layouts plays a crucial role in document design.

Exercises for Chap. 6: Customizing Layouts

6.1 Page Layout, Margins, and Spacing

1. *Adjusting Margins*: Write a LaTeX document that uses the `geometry` package to modify the page margins. Experiment with different margin sizes and explain how they affect the overall layout of the document.

2. *Line Spacing*: Modify the line spacing of a LaTeX document using the `setspace` package. Create a document with single spacing, 1.5 spacing, and double spacing. Include at least two paragraphs in each spacing style.

3. *Page Layout Control*: Create a document where you control the page layout, including margins, headers, and footers. Explain the role of the `geometry` package and its various options in customizing page dimensions.

6.2 Creating Custom Headers and Footers

1. *Basic Headers and Footers*: Write a LaTeX document that uses the `fancyhdr` package to add custom headers and footers. Include the title of the document in the header and the page number in the footer.

2. *Header Customization*: Customize the header to display different content on odd and even pages. For example, display the chapter title on even pages and the section title on odd pages.

3. *Complex Footer Example*: Modify the footer to display the author's name on the left and the page number on the right. Experiment with different footer designs using `fancyhdr`.

6.3 Title Pages, Abstracts, and Table of Contents

1. *Creating a Title Page*: Write a LaTeX document that includes a custom title page. Use the `titlepage` environment to center the title, author, and date.

2. *Adding an Abstract*: Add an abstract to your LaTeX document using the `abstract` environment. Place the abstract between the title and the first section of the document.

3. *Generating a Table of Contents*: Write a LaTeX document with multiple sections and subsections. Use the `\tableofcontents` command to generate an automatic table of contents.

6.4 Footnotes and Endnotes

1. *Using Footnotes*: Create a LaTeX document that includes footnotes using the `\footnote` command. Add at least three footnotes throughout the document and explain how footnotes are managed by LaTeX.

2. *Endnotes with `endnotes` Package*: Write a LaTeX document that uses the `endnotes` package to convert

footnotes into endnotes. Place the endnotes at the end of the document and ensure that they appear correctly.

3. *Customizing Footnotes*: Modify the appearance of footnotes by changing their numbering style (e.g., using symbols instead of numbers). Explain how to achieve this using LaTeX commands.

6.5 Multicolumn Layouts

1. *Basic Two-Column Layout*: Write a LaTeX document that uses the `multicols` package to create a two-column layout. Add multiple sections and paragraphs to demonstrate how content flows across columns.

2. *Three-Column Layout*: Modify the previous document to create a three-column layout. Experiment with different column widths and spacing between the columns.

3. *Mixing Single and Multicolumn Layouts*: Create a document where part of the text uses a single-column layout and another part uses a two-column layout. Use the `\begin{multicols}` environment to control where the columns begin and end.

Chapter 7

LaTeX for Presentations (Beamer)

Contents

Md Aquib, *Fundamentals of LaTeX*, University Texts in the Mathematical Sciences, https://doi.org/10.1007/978-981-96-9318-4_7

Abstract: LaTeX is widely known for its excellence in producing high-quality typeset documents, particularly in scientific and academic settings. Beyond traditional documents, LaTeX also offers powerful tools for creating professional presentations through the `beamer` class. Introduced by Till Tantau in 2003, `beamer` allows users to design visually appealing, content-rich slides with the full typesetting capabilities of LaTeX.

Keywords: Beamer presentations, LaTeX slides, Presentation themes, Frame environment, Beamer templates, Academic presentations

This chapter introduces the `beamer` class and provides a comprehensive overview of how to build and customize presentations in LaTeX. You will learn how to structure a presentation, create frames (slides), apply visual themes, and incorporate various elements such as bullet points, images, tables, equations, and animations.

In addition, we explore advanced features such as overlays for incremental content display, integration of navigation aids, and the use of color and font themes to align with institutional or stylistic guidelines. For users interested in academic posters, we also discuss the `beamerposter` package, which extends `beamer`'s functionality to support large-format poster creation.

By the end of this chapter, you will have the skills to create polished and dynamic presentations suitable for conferences, lectures, and public talks, maintaining the typographic quality that makes LaTeX a favorite among researchers and professionals.

7.1 Introduction to the Beamer Class

The `beamer` class is a robust and flexible LaTeX class designed specifically for creating high-quality presentations. Originally developed by Till Tantau in 2003, it has since become one of the most widely adopted tools for preparing academic and technical slides. Unlike standard presentation software, `beamer` leverages the precision of LaTeX, allowing users to create slides that incorporate complex mathematical notation, bibliographic references, and consistent styling with minimal effort.

What sets `beamer` apart is its structured approach to slide design. Presentations are organized into frames (individual slides), which can contain text, graphics, lists, tables, equations, and overlays, each governed by LaTeX's familiar environment syntax. Because it is a LaTeX class, `beamer` offers fine-grained control over formatting while also supporting modular design, making it ideal for users who value consistency, reusability, and typographic quality.

Another major advantage of `beamer` is its extensive theme system, which allows presenters to apply visual styles, color schemes, and font templates with ease. These themes are especially useful in academic and institutional settings where branding and formal tone are important. Features like navigation bars, section progress markers, and automatically generated tables of contents provide a professional look and feel to every presentation.

In this chapter, we will begin by exploring how to set up a basic `beamer` document, introduce the essential environments and commands, and demonstrate how to build structured, visually effective presentations using only LaTeX. Whether you are preparing a lecture, defending a thesis, or presenting at a conference, `beamer` provides a reliable and elegant platform for creating your slides.

7.1.1 Setting Up a Beamer Presentation

Beamer is a LaTeX document class used for creating high-quality presentations. Unlike typical document classes such as `article` or `report`, the `beamer` class is structured around the concept of "frames," which correspond to individual slides. To begin crafting a Beamer presentation, the very first step is to declare the class in the preamble using:

Declaring the Beamer Class

```
\documentclass{beamer}
```

This declaration informs LaTeX that the output should follow the conventions of a presentation, with visual elements such as slide transitions, titles, navigation bars, and formatting styles typical of slideshows.

A basic Beamer presentation is structured much like a standard LaTeX document in its overarching form but includes elements specific to presentation design. At the beginning of the document, one usually defines the metadata, such as the presentation title, the author's name, and the date of delivery. These declarations use the familiar commands `\title`, `\author`, and `\date`.

Once the document begins, a typical first slide includes the presentation's title page. This is accomplished by wrapping the command `\titlepage` within a frame environment. The title page automatically assembles the title, author, and date into a formatted introductory slide, making it easy to present professional content right from the outset.

Consider the following minimal example of a complete Beamer document:

Minimal Beamer Example

LaTeX Code:

```
\documentclass{beamer}

\title{Introduction to Beamer}
\author{Dr. LaTeX}
\date{\today}

\begin{document}
```

```
\begin{frame}
    \titlepage
\end{frame}

\begin{frame}
    \frametitle{Introduction}
    Welcome to this Beamer
    presentation.
\end{frame}

\end{document}
```

Output:

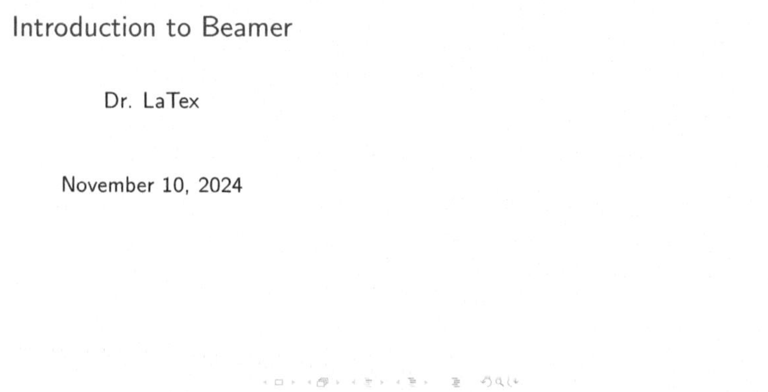

Slide 1: Title Slide

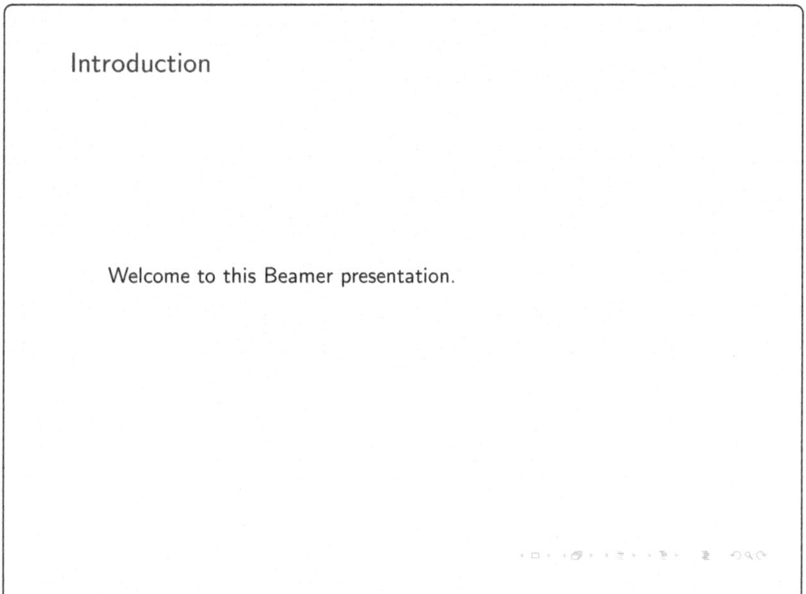

Slide 2: Content Slide

This basic template introduces two frames: The first presents the title slide using the `\titlepage` command, and the second contains a brief welcoming message with a custom title provided by `\frametitle`.

In this early stage, the emphasis is on initializing the structure of the presentation. Later subsections will elaborate on how to construct individual frames with content blocks, insert lists and images, define section-level navigation, and enhance the layout using Beamer themes and templates.

By correctly setting up the Beamer class and structuring metadata at the beginning, one establishes a solid foundation for building an engaging, well-organized presentation entirely within LaTeX.

7.2 Structuring Your Presentation

In Beamer presentations, each slide is called a "frame," and LaTeX provides a structured way to create these frames and organize them into sections and subsections. This section will guide you through creating slides (frames), organizing content with sections and subsections, and how to effectively manage the structure of your presentation using LaTeX.

7.2.1 Creating Frames (Slides)

In the Beamer presentation class, every slide is known as a frame. A frame encapsulates the content that appears on a single slide. Unlike traditional LaTeX documents, where text flows across pages continuously, Beamer explicitly divides content into frames. Each frame is defined using the `frame` environment, and typically, each one carries a title and some body content such as paragraphs, bullet points, figures, or tables.

To define a frame, you wrap its contents between `\begin{frame}` and `\end{frame}`. You can also assign a title to the slide using the `\frametitle` command, which places a header at the top of the slide.

Below is a basic example demonstrating how to create a single frame in a Beamer presentation:

Creating a Basic Frame

LaTeX Code:

```
\begin{frame}
\frametitle{Introduction}
Welcome to this
presentation on Beamer.
```

```
\end{frame}
```

Output:

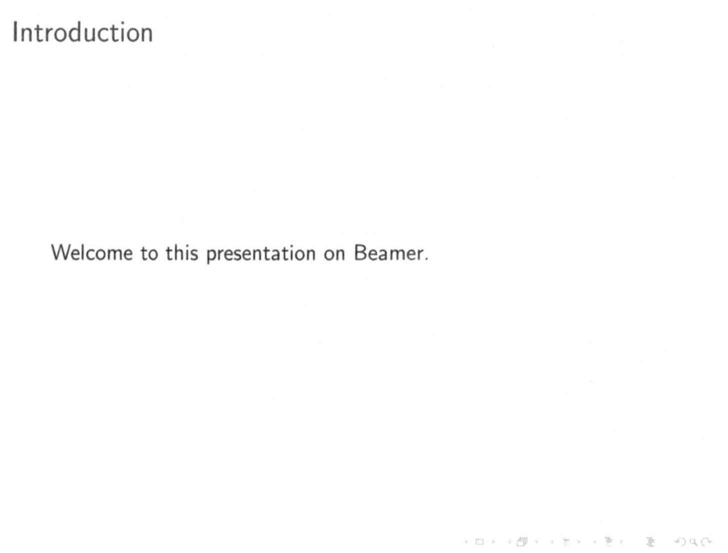

Figure: A slide with a title and text.

In this example, the command `\frametitle{Introduction}` assigns a title to the slide. The body of the frame, here a simple welcoming message, appears below the title in the main content area. Beamer takes care of the slide layout, including margins, font sizes, and navigation bars, depending on the chosen theme.

Once you have established the structure for one frame, creating a complete presentation becomes a matter of adding more frames for each idea or topic. For instance, the following example shows how to define two consecutive slides in a Beamer presentation:

Creating Multiple Frames

LaTeX Code:

```
\begin{frame}
    \frametitle{Introduction to
    LaTeX}
    This slide covers the
    basics of LaTeX.
\end{frame}

\begin{frame}
    \frametitle{Introduction to
    Beamer}
    This slide introduces the
     Beamer class in LaTeX.
\end{frame}
```

Output:

Introduction to LaTeX

This slide covers the basics of LaTeX.

Frame 1: LaTeX basics

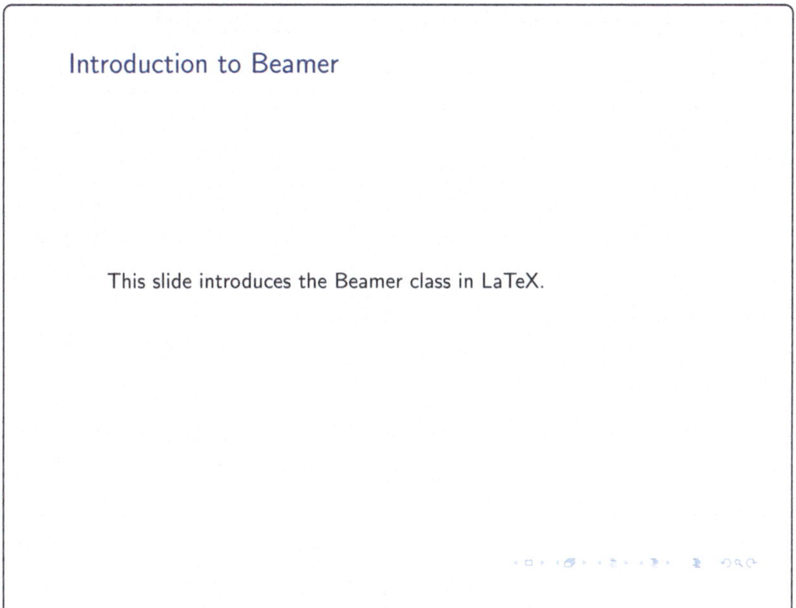

Frame 2: Beamer introduction

Beamer processes each `frame` environment as a new slide. You can define as many frames as needed to convey your content. LaTeX takes care of transitioning from one slide to the next, and you do not need to manage slide numbers or navigation manually, unless you choose to customize it.

At this stage, the focus remains on introducing how to structure content into discrete visual segments using frames. Advanced layout options such as block structures, column alignment, or dynamic overlays will be introduced in the following subsections, allowing greater control over how content is visually distributed within each frame.

Understanding the concept of the frame is foundational to mastering Beamer. Once this building block is familiar, the rest of the presentation structure, sections, blocks, and transitions can be layered on top with ease.

7.2.2 Creating Frames with Blocks

One of the core design features that distinguishes a Beamer presentation from other slide-making tools is its ability to visually organize content into well-defined blocks. These blocks help isolate definitions, results, examples, or any group of ideas that should be framed as a cohesive unit. The `block` environment is used for this purpose and can be included directly within a frame.

The syntax is quite straightforward. A block is initiated using the command `\begin{block}{Title}`, where the argument in curly braces provides a heading for the block. The block's contents are then inserted, followed by `\end{block}`. These blocks are automatically styled by Beamer's theme to visually stand out from the rest of the frame, using borders, backgrounds, and indentation.

The following example demonstrates how blocks are integrated within a slide to structure content:

Basic Frame with Blocks

LaTeX Code:

```
\documentclass{beamer}

\usetheme{Madrid}
\usecolortheme{seagull}

\begin{document}
\begin{frame}
  \frametitle{Introduction}

  \begin{block}{Definition}
  Energy is defined as the
  ability to do work.
  \end{block}
```

```
    \begin{block}{Formula}
    According to Einstein:
    \[
      E = mc^2
    \]
    \end{block}

    This concludes our basic
    example.
\end{frame}

\end{document}
```

Output:

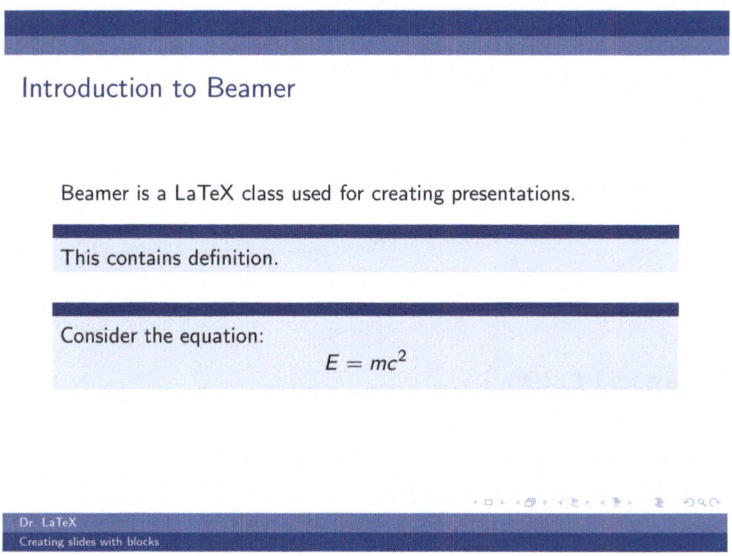

Figure: A slide with two blocks and extra text.

In this example, the slide begins with a title "Introduction" set using the `\frametitle` command. The first block, titled "Definition," is used to enclose a short explanatory sentence. The second block, titled "Formula," includes a mathematical expression rendered using standard LaTeX math syntax. Text outside the blocks can also be added to complement the structured content.

It is also possible to create a block without any visible title by simply leaving the title argument empty. This is useful when you want a content box without labeling it explicitly. For instance:

Untitled Block Example

LaTeX Code:

```
\documentclass{beamer}

\title{Creating slides
with blocks}
\author{Dr. LaTeX}
\date{\today}

\usetheme{Madrid}
\usecolortheme{seagull}

\begin{document}

\begin{frame}

\begin{block}{}
This is an untitled
block, often used for
emphasis or quotations.
\end{block}

\end{frame}
\end{document}
```

Output:

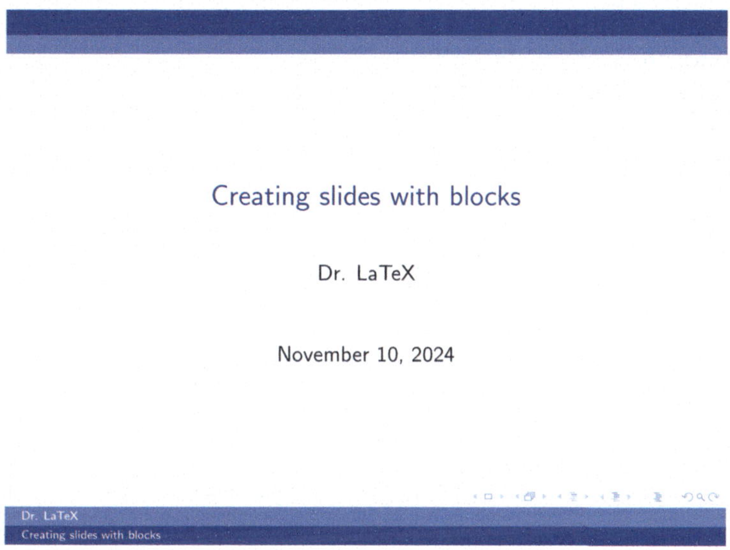

Block Without a Title.

Blocks can be stacked within a single frame or distributed across multiple frames depending on the presentation flow. Their visual structure helps emphasize key ideas, highlight results, or isolate formulas without requiring additional formatting.

While the standard `block` environment is often sufficient, Beamer also offers `alertblock` and `exampleblock` environments for drawing special attention to warnings or illustrative content. These variations will be discussed later when we address custom themes and color schemes.

For now, it is important to understand that blocks form a foundational layout tool in Beamer. Used thoughtfully, they create structure, reduce clutter, and contribute to the overall professionalism of the slide design.

A Presentation with Two Frames

LaTeX Code:

```
\documentclass{beamer}

\title{Creating slides with blocks}
\author{Dr. LaTeX}
\date{\today}

\usetheme{Madrid}
\usecolortheme{seagull}

\begin{document}

\begin{frame}
    \titlepage
\end{frame}

\begin{frame}
\frametitle{Introduction to Beamer}
Beamer is a LaTeX class used for
creating presentations.

 \begin{block}{}
   This contains definition.
 \end{block}

 \begin{block}{}
    Consider the equation:
     \[
            E = mc^2
     \]
    \end{block}

\end{frame}
\end{document}
```

Output:

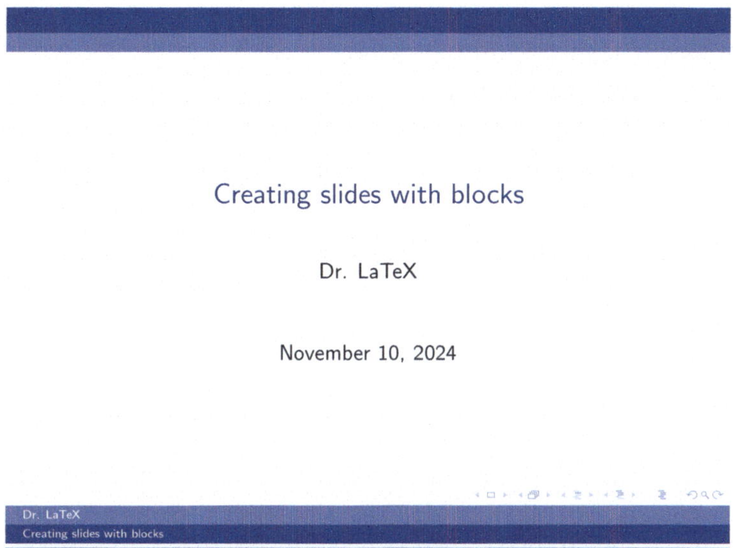

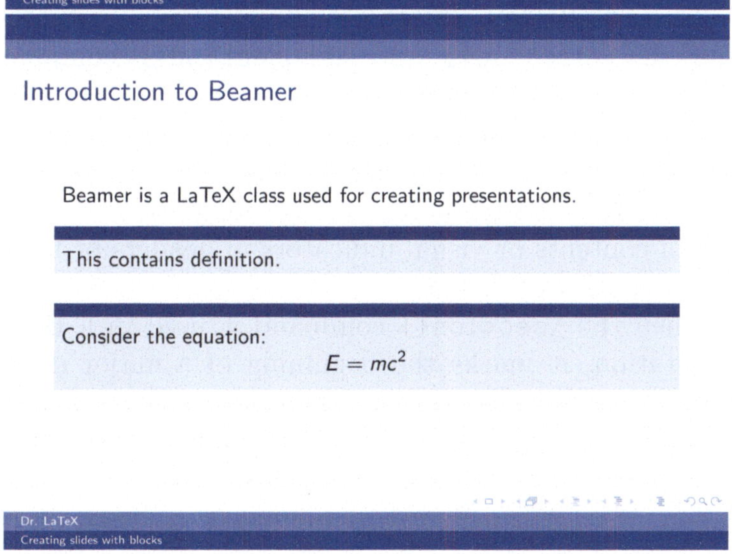

As seen in the output, the first frame generated is the title slide containing the presentation title, author, and date. The second frame, titled "Introduction to Beamer," introduces the topic using two distinct blocks. The first block contains a plain text explanation, while the second displays Einstein's iconic equation in a centered math environment. Both blocks are untitled, demonstrating how you can structure slide content without relying on block headers if they are not needed.

Using blocks in this way enhances the organization and visual clarity of a presentation, particularly when you wish to isolate specific ideas without overwhelming the audience. In longer or more content-heavy presentations, this technique becomes essential for maintaining engagement and helping the viewer process information in digestible sections.

7.2.3 Adding Sections and Subsections

A well-structured presentation not only delivers information clearly but also guides the audience through its logical development. In Beamer, this structural clarity is achieved using the `\section{}` and `\subsection{}` commands. These commands do not produce content slides themselves, but they segment the document internally, allowing LaTeX to group frames into thematic blocks. This grouping can then be utilized to generate navigational aids, such as a table of contents or visual indicators in headers or footers, depending on the theme.

When the `\section{}` command is used in a Beamer presentation, it marks the beginning of a major division within the slide deck. A frame may immediately follow it, typically providing the section's title slide or introductory content. For example, consider the following:

Example: Creating a Section

LaTeX Code:

```
\documentclass{beamer}
\begin{document}
\section{Introduction}
\begin{frame}
\frametitle{Welcome}
Welcome to this
section on
Introduction.
\end{frame}
\end{document}
```

Output:

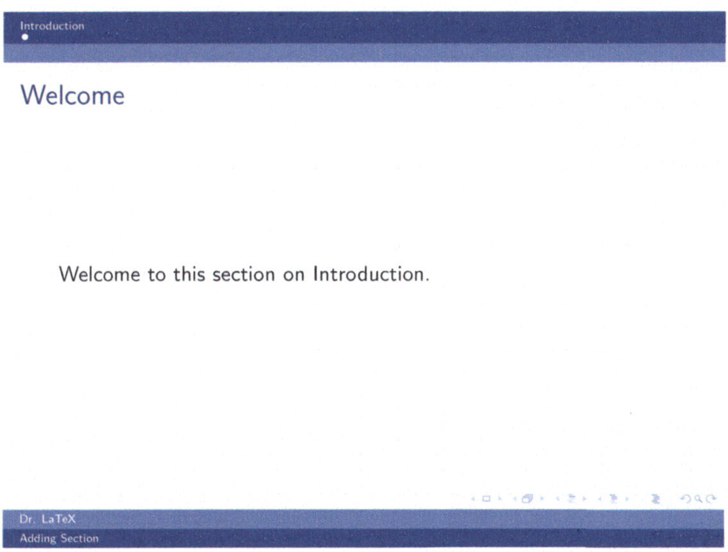

In this example, the presentation moves into a new section titled "Introduction." While the `\section{}` command itself does not render a visible element in the compiled presentation, it informs LaTeX of a new segment's start. The accompanying "frame" contains the first slide within that section.

Subsections are defined in a similar manner using the `\subsection{}` command. These are useful when a section contains several distinct topics or steps that warrant their own frames. Unlike `\section{}`, subsections offer a finer granularity of navigation and structure, especially in presentations that include complex or multistage content. The following code illustrates how multiple subsections can be introduced under a single section:

Example: Adding Subsections

LaTeX Code:

```
\documentclass{beamer}
\begin{document}
\section{Introduction}

\subsection
{What Is LaTeX?}
\begin{frame}
\frametitle{What Is
LaTeX?}
LaTeX is a
typesetting system.
\end{frame}

\subsection
{What Is Beamer?}
\begin{frame}
\frametitle
{What Is Beamer?}
Beamer is a LaTeX class
used for presentations.
\end{frame}
\end{document}
```

Output:

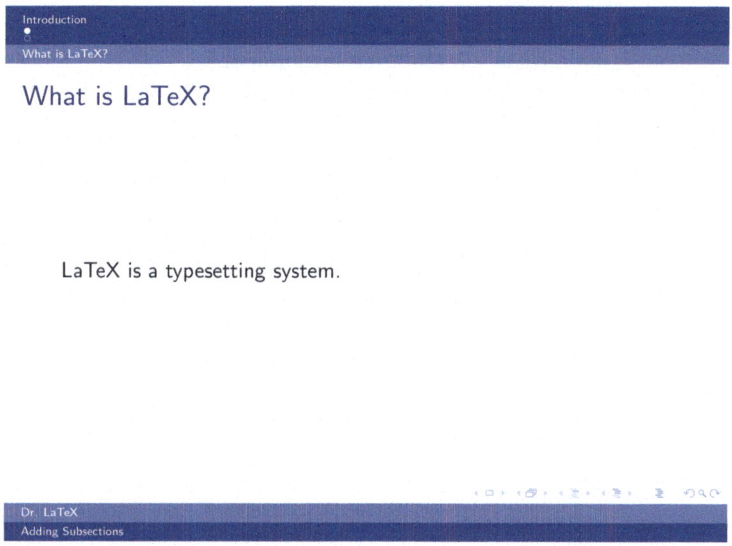

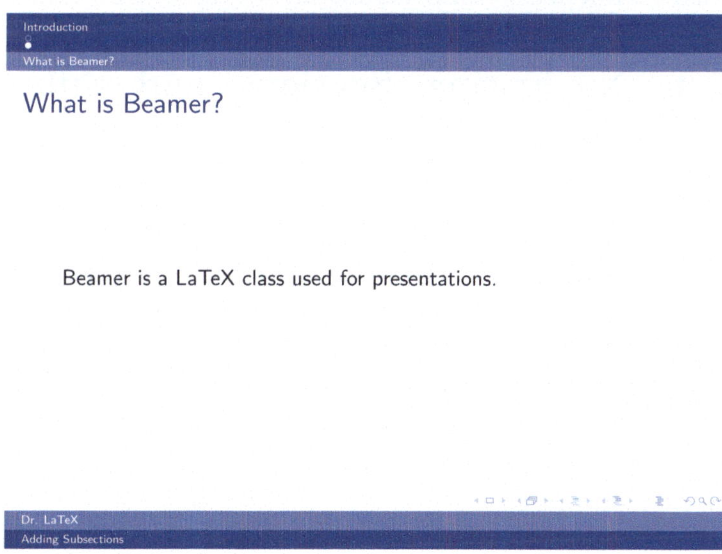

The section "Introduction" in this case contains two distinct topics: one introducing LaTeX, and another introducing Beamer itself. Each subsection is followed by a corresponding frame with a title and content relevant to that topic. When used in combination with a Beamer theme that supports navigation bars or progress indicators, these structural commands help the audience know where they are in the flow of the presentation.

Moreover, these sectioning commands are especially beneficial when generating a table of contents or navigating through slides using keyboard shortcuts. For instance, you can include a frame that automatically displays a list of all sections and subsections using the `\tableofcontents` command, an idea that will be explored further in subsequent subsections related to navigation and structure.

In short, `\section{}` and `\subsection{}` in Beamer do not merely serve formatting purposes; they are integral tools for organizing, navigating, and conceptualizing the narrative arc of a presentation. When thoughtfully used, they contribute significantly to both the author's workflow and the audience's comprehension.

7.2.4 Navigating Sections and Subsections

In a Beamer presentation, organizing content into sections and subsections serves not only a logical function but also a navigational one. Beamer themes typically include a visual navigation bar at the top or bottom of each slide. This bar dynamically updates as the presentation progresses, indicating the current position in the structure. When used thoughtfully, this navigation aid allows both the presenter and the audience to remain aware of the presentation's structure and flow.

To supplement the navigation bar, Beamer provides a built-in `\tableofcontents` command that generates a visual outline of the entire presentation. Including a table of contents slide at the beginning, or before a new section, can help set the agenda and orient the audience.

A basic implementation of the table of contents in Beamer is as follows:

Basic Table of Contents

LaTeX Code:

```
\begin{frame}
    \frametitle{Table of Contents}
    \tableofcontents
\end{frame}
```

This command generates a list of all sections and subsections previously declared using `\section{}` and `\subsection{}`. If the presentation has multiple parts, this table provides a comprehensive view of the slide deck's layout.

In some cases, it is helpful to display a subset of the table of contents that focuses on the current section or subsection. This technique is especially useful for long presentations, where repeatedly listing the full contents may distract from the immediate topic. To achieve this, Beamer offers modifiers such as `\tableofcontents[currentsection]` or `\tableofcontents[currentsubsection]`. These options render a condensed version of the full contents with emphasis on the relevant part.

The following example demonstrates how to highlight the current section in a table of contents slide:

Highlighting the Current Section

LaTeX Code:

```
\begin{frame}
    \frametitle{Overview}
    \tableofcontents[currentsection]
\end{frame}
```

This command is typically used at the beginning of each major section to help the audience understand what will follow. It highlights only the slides that belong to the currently active section, presenting them in a focused way that reinforces the structure without overwhelming the audience with too much context.

Beamer's automated navigation system offers a smooth and professional experience when moving through the content. With minimal manual effort, a well-organized document results in a well-guided presentation. When used alongside the `\section{}` and `\subsection{}` commands discussed earlier, these features provide a cohesive way to structure and navigate a talk.

In the next sections, we will examine how to enhance frame content with lists and bullet points, which are essential tools for pacing and presenting detailed information.

7.2.5 Adding Lists to Frames

Presentations often rely on structured points to communicate information clearly and sequentially. Beamer, as a LaTeX class designed for presentations, supports both itemized and enumerated lists in a manner similar to standard LaTeX documents. Within the `frame` environment, lists can be embedded using the `itemize` or `enumerate` environments to highlight key ideas, steps, or features on a slide.

An itemized list is ideal for unordered points where the sequence is not critical. For example, consider a slide that introduces the main advantages of using Beamer. The following code illustrates how to embed such a list into a single frame:

Creating an Itemized List in Beamer

LaTeX Code:

```
\begin{frame}
    \frametitle{Advantages of Beamer}
    \begin{itemize}
        \item Easy to use
        \item Highly customizable
        \item Integrates with LaTeX
    \end{itemize}
\end{frame}
```

In this example, a frame titled "Advantages of Beamer" contains an itemized list of three concise bullet points. These are formatted using the `itemize` environment, which by default uses simple circular bullets to mark each item. The layout is clean and emphasizes clarity, making it particularly effective for presenting overviews, benefits, or features.

For lists where order is important, such as outlining steps in a process or presenting a ranked set of principles, one can use the `enumerate` environment. It behaves similarly but replaces bullet symbols with sequential numbers or letters depending on the depth level.

Lists can also be nested, allowing for hierarchical organization of ideas. For example, an item in a list might include a sublist that provides further details or subcategories. While Beamer handles this automatically, it is a good practice to keep nested lists visually compact to avoid overwhelming the audience on a single slide.

It is worth noting that lists in Beamer are often combined with overlay techniques to reveal items one by one, which helps maintain focus and pacing during live presentations. However, these incremental effects are covered separately under the topic of overlays and should not be confused with the basic list structure discussed here.

When used thoughtfully, lists can significantly enhance the clarity and structure of a Beamer presentation, allowing complex information to be broken into digestible, well-organized points. They are a core component of most presentation slides and are fully compatible with the broader stylistic and structural tools offered by Beamer.

7.2.6 Incremental Slides and Overlays

A major strength of the Beamer class lies in its ability to control the pacing of information delivery through incremental reveals and overlays. Rather than overwhelming the audience with all the content at once, you can guide their attention step by step, unveiling each element of a slide as needed. This is especially valuable in situations where you want to emphasize individual points, build suspense, or encourage focused discussion.

The most common use of incremental overlays occurs in list environments, such as `itemize` or `enumerate`. Beamer offers a convenient mechanism to control when each item in a list appears. This is achieved using the overlay specification syntax `<n->`, where `n` denotes the slide number from which the item becomes visible.

The following example illustrates how this works in practice. Each item in the list is revealed one at a time as you navigate through the slide:

Incremental Reveal in a List

LaTeX Code:

```
\begin{frame}
\frametitle{Advantages of LaTeX}
 \begin{itemize}
\item<1-> High-quality typesetting
\item<2-> Easy to create complex
          documents
```

```
\item<3-> Extensible with packages
\end{itemize}
\end{frame}
```

In this frame, the first item appears on the first display of the slide, the second on the next click or forward action, and the third after that. This pacing mechanism is invaluable for interactive teaching or presentations, allowing the speaker to explain each point before moving on to the next.

In addition to lists, Beamer offers even finer control over slide elements using the `\onslide` command. This command can be wrapped around any content, not just list items, to specify exactly when it should appear. The syntax `<n->` again indicates that the enclosed content should be shown starting from the `n`-th step of the slide onward.

Below is an example where three lines of text are revealed one after another, without using the `itemize` environment:

Stepwise Text Using \onslide

LaTeX Code:

```
\begin{frame}
    \frametitle{Step-by-Step Process}
    \onslide<1-> First, we do this.

    \onslide<2-> Then, we do this.

    \onslide<3-> Finally, we do this.
\end{frame}
```

This method is especially useful when narrating a process, walking through derivations, or breaking down visual explanations. Any part of the slide content can be wrapped with `\onslide` to fine-tune the timing of its appearance.

There are many additional overlay tools available in Beamer, including commands such as `\only`, `\visible`, and `\uncover`, each offering a slightly different behavior. However, `\onslide` and the `<n->` syntax remain among the most commonly used because of their simplicity and effectiveness.

7.2.7 Structuring a Complex Presentation

When working with larger presentations in Beamer, proper structural organization becomes essential. As the number of slides increases, managing the content through well-defined sections and subsections not only enhances navigation but also improves the overall readability and logic of the presentation.

Beamer provides dedicated commands to define this structure: `\section{}` is used to declare major thematic divisions of your talk, while `\subsection{}` allows further subdivision within each section. These declarations serve two purposes: They visually organize the presentation in the source code, and they enable Beamer to generate useful navigation aids such as progress bars or tables of contents during the presentation.

Importantly, these sectioning commands do not create slides on their own, they act as structural markers. However, once they are defined, any `frame` environment that follows is automatically associated with the most recently declared section or subsection.

Here is a clear example demonstrating how a presentation might be logically structured using these commands:

Presentation with Multiple Slides

```
\section{Introduction}
\subsection{What Is LaTeX?}
\begin{frame}
    \frametitle{What Is LaTeX?}
    LaTeX is a powerful typesetting system.
\end{frame}

\section{Creating Documents}
\subsection{Using LaTeX}
\begin{frame}
    \frametitle{Using LaTeX}
    LaTeX allows you to create complex
    documents with ease.
\end{frame}

\section{Beamer Presentations}
\subsection{What Is Beamer?}
\begin{frame}
    \frametitle{What Is Beamer?}
    Beamer is a LaTeX class for creating
    presentations.
\end{frame}
```

In this structure, the presentation is divided into three coherent sections: "Introduction," "Creating Documents," and "Beamer Presentations." Each section is further refined by meaningful subsections that contain individual frames.

This logical hierarchy is not only useful for presenters, but it also improves the viewing experience for the audience, especially when combined with Beamer's ability to generate navigation cues and automatic outlines. In more advanced cases, sections and subsections can also be used in conjunction with progress indicators or dynamically updated tables of contents that reflect the audience's current position in the talk.

As your presentation becomes more complex, embracing this structural discipline early on will greatly simplify editing, reviewing, and extending your material over time.

7.2.8 Full LaTeX Example

To illustrate how a Beamer presentation is structured, we present a complete example that creates six slides. Each slide is displayed with its LaTeX source on the left and the corresponding output on the right.

This Beamer presentation titled *Creating Slides and Sections* introduces the foundational concepts of using LaTeX for designing professional presentations. It is structured into six slides and styled with the `Bergen` theme and the `orchid` color scheme to provide a visually clean and modern layout. The presentation opens with a title slide that automatically formats and displays the title, author, and date using the `\titlepage` command.

The subsequent slides walk through core LaTeX concepts, starting with a brief explanation of what LaTeX is, followed by a concise description of the Beamer class. It then introduces reasons for using LaTeX, presented as an itemized list with incremental reveals enabled through overlay commands such as `<1->`, `<2->`, and so on. A dedicated slide then summarizes the current section using the `\tableofcontents[currentsection]` command, which dynamically updates the viewer's orientation within the presentation. The final slide highlights the strengths of Beamer as a tool for creating structured and professional slides, thus rounding out the presentation with a clear emphasis on Beamer's utility within the LaTeX environment.

First Three Slides

LaTeX Code:

```
\documentclass{beamer}
\title{Creating Slides
       and Sections}
\author{Dr. LaTex}
\date{\today}

\usetheme{Bergen}
\usecolortheme{orchid}

\begin{document}

\begin{frame}
    \titlepage
\end{frame}

\section{Introduction}
\subsection
{What Is LaTeX?}
\begin{frame}
\frametitle{What
Is LaTeX?}
LaTeX is a
typesetting system.
\end{frame}

\subsection{What Is
Beamer?}
\begin{frame}
\frametitle
{What Is Beamer?}
Beamer is a LaTeX
class for creating
presentations.
\end{frame}
```

Output:

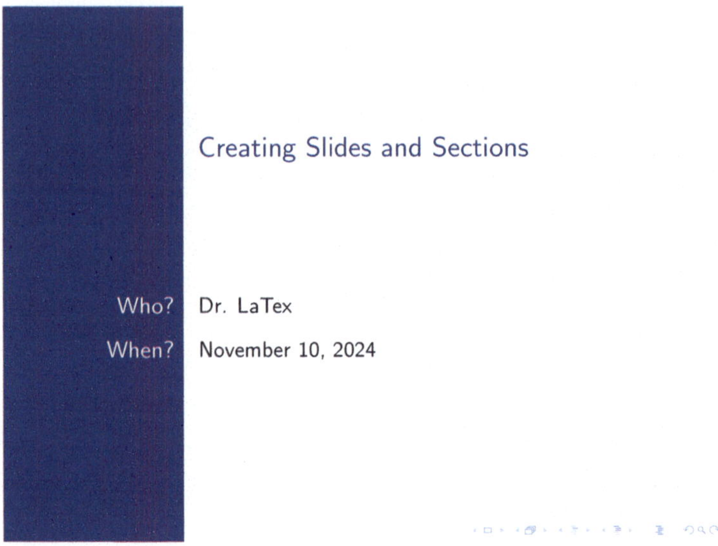

Slide 1

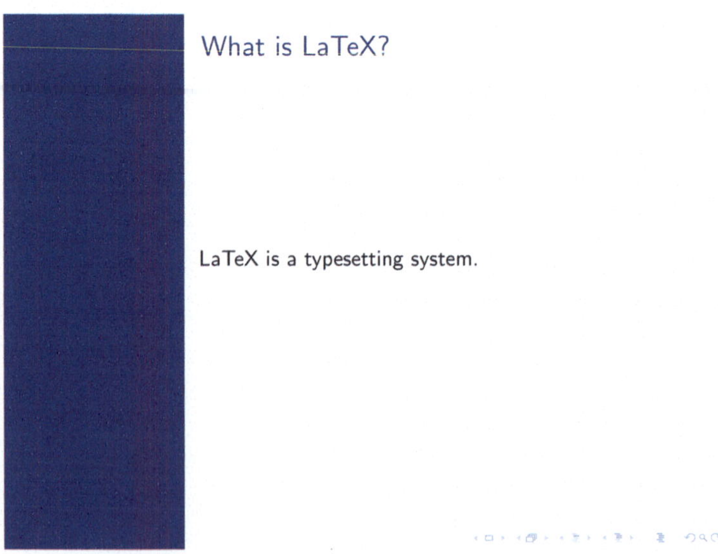

Slide 2

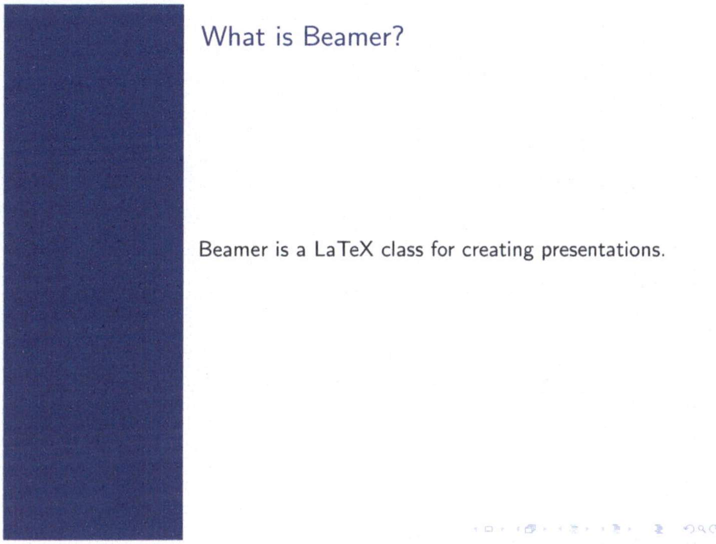

Slide 3

Presentation Continue

LaTeX Code:

```
\section
{Creating Documents}
\subsection
{Why Use LaTeX?}
\begin{frame}
\frametitle
{Why Use LaTeX?}
\begin{itemize}
\item<1-> High-quality
         typesetting
\item<2->
Easy to create
complex documents
```

```
\item<3->
Supports mathematical
typesetting
\end{itemize}
\end{frame}

\section
{Beamer Presentations}
\begin{frame}
\frametitle{Overview}
\tableofcontents
[currentsection]
\end{frame}

\begin{frame}
\frametitle{Beamer
      Features}
Beamer allows you to
create professional
presentations in LaTeX.
\end{frame}
```

Output:

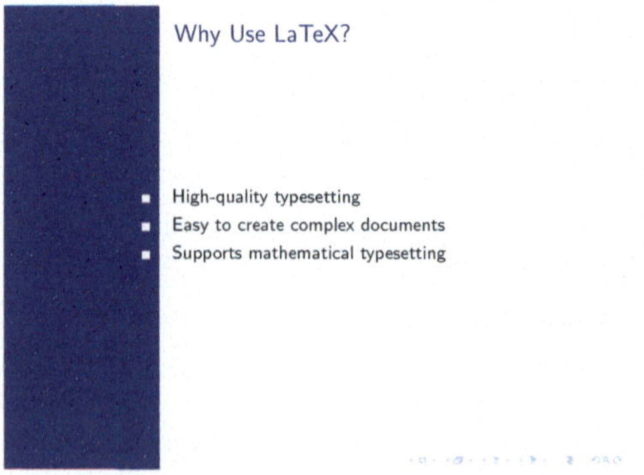

Slide 4

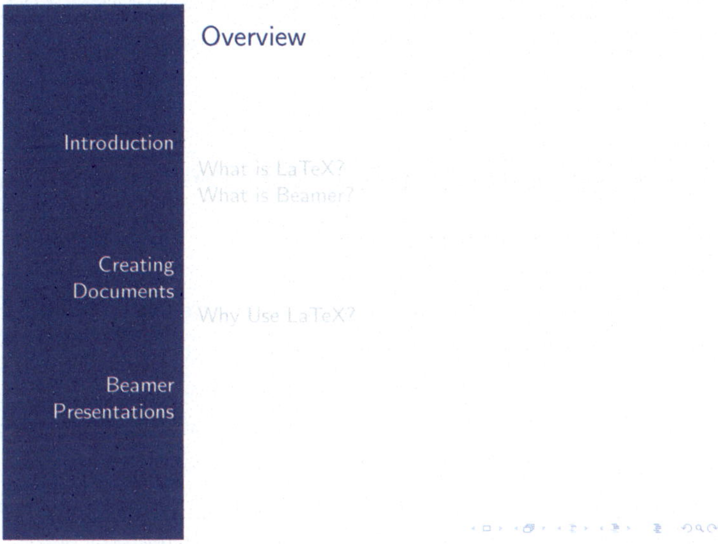

Slide 5

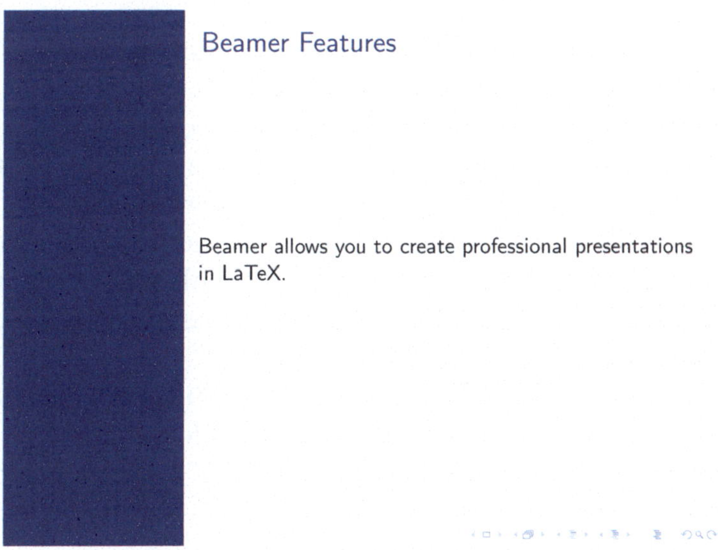

Slide 6

Note that in Slide 4, the three list items are revealed incrementally during the presentation, thanks to the overlay specifications `<1->`, `<2->`, and `<3->`.

7.3 Customizing Slide Themes and Colors

One of the best features of Beamer is its flexibility in terms of presentation design. Beamer offers various predefined themes and color schemes, but it also allows you to customize both themes and colors to suit your personal style or presentation requirements. This section will guide you through the process of customizing Beamer themes, colors, and other visual aspects of your slides.

7.3.1 Using Predefined Themes

Beamer offers a wide variety of predefined themes that significantly influence the visual style and structure of a presentation. These themes govern how content is laid out on each slide, the formatting of titles and headers, the positioning of navigation bars, and other stylistic details that contribute to a polished and professional appearance. Selecting an appropriate theme not only enhances the aesthetic appeal but also improves audience engagement and clarity.

To use a predefined theme, one must invoke the `\usetheme{}` command in the preamble of the LaTeX document. For example, applying the popular `Madrid` theme would look as follows:

Applying a Beamer Theme

LaTeX Code:

```
\usetheme{Madrid}
```

Description: This command activates the `Madrid` layout, which features a compact title banner, clean fonts, and a standard navigation bar at the top.

Beamer includes many themes to choose from, each offering distinct layout characteristics. For instance, `Berlin`, `Copenhagen`, `Warsaw`, and `Bergen` all exhibit unique arrangements of slide headers, itemization styles, and navigation elements. While `Bergen` favors a minimalistic style, `Warsaw` introduces colored navigation bars and frames. Some themes also support sidebar navigation (`Darmstadt`, `Ilmenau`), while others emphasize simplicity (`AnnArbor`, `Pittsburgh`). However, Beamer provides many such themes, each with a distinctive style. The following table lists several popular visual themes available in Beamer:

Beamer Theme	**Beamer Theme**	**Beamer Theme**
Berlin	Copenhagen	Madrid
Warsaw	Ilmenau	Darmstadt
Metropolis	Singapore	Bergen
Szeged	Malmoe	Dresden
Boadilla	CambridgeUS	AnnArbor
EastLansing	Rochester	Antibes

To enhance the appearance further, one can pair a visual layout theme with a color scheme using the

`\usecolortheme{}` command. This option affects the palette used for titles, backgrounds, bullets, and structural elements, making it possible to align the presentation with institutional or branding requirements.

Combining Visual and Color Themes

LaTeX Code:

```
\usetheme{Madrid}
\usecolortheme{seagull}
```

Description: This example applies the `Madrid` theme and the `seagull` color palette, resulting in a balanced design with muted shades and a subtle accent for navigation elements.

Among the many color themes available, `orchid`, `beaver`, `whale`, and `wolverine` are widely used for their distinct tones. For example, `dolphin` provides soft grayscale contrast, while `rose` emphasizes rich reddish tones. By pairing a theme with a suitable color scheme, presenters can fine-tune the tone and readability of their content to suit formal or informal settings.

It is recommended to experiment with different theme combinations early in the document preparation process, as some themes may influence not only appearance but also structural elements like slide titles, navigation bars, and bullet styles. Keep in mind that theme compatibility can vary slightly depending on which additional customization packages are being used.

The table below lists some commonly used color themes in Beamer:

Color Theme	**Color Theme**
Albatross	Beaver
Beetle	Crane

Dolphin	Dove
Fly	Lily
Orchid	Rose
Seagull	Seahorse
Sidebartab	Structure
Whale	Wolverine

Using predefined themes and color themes in Beamer allows you to focus on your content while ensuring that your presentation maintains a professional and visually pleasing appearance. These themes are particularly useful for academic and scientific talks, where clarity and structure are paramount.

7.3.2 Customizing Colors

In addition to using predefined color themes, Beamer provides extensive support for manually customizing the colors of different slide components. This flexibility allows authors to align the visual identity of their presentation with institutional guidelines or personal preferences. Customizing colors in Beamer is accomplished using the `\setbeamercolor` command, which lets you adjust the foreground (text) and background colors of various elements such as frames, titles, and body text.

To start, you might want to change the background color of the slides and the appearance of frame titles. This can be done by modifying the `background canvas` and `frametitle` elements. For instance, consider the following configuration:

Customizing Background and Frame Title

LaTeX Code:

```
\setbeamercolor{background canvas}
               {bg=lightgray}
\setbeamercolor{frametitle}{fg=blue}
```

Effect:
This configuration will apply a light gray background to every slide and render all frame titles in blue text.

In the code above, `bg` stands for "background" and `fg` refers to the "foreground," which typically means the text color. The `background canvas` refers to the full slide background, while `frametitle` targets only the area that displays the title at the top of each frame.

Beyond structural elements, you may also want to control the color of your main body text and any emphasized content. For instance, to set normal text to black and make alerted text appear red, you could include the following:

Setting Text and Alert Colors

LaTeX Code:

```
\setbeamercolor{normal text}{fg=black}
\setbeamercolor{alerted text}{fg=red}
```

Effect:
All standard text will appear in black, while highlighted text—wrapped in the `{}` command—will appear in red.

To apply this alerted text in a frame, the following frame demonstrates the use of the `\alert{}` command to emphasize key phrases:

Using Alerted Text

LaTeX Code:

```
\begin{frame}
\frametitle{Key Points}
  Here is an important \alert{note}.
\end{frame}
```

Effect:
The word "note" will be rendered in red to draw attention.

Alternatively, if you prefer more general control over inline text color, the `\color{}` command may be used. This method does not rely on the Beamer alert system but provides manual coloring for specific words or phrases. For instance:

Using Inline Text Color

LaTeX Code:

```
\begin{frame}
\frametitle{Key Points}
  Here is an important
  {\color{red}{note}}.
\end{frame}
```

Effect:
Again, the word "note" appears in red, but this time using the more generic LaTeX color command.

This method is especially useful when you need to apply specific colors not tied to Beamer's alerting system or when dealing with multi-word spans.

7.3.3 Customizing Font Styles and Sizes

Beamer offers a flexible set of tools for customizing the appearance of fonts in your presentation. Whether your goal is to emphasize section titles, align the design with institutional formatting guidelines, or simply enhance the overall readability of your slides, Beamer's font management system allows detailed control over both font size and style.

One of the primary ways to adjust text formatting is by using the `\setbeamerfont` command, which takes as arguments the target element (such as `frametitle`, `title`, `subtitle`, `item`, etc.) and the desired font properties. For example, to increase the font size of frame titles, you might apply the following customization:

Customizing Font Size in Frame Titles

LaTeX Code:

```
\setbeamerfont{frametitle}{size=\large}
```

Effect:
This will render the frame title in a slightly larger font than the default. You can substitute `\large` with other LaTeX size commands such as `\small`, `\normalsize`, `\footnotesize`, or even `\Huge`, depending on your preferences and slide layout.

It is important to choose font sizes judiciously, especially in a slide-based format where visual clarity is essential. Overly large fonts can disrupt slide layout, while very small text may be unreadable from a distance.

In addition to adjusting font size, Beamer also supports changing font families, allowing you to set whether text appears in serif, sans-serif, or monospaced (typewriter-style) fonts. This is useful when emphasizing structure (e.g., using monospaced fonts for code), or when harmonizing slide design with a broader theme or branding style. To apply a sans-serif font to all frame titles, the following code may be used:

Customizing Font Family in Frame Titles

LaTeX Code:

```
\setbeamerfont{frametitle}
        {family=\sffamily}
```

Effect:
This command changes the frame title font to a sans-serif typeface, which is typically more modern and easier to read on-screen. You may also use `\rmfamily` for traditional serif fonts or `\ttfamily` for monospaced fonts when appropriate.

These font customizations can be applied not only to frame titles but also to other slide elements such as item labels, footnotes, subtitles, and captions. When applied consistently, they can dramatically enhance the visual tone of the presentation.

While Beamer offers broad control through its internal font commands, additional font selection and styling capabilities, especially for using system fonts or OpenType features, can be accessed by compiling with XeLaTeX or LuaLaTeX and loading the `fontspec` package. However, those techniques fall under advanced font management and are covered in a separate section.

7.3.4 Adding a Custom Logo

In many professional or academic presentations, it is often desirable to include an institutional or organizational logo on each slide. Beamer makes this task straightforward by providing the `\logo` command, which allows you to embed an image, typically a logo, into a predefined position on every slide in your presentation.

To include a logo, the command is placed in the preamble or immediately before the `\begin{document}` line. It expects a LaTeX box as its argument, which means you can use the `\includegraphics` command (from the `graphicx` package, which is loaded by default in Beamer) to import an image. The logo typically appears in the lower right or upper right corner, depending on the theme.

For example, the following code snippet places a logo image named `logo.png` on each slide:

Placing a Logo on Every Slide

LaTeX Code:

```
\logo{\includegraphics
    [height=1cm]{logo.png}}
```

Effect:
The specified logo will be scaled to 1 cm in height and automatically positioned according to the default placement of the chosen Beamer theme. The image file `logo.png` should be located in the same directory as the `.tex` file or an accessible path.

Note that the actual placement of the logo, whether it appears in the top right, bottom corner, or side margin, varies depending on the visual theme used in the presentation. Some themes integrate the logo prominently into the header, while others may display it more subtly.

For best results, use a logo image with a transparent background and appropriate resolution to ensure visual clarity without overwhelming the slide content. If necessary, you can adjust the height or width further using `\includegraphics[height=..., width=...]` options.

Advanced customizations, such as placing the logo only on the title slide or changing its position using `\setbeamertemplate{logo}`, are discussed in later sections focusing on layout and template control.

Adding a logo in this manner not only reinforces visual branding but also lends a polished and professional appearance to the presentation.

7.3.5 Customizing Navigation Bars

In Beamer presentations, navigation symbols and progress indicators are often displayed by default, typically appearing at the lower corners or top edges of the slides depending on the theme in use. These navigation elements include clickable icons such as arrows for navigating between slides, as well as small dots representing individual frames. While these can be useful for interactive presentations, there are many cases, especially in academic or formal settings, where you may prefer to remove or customize these symbols to achieve a cleaner aesthetic.

To remove the navigation symbols entirely from all slides, Beamer provides a straightforward command that can be placed in the preamble of your document. The following line suppresses all default navigation symbols:

Removing Navigation Symbols

LaTeX Code:

```
\setbeamertemplate
{navigation symbols}{}
```

Effect:
This command removes all navigation icons from the slides, resulting in a presentation that appears more minimal and distraction-free.

This minimal configuration is especially beneficial when your presentation is designed for print, or when slides are being recorded or projected in contexts where such symbols offer no functional advantage.

Beyond removing them, Beamer also allows full customization of the navigation bar elements using the `navigation symbols` template. You may define a custom version containing only the icons you need or modify their position, size, and style. This level of customization, however, requires a deeper understanding of Beamer templates and is best addressed in an advanced section dedicated to modifying slide templates and overlays.

To demonstrate how the navigation bar, along with other theme and style customizations, integrates into a complete presentation, consider the following example. It combines several Beamer features, custom color themes, font styles, and a logo with the removal of navigation symbols to produce a streamlined, professional slide deck.

7.3.6 Full LaTeX Example with Slide-by-Slide Explanation

Beamer allows users to design rich presentations with complete control over themes, colors, fonts, and layout. In the example below, we walk through a complete Beamer document, illustrating how customization options affect each slide.

Slide 1: Title Page

LaTeX Code:

```
\documentclass{beamer}

\usetheme{Warsaw}
\usecolortheme{seahorse}
```

```
\setbeamercolor{background canvas}
               {bg=lightgray}
\setbeamercolor{frametitle}{fg=blue}
\setbeamercolor{normal text}{fg=black}
\setbeamercolor{alerted text}{fg=red}

\setbeamerfont{frametitle}
{size=\large, family=\sffamily}

\logo{\includegraphics[height=1cm]
                      {logo.png}}

\setbeamertemplate{navigation symbols}{}

\title{Customizing Beamer Themes and
Colors}
\author{Dr. LaTex}
\date{\today}

\begin{document}

\begin{frame}
    \titlepage
\end{frame}
```

Output:

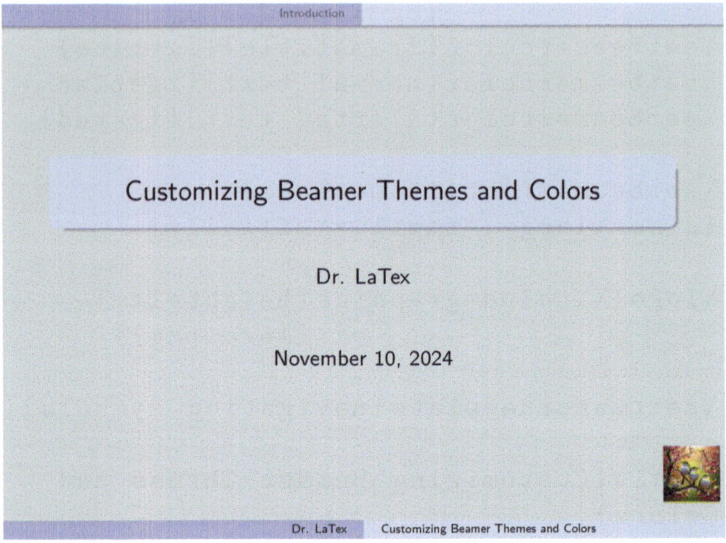

This slide serves as the title page, styled with the "Warsaw" theme and "seahorse" color scheme. The background is light gray, and a logo is positioned in the lower right corner (This will appear on each slide). The navigation bar has been removed for a clean aesthetic.

Slide 2: Introduction Slide

LaTeX Code:

```
\section{Introduction}
\begin{frame}
\frametitle
{Beamer Customization}
In this presentation,
we will learn how to
customize Beamer
themes and colors.
\end{frame}
```

Output:

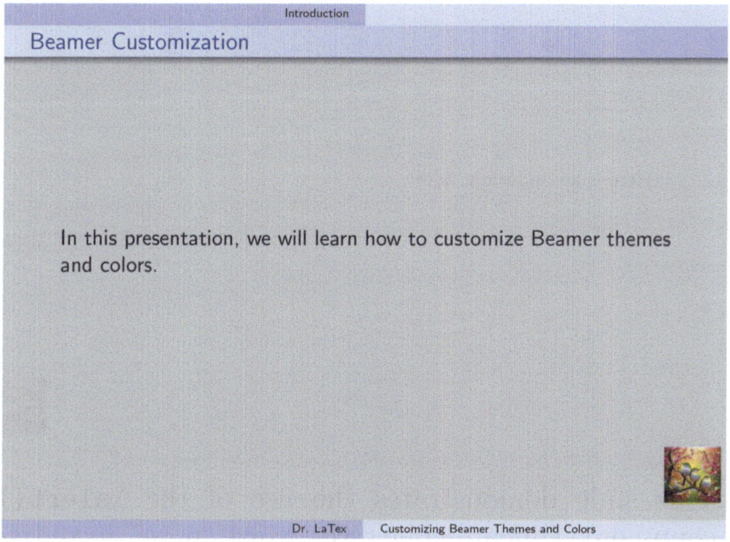

The second slide introduces the topic of customization. The frame title is styled in blue, and the body text appears in black. The layout inherits the same gray background and sans-serif font family.

Slide 3: Highlighted Text

LaTeX Code:

```
\begin{frame}
\frametitle{Key Points}
Here is an important
\alert{note}.
\end{frame}

\end{document}
```

Output:

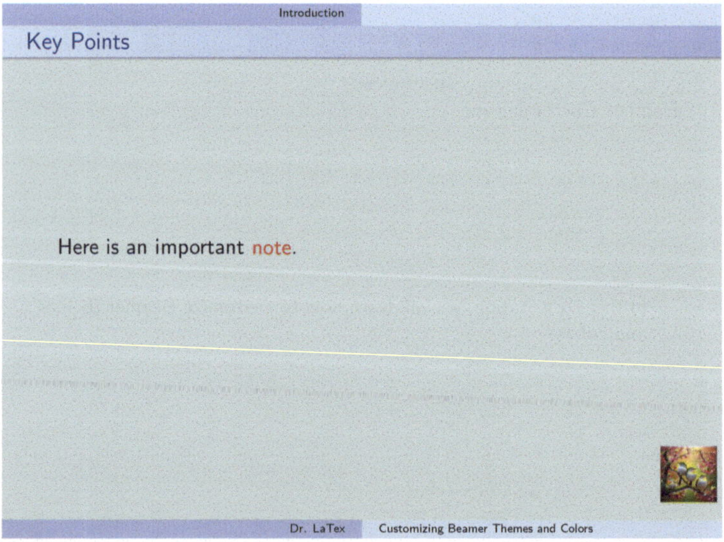

This slide demonstrates the use of the `\alert{}` command, which displays the word "note" in red as defined by the customized alerted text color.

Through thoughtful control of navigation elements, Beamer allows presenters to tailor the visual behavior of their slides. Whether your goal is to reduce distraction, align with institutional branding, or simply refine the visual language of your presentation, mastering navigation bar customization is an important step in producing clean, engaging slides.

7.4 Adding Figures, Tables, and Equations in Slides

In Beamer presentations, visual and mathematical elements are key to making your slides engaging and informative. Whether you are inserting images, creating tables, or adding equations, Beamer provides flexible and powerful tools for handling figures, tables, and math content. In this section, we will cover how to insert figures, create tables, and format mathematical equations in your slides.

7.4.1 Inserting Figures into Slides

Incorporating figures into a Beamer presentation is essential for delivering visually engaging and informative content. Beamer supports all standard image-handling features provided by the `graphicx` package, and with the right use of environments and scaling options, you can achieve clean and professional layouts.

To begin with, images are typically inserted using the `\includegraphics` command, which accepts a variety of scaling and positioning options. When used within the `figure` environment, images are automatically centered and may be accompanied by captions. This is the most common method for placing figures on slides, especially when clarity and alignment are critical.

The following example demonstrates the standard way to embed a figure within a Beamer slide:

Inserting an Image with Caption

LaTeX Code:

```
\begin{frame}
\frametitle
{Inserting an Image}
\begin{figure}
\centering
\includegraphics[width=
0.7\textwidth]
{example-image}
\caption{An example
image}
\end{figure}
\end{frame}
```

Output Preview

This slide displays the image centered at 70% of the text width, with a caption aligned beneath it. The `figure` environment ensures that the content remains properly positioned and captioned throughout.

The width of the image here is defined using the relative parameter `0.7\textwidth`, which allows the image to adapt naturally across different screen or print sizes. Instead of defining absolute units, using relative widths ensures consistent scaling throughout the presentation.

In scenarios where the height of the image must be constrained, you can modify the image size using the `height` option instead. The following snippet scales the image vertically:

Resizing with Fixed Height

LaTeX Code:

```
\includegraphics[height=4cm]
            {example-image}
```

Output Preview

The image is scaled so that its height is exactly 4cm. The width is automatically adjusted to preserve the original aspect ratio, preventing distortion.

In cases where both height and width need to be specified—usually when exact placement is necessary for design purposes, LaTeX will override the aspect ratio unless otherwise specified. This can lead to image distortion, which should be used with caution:

Custom Height and Width

LaTeX Code:

```
\includegraphics[height=4cm, width=5cm]
                {example-image}
```

Output Preview

Here, both height and width are explicitly set. Beamer applies both values, even if it alters the proportions of the image.

It is a good practice to use relative sizing (e.g., `width=0.6\textwidth`) for most slides to ensure layout flexibility. Images should also be stored in a well-structured directory (e.g., `figures/`) and included using consistent naming schemes for clarity and reusability.

7.4.2 Creating Tables in Slides

Tables offer a compact and structured way to present data, particularly in technical or academic presentations where clarity is paramount. In Beamer, the process of creating tables is similar to that in any LaTeX document. The primary environment used is `tabular`, often enclosed within a `table` environment to enable captions and positioning.

To begin with, a simple table can be constructed using three centered columns with vertical lines between them. The following slide demonstrates a standard layout where rows of data are organized beneath a horizontal header row.

Basic Table Slide

LaTeX Code:

```
\begin{frame}
\frametitle{Example Table}
\begin{table}
\centering
\begin{tabular}{|c|c|c|}
\hline
Column 1 & Column 2 & Column 3\\
\hline
Data 1 & Data 2 & Data 3 \\
Data 4 & Data 5 & Data 6 \\
\hline
\end{tabular}
\caption{An example table}
\end{table}
\end{frame}
```

Expected Output

A neatly formatted table appears, displaying three columns and two rows of data beneath a header. Horizontal rules divide the content for readability, and the caption "An example table." appears just below the table.

The table is constructed using the `tabular` environment with column alignment options. In this case, `c` centers the content within each column, and vertical bars (`|`) define column borders. Horizontal lines (`\hline`) are added above the header, between rows, and at the bottom to clearly distinguish table content.

For more sophisticated layouts, Beamer also supports multicolumn and multi-row cells, useful when summarizing hierarchical or grouped data. The next example introduces the `multicolumn` and `multirow` commands, available from the `multirow` package, to demonstrate how cells can span across rows or columns.

Merged Row and Column Table

LaTeX Code:

```
\begin{frame}
\frametitle{Complex Table}
\begin{table}
\centering
\begin{tabular}{|c|c|c|}
\hline
\multicolumn{2}{|c|}{Merged Columns}
                & Column 3 \\
\hline
\multirow{2}{*}{Row Spanning}
         & Data 1 & Data 2 \\
         & Data 3 & Data 4 \\
\hline
\end{tabular}
\caption{A table with merged
rows and columns}
\end{table}
\end{frame}
```

Expected Output

The header row includes a merged cell that spans two columns, labeled "Merged Columns," followed by a third column. In the body, the phrase "Row Spanning" occupies the height of two rows in the first column, while the other two rows continue independently.

The `\multicolumn{2}{|c|}{Merged Columns}` command merges two columns into a single cell, aligned centrally. The syntax requires specifying how many columns are merged (2), how they are aligned and bounded (`|c|`), and the content of the cell ("Merged Columns").

Similarly, the `\multirow{2}{*}{Row Spanning}` command spans two rows. The second argument `*` indicates that LaTeX should automatically calculate the appropriate width for the multirow cell.

These techniques are essential for creating complex tables in Beamer, especially when your data involves grouped or hierarchical categories. When designing tables, it is crucial to maintain readability by avoiding excessive detail or overcrowding. Instead, present only the most relevant data, and consider spreading complex tables across multiple slides if needed.

7.4.3 Adding Equations to Slides

Mathematics is an integral part of many technical and scientific presentations. Beamer, being a LaTeX-based class, supports all the powerful mathematical typesetting features provided by LaTeX, including inline math, display equations, numbered expressions, and aligned multiline equations. The use of mathematical notation in slides not only enhances clarity but also ensures consistency and precision in presentation content.

To include mathematical content in a slide, one may use inline or display math environments depending on whether the expression should appear within a sentence or centered as a separate entity.

1. Inline Math

Inline mathematics is typically used when an expression is embedded in a line of text. The simplest and most common syntax for this is to wrap the expression in dollar signs. For example:

Inline Math Example

LaTeX Code

```
\begin{frame}
\frametitle{Inline Math Example}
The famous equation $E = mc^2$
describes the relationship
between energy and mass.
\end{frame}
```

Expected Output

The sentence appears as part of a slide, with the equation $E = mc^2$ typeset neatly within the running text.

2. Display Math

When the expression needs to stand out or is too large to fit inline, display math is preferred. This places the equation on its own line and centers it. There are multiple syntaxes for this, such as `\[ ... \]`, `$$ ... $$`, or using the `equation` environment.

Display Math Example

LaTeX Code

```
\begin{frame}
\frametitle
{Display Math Example}
  \[
  E = mc^2
  \]
\end{frame}
```

Expected Output

The equation is displayed prominently and centered on the slide. No equation number appears in this case.

3. Numbered Equations

When you need to reference equations later in the slide deck, the `equation` environment provides automatic numbering.

Numbered Equation Example

LaTeX Code

```
\begin{frame}
\frametitle
{Numbered Equation}
  \begin{equation}
    E = mc^2
  \end{equation}
\end{frame}
```

Expected Output

The equation $E = mc^2$

is centered and numbered, allowing later references like "as shown in Equation (1)."

4. Aligned Multiline Equations

For multiline equations or systems that should align on a common symbol such as the equals sign, the `align` environment from the `amsmath` package is ideal. This provides both vertical alignment and optional numbering for each line.

Aligned Equations Example

LaTeX Code

```
\begin{frame}
\frametitle
{Aligned Equations}
  \begin{align}
    a + b &= c \\
    x + y &= z
  \end{align}
\end{frame}
```

Expected Output

Two equations are

displayed, aligned at the equals sign. Each is independently numbered unless numbering is suppressed.

These mathematical environments offer the flexibility required for academic and technical presentations. The combination of inline expressions, display formulas, and aligned equations allows presenters to structure complex mathematical content with clarity and professionalism.

7.4.4 Full LaTeX Example of a Presentation

Slide 1: Title Page

LaTeX Code:

```
\documentclass{beamer}
\usepackage{graphicx}
\usepackage{multirow}
\usetheme{Copenhagen}
\usecolortheme{albatross}

\title{Adding Figures, Tables,
and Equations}
\author{Dr. LaTex}
\date{\today}

\begin{document}
\begin{frame}
    \titlepage
\end{frame}
```

Output:

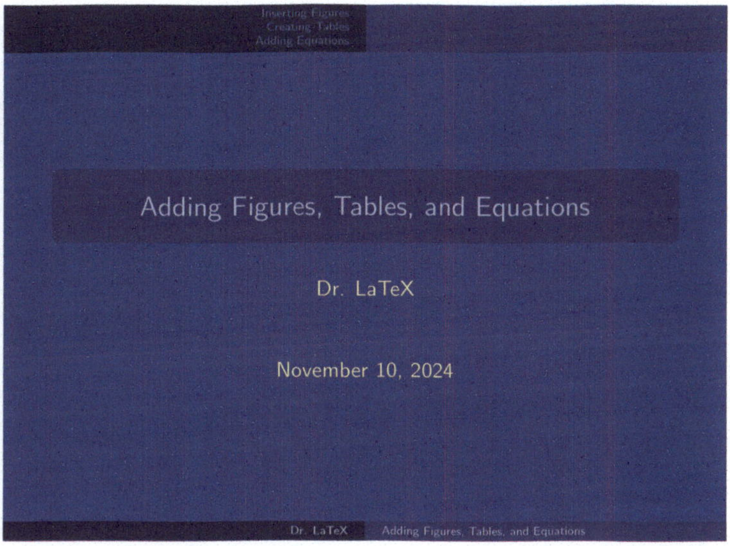

Slide 2: Inserting a Figure

LaTeX Code:

```
\section
{Inserting Figures}
\begin{frame}
\frametitle
{Inserting an Image}
\begin{figure}
\centering
\includegraphics[width=0.7
\textwidth]{example - image}
\caption{An example image}
\end{figure}
\end{frame}
```

Output:

Slide 3: Basic Table

LaTeX Code:

```
\section{Creating Tables}
\begin{frame}
\frametitle{Example Table}
\begin{table}
\centering
\begin{tabular}{|c|c|c|}
\hline
Column 1 & Column 2 & Column 3 \\
\hline
Data 1 & Data 2 & Data 3 \\
Data 4 & Data 5 & Data 6 \\
\hline
\end{tabular}
\caption{An example table}
```

```
\end{table}
\end{frame}
```

Output:

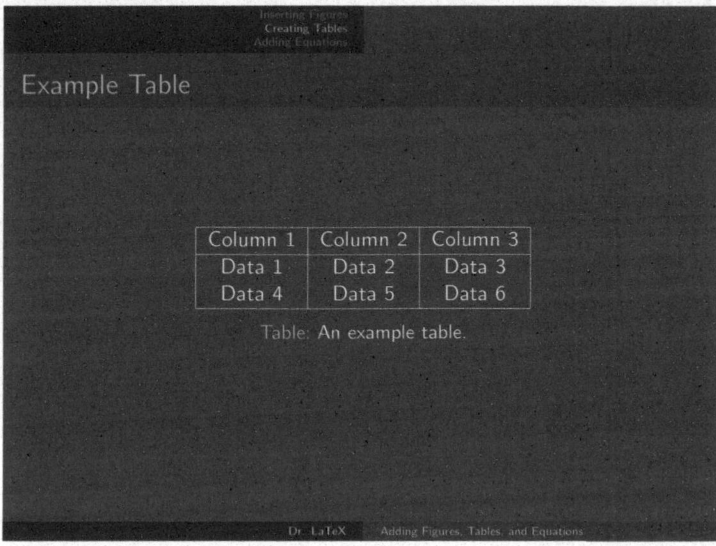

Slide 4: Inline Math

LaTeX Code:

```
\section
{Adding Equations}
\begin{frame}
\frametitle
{Inline Math Example}
The famous equation
$E = mc^2$ describes
the relationship
between energy and mass.
\end{frame}
```

Output:

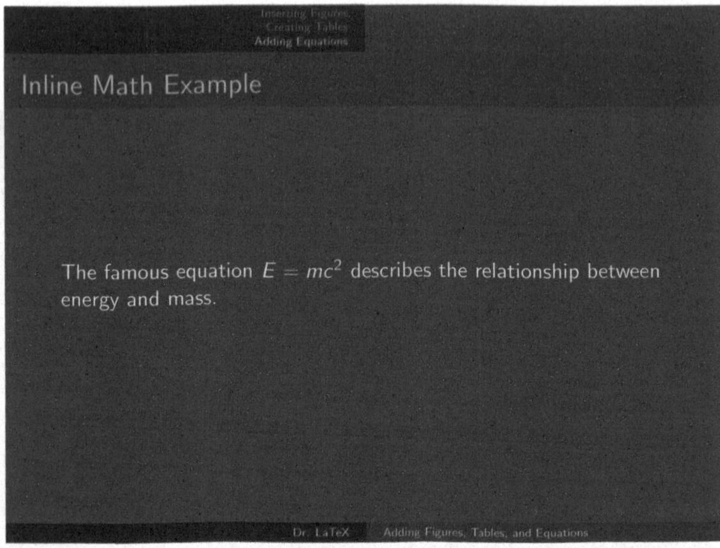

Slide 5: Display Math

LaTeX Code:

```
\begin{frame}
\frametitle
{Display Math Example}
    \[E = mc^2\]
\end{frame}
```

Output:

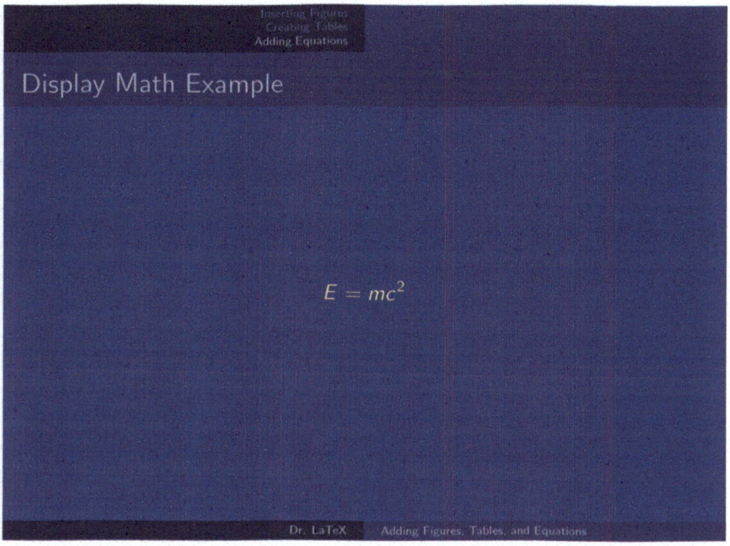

Slide 6: Numbered Equation

LaTeX Code:

```
\begin{frame}
\frametitle
{Numbered Equation}
    \begin{equation}
        E = mc^2
    \end{equation}
\end{frame}
```

Output:

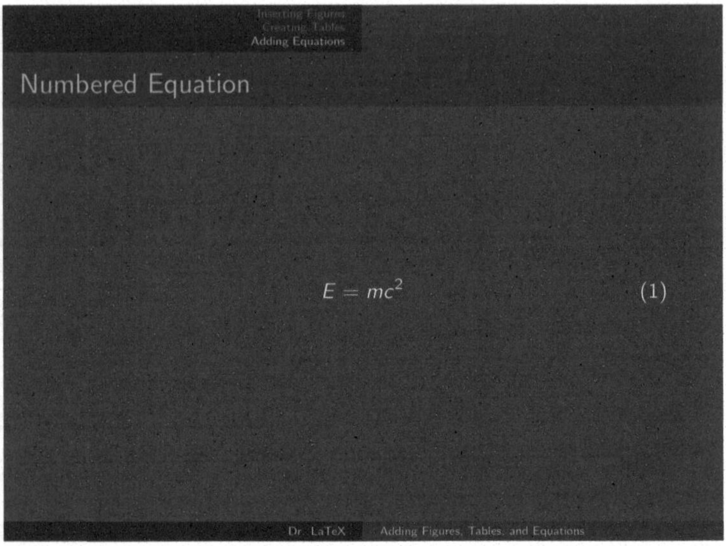

Slide 7: Aligned Equations

LaTeX Code:

```
\begin{frame}
\frametitle
{Aligned Equations}
    \begin{align}
        a + b &= c \\
        x + y &= z
    \end{align}
\end{frame}
```

Output:

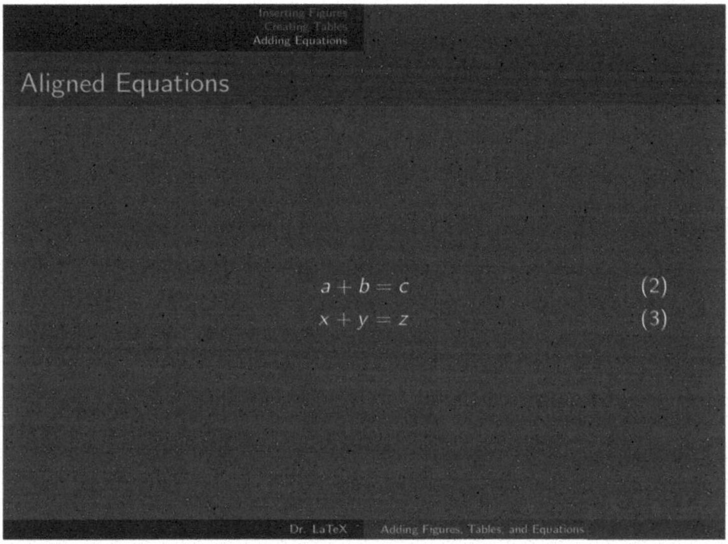

Exercises for Chap. 7: LaTeX for Presentations (Beamer)

7.1 Introduction to Beamer Class

1. *Basic Beamer Presentation*: Create a simple presentation using the `beamer` class. Include a title slide, a few slides with section headers, and some basic content such as bullet points or text.

2. *Presentation Structure*: Explain the basic structure of a `beamer` presentation. Identify the role of `\frametitle`, `\framesubtitle`, and `\section`.

3. *Document Class Options*: Experiment with different `beamer` document class options. Change the aspect

ratio of the slides (e.g., `aspectratio=169`) and observe how it affects the presentation layout.

7.2 Creating Slides and Sections

1. *Creating Sections*: Write a `beamer` presentation with multiple sections and subsections. Create at least three sections, each with a few slides of content.

2. *Adding Content to Slides*: Create a slide with a list of bullet points and another slide with an enumerated list. Experiment with different list structures and add text to each item.

3. *Slide Navigation*: Add `\tableofcontents` at the beginning of your presentation and ensure that section headers are clickable in the generated PDF. Test how `beamer` handles slide navigation.

7.3 Customizing Slide Themes and Colors

1. *Applying Themes*: Write a `beamer` presentation and apply different `beamer` themes such as `Warsaw`, `Madrid`, and `Copenhagen`. Compare how each theme affects the appearance of the presentation.

2. *Customizing Colors*: Customize the colors of a `beamer` presentation by modifying the theme colors. Change the background, title, and block colors using commands such as `\setbeamercolor`.

3. *Customizing Fonts*: Modify the font sizes and types in a `beamer` presentation. Change the font size for titles, subtitles, and slide content using `\setbeamerfont`.

7.4 Adding Figures, Tables, and Equations in Slides

1. *Inserting Figures*: Create a slide that includes an image using the `\includegraphics` command. Add a caption to the image and adjust its size to fit the slide.

2. *Adding Tables*: Create a slide that includes a table with at least three rows and three columns. Use the `tabular` environment and experiment with different alignments for the table.

3. *Equations in Slides*: Write a slide that includes a mathematical equation. Use both inline and display math mode to show the equation on the slide. Test how the equation is displayed in the presentation.

Chapter 8

Packages and Custom Commands

Contents

Md Aquib, *Fundamentals of LaTeX*, University Texts in the Mathematical Sciences,
https://doi.org/10.1007/978-981-96-9318-4_8

Abstract: One of the most powerful features of LaTeX is its extensibility through packages and user-defined commands. Though the core functionality of LaTeX provides everything needed to create basic documents, most real-world documents require additional features, such as advanced mathematical notation, customized formatting, colorful diagrams, or refined bibliography handling, that are made possible through the use of packages.

Keywords: LaTeX packages, Custom commands, `\newcommand`, Package management, Command definitions, LaTeX customization

In this chapter, we explore how to harness the vast ecosystem of LaTeX packages to expand the capabilities of your documents. You will learn how to load and configure commonly used packages, understand package dependencies, and identify the right package for a specific task. Special attention is given to essential packages like `amsmath`, `graphicx`, `hyperref`, `geometry`, and many others that are indispensable for academic and professional typesetting.

In addition to packages, this chapter also covers the creation of custom commands using `\newcommand`, `\renewcommand`, and related macros. These tools allow you to define shortcuts for frequently used expressions, tailor the document's appearance, and build reusable structures that improve both efficiency and consistency in your writing.

By mastering packages and custom commands, you will not only streamline your workflow but also unlock the full potential of LaTeX for producing complex, elegant, and highly personalized documents.

8.1 Introduction to LaTeX Packages

In LaTeX, packages are essential tools that extend the core functionality of the system. They provide additional commands, environments, and features that make LaTeX more powerful and versatile for different use cases. Whether you are adding graphics, customizing layouts, or including advanced mathematical notation, packages allow you to streamline your workflow and enhance your documents. This section introduces LaTeX packages, explains how to load them, and highlights some commonly used packages.

8.1.1 What Are LaTeX Packages?

At its core, LaTeX is a powerful typesetting system that excels in producing high-quality documents, particularly in academic and scientific writing. However, its core distribution is intentionally kept minimal, offering only the most essential features needed to create a document. To extend its functionality and adapt it for various tasks and disciplines, LaTeX relies on modular components known as packages.

A LaTeX package is essentially an add-on that provides additional macros, environments, styles, or tools beyond what is available by default. These packages are typically developed by the TeX community and are freely available through comprehensive repositories such as CTAN (Comprehensive TeX Archive Network). By including the appropriate packages in the preamble of your document, you can significantly enhance its capabilities and streamline your workflow.

For instance, if you need to include images in your document, the `graphicx` package offers intuitive commands for inserting and scaling graphics. Similarly, for creating colored text or backgrounds, the `xcolor` package provides a robust interface for defining and applying colors. More advanced packages, such as `amsmath` or `mathtools`, enrich LaTeX's mathematical typesetting by introducing new symbols and structured equation environments.

One of the greatest advantages of LaTeX packages is their modularity. You only load what you need, keeping your document lightweight and minimizing potential conflicts. Each package focuses on a specific domain: tables, figures, layout customization, citations, headers and footers, font management, multilingual support, and so forth.

For example, consider a scenario where a user wishes to add hyperlinks to their document. This functionality is not included in base LaTeX, but by loading the `hyperref` package, hyperlinks can be enabled for cross-references, citations, table of contents entries, and URLs. This transformation occurs with a single command in the preamble:

Basic Package Loading Example

```
\usepackage{hyperref}
```

Once loaded, all cross-referencing commands such as `\ref` and `\cite` are automatically enhanced to become clickable links in the PDF output.

Packages are a fundamental component of the LaTeX ecosystem. They allow users to customize their document's behavior and appearance to a high degree, often with minimal effort. Whether you are typesetting a thesis, preparing a research article, or designing a résumé, LaTeX packages empower you to tailor the document to your exact needs. As you become more familiar with LaTeX, learning how to identify and use the right packages becomes an essential skill in mastering this typesetting system.

8.1.2 Loading Packages in LaTeX

To take full advantage of LaTeX's extensibility, users commonly rely on packages, modular components that add new commands, environments, or stylistic capabilities. Before any of these features can be used in your document, the relevant package must first be loaded in the preamble, which is the section before `\begin{document}`.

The primary command used to load a package is `\usepackage`. This command accepts the package name as its argument and should be placed in the preamble of your document. For instance, to work with images in your document, one would typically load the `graphicx` package as shown below:

Basic Example of Package Loading

```
\documentclass{article}
\usepackage{graphicx}

\begin{document}

% Your content goes here

\end{document}
```

In this example, the package `graphicx` is loaded, enabling commands like `\includegraphics` that allow the insertion and adjustment of images in the document. Without this package, such commands would not be recognized by the compiler.

It is also common for documents to require the functionality provided by multiple packages. In such cases, each package should be loaded with its own `\usepackage` command, all placed sequentially in the preamble. For example, a document that requires enhanced mathematical notation, hyperlinks, and image inclusion might begin as follows:

Loading Multiple Packages

```
\usepackage{amsmath}
% Mathematical environments and symbols
\usepackage{hyperref}
% Hyperlinks and clickable references
\usepackage{graphicx}
% Image insertion and manipulation
```

Each of these packages contributes a different set of features to the document. The order of loading usually does not matter, although there are exceptions when packages interact with each other, particularly in layout and styling. In such cases, careful attention to package documentation can help determine the correct loading sequence.

What is important to note is that package loading is not a cosmetic step, it is foundational. A command from a package cannot be used unless that package has been explicitly loaded. Attempting to use such a command otherwise will typically result in an error during compilation.

8.1.3 Specifying Package Options

One of the key strengths of LaTeX packages lies in their configurability. Most packages provide options that allow users to customize their behavior or appearance to suit particular needs. These options are passed directly to the package via the optional argument of the `\usepackage` command. This argument is enclosed in square brackets and precedes the name of the package.

For example, consider the `geometry` package, which is widely used to control page layout, especially margins. To set uniform margins of one inch on all sides, the package can be loaded as follows:

Setting Uniform Margins with **geometry**

```
\usepackage[margin=1in]{geometry}
```

In this example, the `margin=1in` option configures the layout to maintain a one-inch space on all four sides of the page. This method of passing options applies to most packages in LaTeX and is particularly valuable when you want to achieve specific formatting goals without redefining commands manually.

Multiple options can be passed to a single package by separating them with commas. A good illustration of this is the `hyperref` package, which provides hyperlinking capabilities. Suppose you want to ensure that links are colored rather than boxed, and you wish to customize their appearance. You might load the package like this:

Customizing Hyperlink Colors with **hyperref**

```
\usepackage[
    colorlinks=true,
    linkcolor=blue,
    urlcolor=red
]{hyperref}
```

Here, the `colorlinks=true` option tells LaTeX to display links in color rather than with colored boxes. The `linkcolor=blue` option sets the color of internal document links, such as section references, to blue. Meanwhile, `urlcolor=red` defines the color of external hyperlinks.

The order of the options is generally flexible, though it is advisable to follow the conventions recommended by the package documentation. Not all packages support options, but for those that do, this mechanism provides a clean and efficient way to control their functionality.

Using options effectively not only gives you greater control over the document's appearance and behavior but also contributes to the clarity and modularity of your code. Instead of redefining parameters inside the document body, you encapsulate configurations cleanly within the preamble, resulting in better-organized source files.

8.1.4 Finding and Installing Packages

As you continue working with LaTeX, you will inevitably reach a point where the built-in commands are not sufficient for your needs. Whether you want to draw diagrams, typeset chemical equations, or manage bibliographies, the solution usually lies in loading the appropriate package. Fortunately, the LaTeX ecosystem is vast, and thousands of packages have been developed and made publicly available.

Most of these packages are hosted on the Comprehensive TEX Archive Network (CTAN), which is the central repository for all things related to LaTeX. The CTAN website at https://ctan.org allows you to browse, search for, and read documentation for any package. If you already know the name of a package, simply entering it in the search bar will take you directly to its information page. If you are looking for a package by function, say, something that manages glossaries, you can search using keywords, and CTAN will return a list of matching packages.

For users of TEX distributions such as TEXLiveor MiKTEX, installing packages is usually straightforward. TEXLiveincludes most commonly used packages by default. If a package is missing, you can use the `tlmgr` utility (short for TEX Live Manager) to install it. For example, in a terminal or command prompt, you might run:

```
tlmgr install lipsum
```

This command installs the `lipsum` package, which generates dummy text useful for testing layouts.

Users of MiKTEXtypically benefit from on-the-fly installation. When you compile a document that uses a package not currently installed, MiKTEXwill prompt you to install it automatically. This behavior can be adjusted through the MiKTEXsettings panel.

If you are working in Overleaf, an online LaTeX editor, you generally do not need to install packages manually. Overleaf maintains a large set of preinstalled packages that are updated regularly. If you try to use a package that is not supported, Overleaf will typically generate a compilation error, at which point you can check their documentation or contact support to request its inclusion.

To summarize, once you have found a package you want to use, you simply load it in your document preamble using the `\usepackage` command. For example, if you have located the `csquotes` package for advanced quotation formatting, you would include:

Example: Loading an Installed Package

```
\documentclass{article}
\usepackage{csquotes}

\begin{document}
\enquote{This is a properly formatted
        quotation.}
\end{document}
```

Once a package is installed, it becomes available system-wide and can be used in any LaTeX document you create. Always remember to check the package documentation for detailed usage instructions, as many packages offer a wide array of configuration options and commands that go far beyond what is introduced in simple examples.

Steps to Install a Package (If Needed)

1. Visit https://ctan.org/ and search for the package you need.

2. Download the package files.

3. Follow the instructions provided with the package to install it manually, if required (most distributions handle package installation automatically).

8.1.5 Package Conflicts

While LaTeX's extensibility through packages is one of its greatest strengths, it occasionally leads to complications when multiple packages attempt to redefine the same internal commands or settings. Such clashes are referred to as package conflicts, and they can result in unexpected behavior, compilation errors, or inconsistencies in formatting.

Package conflicts most often occur when two packages offer overlapping functionality or modify similar document structures, such as headers, footnotes, or mathematical typesetting. For instance, if two packages both attempt to control hyperlink behavior or manipulate document geometry, LaTeX may not be able to reconcile their instructions unless guided properly.

One important strategy to minimize the likelihood of conflicts is to load packages in a deliberate and informed order. Because LaTeX processes packages sequentially, the order in which packages are declared using the `\usepackage` command can influence the outcome. If you encounter errors or formatting anomalies, experimenting with the order of package loading can often resolve the issue.

Another strategy involves consulting package documentation. Many popular packages, such as `hyperref`, `amsmath`, or `geometry`, include detailed documentation that outlines known incompatibilities or suggests options for coexisting with other packages. For example, the `hyperref` package, which adds hyperlink functionality to references and citations, is known to be sensitive to where it is placed in the preamble. The general recommendation is to load it last, after most other packages, to ensure that it correctly patches links into the structures already defined.

Some conflicts are not resolvable simply by reordering packages. In such cases, many packages offer specific options to modify their behavior and reduce incompatibilities. For instance, a package might have a compatibility mode or a setting that disables conflicting features.

Below is a working example of a document that loads several commonly used packages. It demonstrates proper sequencing and the use of options to avoid common issues such as link color inconsistencies or overlapping margins.

Example: Avoiding Package Conflicts

```
\documentclass{article}
% Load general-purpose packages first
\usepackage{amsmath}
% Advanced mathematical typesetting
\usepackage{graphicx}
% Image inclusion and manipulation
\usepackage{xcolor}
% Enable color definitions
% Layout and page setup
\usepackage[margin=1in]{geometry}
% Set 1-inch margins
% Load hyperref last to avoid conflicts
\usepackage[colorlinks=true,
linkcolor=blue, urlcolor=red]{hyperref}
\begin{document}
```

```
\title{Managing LaTeX Packages and
      Conflicts}
\author{Dr. LaTeX}
\date{\today}
\maketitle
\section{Introduction}
LaTeX documents often require additional
functionality provided by external
packages. With great power comes the
possibility of conflict, especially
when multiple packages interact with
document elements like hyperlinks,
fonts, or layout settings.
\section
{Package Loading and Compatibility}
In this example, we use \texttt{amsmath}
for mathematical formatting,
\texttt{graphicx} to include images, and
\texttt{hyperref} to create hyperlinks.
Loading \texttt{hyperref} after all
other packages ensures that it modifies
the document safely without interfering
with other features.
\end{document}
```

Understanding and resolving package conflicts is part of mastering LaTeX. By learning how packages interact and being attentive to documentation and loading order, users can prevent most issues and confidently build complex documents that combine powerful features without compromising stability.

8.2 Common Packages for Mathematics, Graphics, and Formatting

One of the great strengths of LaTeX lies in its modular design, where additional functionality is made available through packages. For most documents, especially those in academic and scientific domains, three key areas require special attention: mathematics, graphics, and document formatting. In this section, we will explore some of the most widely used packages in each of these categories and demonstrate their application through well-documented examples.

8.2.1 Mathematical Typesetting Packages

Mathematics is at the heart of many LaTeX documents, and its built-in support is already robust. However, packages developed by the AMS (American Mathematical Society) and others further enhance its capabilities.

`amsmath`

The `amsmath` package is the cornerstone of advanced mathematical typesetting. It provides additional environments for multiline equations, improved alignment, and semantic structure for mathematical content.

The align environment from amsmath

LaTeX Code:

```
\usepackage{amsmath}

\begin{document}
```

```
\begin{align}
  f(x) &= x^2 + 2x + 1 \\
       &= (x + 1)^2
\end{align}

\end{document}
```

This environment automatically aligns equations at the equal sign, making mathematical derivations clear and easy to follow.

`amssymb` and `mathtools`

The `amssymb` package introduces a broader range of mathematical symbols, including logic symbols, blackboard bold fonts, and additional relation signs. The `mathtools` package builds upon `amsmath`, providing enhancements such as `\coloneqq` for defining equalities and refined spacing options.

8.2.2 Packages for Including Graphics

Visuals such as figures, diagrams, and plots are essential in many types of documents. LaTeX provides several packages to support the inclusion and manipulation of graphics, the most foundational of which is `graphicx`.

`graphicx`

The `graphicx` package allows users to insert external image files in various formats (e.g., PNG, PDF, JPG, EPS) and control their size, rotation, and placement.

Example: Inserting an Image

LaTeX Code:

```
\usepackage{graphicx}

\begin{document}

\includegraphics[width=0.5\textwidth]
                {example-image}

\end{document}
```

This code will scale the image to occupy 50% of the text width. You can also specify height, rotate images with the `angle` option, or clip images if needed.

`float` and `caption`

While `graphicx` handles image inclusion, the `float` package enhances control over figure placement using the `[H]` option. The `caption` package allows customization of figure and table captions, including formatting style, font size, and label positioning.

8.2.3 Formatting and Layout Packages

Beyond content, presentation matters. LaTeX offers packages that allow users to configure margins, line spacing, and text appearance.

`geometry`

The `geometry` package allows fine control over page layout. Rather than redefining margins manually, users can specify all dimensions in a single command:

Set Custom Margins with geometry

```
\usepackage[margin=1in]{geometry}
```

This command sets one-inch margins on all four sides of the page, which is often required by institutions for theses or reports.

fancyhdr

To customize headers and footers, the `fancyhdr` package is a flexible and powerful tool. It allows you to define different styles for left, center, and right portions of the header and footer areas.

xcolor

The `xcolor` package provides access to an extensive palette of colors and allows users to define their own. It supports coloring of text, table cells, boxes, and background areas.

Coloring Text with xcolor

LaTeX Code:

```
\usepackage{xcolor}

\begin{document}

\textcolor{red}{This is red text.}

\end{document}
```

Colors can also be applied to tables, rules, or entire environments with additional commands supported by `xcolor`.

8.3 Creating and Using Custom Commands

One of the most powerful features of LaTeX is its ability to define custom commands. By creating custom commands, you can simplify repetitive tasks, ensure consistency in your documents, and make your LaTeX code more readable. Whether you want to shorten a frequently used command or create a new macro that combines multiple commands, custom commands in LaTeX offer great flexibility. In this section, we will explore how to define and use custom commands.

8.3.1 Defining Custom Commands

One of the most powerful features of LaTeX is the ability to define your own commands. This feature not only reduces repetition in long documents but also improves readability, ensures consistency, and enables greater flexibility in formatting. At its core, defining a custom command in LaTeX allows you to create a shorthand representation for any piece of text or formatting instruction you frequently use.

The most basic way to define a new command is through the `\newcommand` macro. This macro creates a new LaTeX command with a specific name and associates it with a definition that LaTeX will substitute each time the command is invoked.

The general syntax for creating such a command is as follows:

```
\newcommand{\commandname}{definition}
```

Here, `\commandname` is the name of your new command, and `definition` is the content that should be inserted whenever the command is used. It is important to note that all command names in LaTeX begin with a backslash, and your custom command name should follow the same rule. Additionally, this basic form does not include any arguments, and that topic will be addressed in the next subsection.

To illustrate how this works in practice, consider a document in which you frequently refer to the phrase "First Law of Thermodynamics." Instead of typing this full phrase repeatedly, you can define a custom command to represent it:

Simple Custom Command

LaTeX Code:

```
\newcommand{\firstlaw}
{First Law of
Thermodynamics}

The \firstlaw{} is a
statement of energy
conservation.
```

Output:

The First Law of Thermodynamics is a statement of energy conservation.

In this example, the command `\firstlaw` acts as a shortcut that expands to the full phrase. This is particularly helpful in documents where the same terminology is referenced repeatedly. If, at a later stage, the phrasing needs to change (e.g., switching to "Law of Conservation of Energy"), it can be done in a single place, in the definition of the command, saving time and avoiding inconsistencies.

Another common use case is applying formatting uniformly. For example, if your document includes frequent references to a specific book title or product name that should always appear in italics, you can define a command to apply that formatting automatically:

Formatting Text with a Custom Command

LaTeX Code:

```
\newcommand{\turing}{
\textit{Turing Machine}}

The \turing{} is a model
of computation.
```

Output:

The *Turing Machine* is a model of computation.

Custom commands in this form are limited to fixed substitutions with no flexibility for inputs. If your command needs to behave dynamically, accepting one or more arguments, then you would use an extended version of `\newcommand`, which we will cover in the next subsection. For now, this foundational concept of defining static commands forms the building block for more sophisticated macros and document automation techniques in LaTeX.

Defining commands at the start of your document or in a separate style file is also a good practice. It centralizes the control of frequently used elements and makes your document more modular and easier to maintain. Additionally, this technique can greatly simplify collaborative writing by ensuring standardized terms and formatting across co-authors

8.3.2 Creating Simple Commands

After understanding how to define a basic custom command, the next logical step is learning how to use this capability to simplify your LaTeX documents. A simple command in LaTeX is one that acts as a fixed replacement, essentially a macro with no input parameters. These are especially useful when you need to repeatedly insert the same phrase, symbol, or formatting style across your document.

One common use case is defining a shorthand for a frequently used term or phrase. For instance, suppose you are working on a report that often references a LaTeX document. Instead of typing this phrase over and over, you can define a simple custom command to represent it. The definition might look like this:

Simple Custom Command Example

LaTeX Code:

```
\newcommand{\LaTeXdoc}
 {\LaTeX~document}
```

Usage:

This is a \LaTeXdoc.

Output:

This is a $\LaTeX$ document.

In this definition, `\LaTeXdoc` is a new command that substitutes the phrase `\LaTeX` document every time it appears. The tilde character ~ ensures a non-breaking space between `\LaTeX` and "document," preventing the two words from being split across lines in the output. This subtle touch preserves typographic quality, especially in formal documents.

Simple commands like this are most effective for standardizing terminology or formatting across a large document. They can also help maintain consistency in naming conventions. For example, if your document frequently mentions a product name, journal title, or key concept, defining it as a simple command ensures uniform presentation and makes it easier to update later if needed.

Here is another practical example. Suppose you are referring to a conference name multiple times throughout a paper:

Shorthand for a Conference Name

LaTeX Code:

```
\newcommand{\NeurIPS}
 {NeurIPS 2025}
```

Usage:

```
The results were published in \NeurIPS.
```

Output:

The results were published in NeurIPS 2025.

This approach not only saves typing but also reduces the risk of inconsistency, especially if the name or formatting needs to change, say, updating the year of the conference.

It is good practice to define simple commands near the beginning of your document (typically in the preamble) or in a separate file if you are managing a large project. This way, you create a modular structure that makes your document easier to maintain and modify over time.

While simple commands do not take any inputs, their real power becomes more evident when you extend them to accept arguments. This allows you to define reusable formatting or labeling patterns, which we will explore in the next subsection.

For now, mastering simple commands provides a foundation for writing cleaner, shorter, and more maintainable LaTeX documents.

8.3.3 Custom Commands with Arguments

As you continue to build more expressive LaTeX documents, you will often encounter scenarios where a custom command needs to vary its output depending on the input it receives. LaTeX allows you to define such flexible commands using arguments. Unlike simple commands, which perform static substitutions, commands with arguments can dynamically insert different content based on user input.

The general form for creating a command with arguments in LaTeX is:

\newcommand{\commandname}[num]{definition}

Here, `num` represents the number of arguments the command will accept (from 1 to 9), and the placeholders `#1`, `#2`, etc., refer to the values of those arguments within the command definition. This approach enables the creation of reusable formatting templates, semantic labels, or even structural elements that adapt to content.

To illustrate the power of this feature, consider the task of emphasizing text in both bold and italics. Rather than writing `\textbf{\textit{...}}` every time, you can define a command that takes the target phrase as an argument:

Command with One Argument

LaTeX Code:

```
\newcommand{\bi}[1]
{\textbf{\textit{#1}}}

This is \bi{important}
text.
```

Output:

This is ***important*** text.

In this definition, the command `\bi` takes one argument, denoted by `#1`, and wraps it with both bold and italic formatting commands. The result is cleaner syntax and consistent styling throughout the document.

Commands with multiple arguments follow the same structure. Each argument is referred to sequentially using #1, #2, and so forth. For example, let us define a custom command to create a citation-style phrase like "Author (Year)":

Command with Two Arguments

LaTeX Code:

```
\newcommand{\citeinline}[2]{#1 (#2)}

According to \citeinline{Smith}{2023},
data integrity is essential.
```

Output:

According to Smith (2023), data integrity is essential.

In this case, #1 holds the author's name, and #2 holds the publication year. This pattern is particularly useful in disciplines where different citation styles must be maintained. If the format of citations needs to change later (e.g., switching to "(Author, Year)"), only the command definition must be updated, LaTeX will propagate the change everywhere the command is used.

It is worth noting that commands with arguments must be written carefully. Every instance of an argument, such as #1, must be placed inside curly braces if used within another command or as part of formatting. In addition, LaTeX will produce an error if you try to define a command with arguments but forget to include the square brackets that specify the argument count.

Custom commands with arguments strike a balance between simplicity and adaptability. They allow authors to build semantic macros that clarify intent and simplify document maintenance. While the examples shown here deal with one or two arguments, LaTeX supports up to nine arguments for any given command, making it possible to design fairly complex macros within the `\newcommand` framework.

In the next subsection, we will explore how to go one step further by introducing optional, default values for arguments, enabling even greater flexibility in command design.

8.3.4 Default Values for Arguments

Custom commands in LaTeX become even more powerful when you introduce optional arguments with default values. This feature allows you to design flexible commands that behave differently depending on whether the user provides all arguments or not, without requiring a separate command for each variation.

The syntax for defining a command with a default value differs slightly from that of a standard command. You must indicate the number of arguments using the optional square-bracket notation, and immediately after that, specify the default value for the first argument. LaTeX will then substitute this default whenever the user omits the first argument.

To demonstrate this concept, consider the task of placing a piece of text inside a colored frame. Suppose you want the command to default to a red border but allow the user to change the color when desired. This can be accomplished with the following definition:

Custom Command with Optional Argument

LaTeX Code:

```
\newcommand{\colbox}[2][red]{
  \fcolorbox{#1}{white}{#2}
}
```

```
% Usage examples:
\colbox{This is a red box.}

\colbox[blue]{This is a blue box.}
```

Output:

Two framed text boxes:

- The first is outlined in red.
- The second is outlined in blue.

In this definition, the command `\colbox` takes two arguments. The first argument is optional and has the default value `"red"`; the second argument is mandatory and represents the text to be boxed. The `\fcolorbox` command from the `xcolor` package is used to draw the colored border.

When the command is called with just one argument, as in `\colbox{...}`, LaTeX substitutes `"red"` for the missing color. When called with two arguments, as in `\colbox[blue]{...}`, the user-specified color overrides the default.

This approach provides the best of both worlds: A convenient default for most cases and flexibility when variation is required. It also keeps your source code clean and avoids repetitive definitions for similar commands with slight variations.

Although LaTeX allows only one optional argument (which must be the first), this constraint can be managed creatively to design versatile commands. For instance, you can define commands that accept options like font size, color, alignment, or caption labels, all defaulting to common values but customizable on demand.

When using default arguments, it is also good practice to ensure that the command remains readable even when extended by collaborators or used in documents with different formatting expectations. Clear naming, consistent usage, and brief documentation near the command definition all contribute to this goal.

As with earlier examples, such commands are best placed in the preamble or in a separate style file if you are developing a larger document or template. This helps ensure modularity and makes it easy to update default values across a project.

The ability to define custom commands with optional arguments represents a natural progression in building intelligent LaTeX documents. It allows for elegant abstraction and reusable formatting, supporting both personal convenience and professional document design.

8.3.5 Combining Multiple Formatting Commands

In LaTeX, formatting commands can be composed, one nested within another, to apply multiple styles to a single piece of content. This feature becomes especially powerful when building custom commands that standardize a specific visual style across a document. By combining existing LaTeX formatting commands such as `\textbf` (for bold), `\textit` (for italics), and `\textcolor` (for color), authors can encapsulate complex visual instructions into a single, reusable macro.

Consider a situation where you want certain terms to be displayed in a visually prominent way, bold, italicized, and in red text. Writing all three formatting commands each time would quickly become tedious and error-prone. A better approach is to define a custom command that handles all the formatting internally and accepts the target text as an argument.

Here is how such a command might be defined:

Combining Bold, Italic, and Color Formatting

LaTeX Code:

```
\newcommand{\fancytext}
[1]{\textbf{\textit{\textcolor{red}
{#1}}}}

This is \fancytext{fancy} text.
```

Output:

This is ***fancy*** text.

In this example, the custom command `\fancytext` takes one argument, represented by `#1`, and wraps it with three layers of formatting. The innermost command, `\textcolor{red}{#1}`, colors the text red. This result is then passed to `\textit` to italicize it, and finally to `\textbf` to apply boldface. The nesting of commands follows a clear and logical structure: innermost first, outermost last. LaTeX processes these from the inside out, applying the formatting in the correct order.

This method is particularly useful in long documents such as dissertations, books, or technical manuals, where visual consistency is important. Instead of memorizing or repeating the formatting each time, the author simply calls `\fancytext` wherever needed. Moreover, if the formatting needs to change, for example, switching from red to blue or removing italics, it can be done in one place: the command definition.

While building such composite commands, it is essential to follow good design practices. First, always choose meaningful names for your commands that reflect their purpose. For example, `\highlightterm` might be more descriptive than `\ht`. Second, test your command thoroughly, especially when it involves nested formatting or color. Overlapping or conflicting instructions may lead to unexpected behavior. Lastly, avoid redefining existing LaTeX commands unless absolutely necessary, as this can lead to compatibility issues or override critical functionality.

These small steps, choosing clear names, layering styles thoughtfully, and encapsulating design logic, contribute to the overall structure and maintainability of a LaTeX document. As your documents grow in length and complexity, these habits will save you time, reduce redundancy, and ensure typographic consistency throughout your work.

To consolidate the concepts explored in the preceding sections, it is helpful to examine a complete LaTeX document that demonstrates several types of custom commands. The following example brings together commands for defining static phrases, styling text with arguments, using default values, and layering multiple formatting instructions.

Complete LaTeX Document with Custom Commands

LaTeX Code:

```
\documentclass{article}
\usepackage{xcolor}
\usepackage{amsmath}

% Custom commands
\newcommand{\LaTeXdoc}
 {\LaTeX~document}
\newcommand{\bi}[1]{\textbf
 {\textit{#1}}}
\newcommand{\fraction}[2]
 {\frac{#1}{#2}}
\newcommand{\colbox}[2][red]{
```

```
  \fcolorbox{#1}{white}{#2}}
\newcommand{\fancytext}[1]{%
  \textbf{\textit{
  \textcolor{red}{#1}}}
}

\begin{document}

\section{Using Custom Commands}

This is a \LaTeXdoc.

Here is some \bi{important} text.

The fraction is \fraction{3}{4}.

\colbox{This is a red box.}

\colbox[blue]{This is a blue box.}

This is \fancytext{fancy} text.

\end{document}
```

Description:

- "LaTeX document" is typeset with a non-breaking space using the `\LaTeXdoc` command.
- "Important" appears in bold italic via `\bi`.
- The fraction $\frac{3}{4}$ is rendered using the custom `\fraction` macro.
- The text "This is a red box." is framed in red using `\colbox`.

- The next box changes the border color to blue using an optional argument.
- "Fancy" appears in bold, italic, and red using `\fancytext`.

This self-contained document exemplifies how custom commands allow authors to abstract away repetitive formatting tasks. Each macro enhances modularity, enabling changes to be made in one place and reflected throughout the entire text. This approach is particularly beneficial in larger projects such as academic theses, books, or technical documentation, where formatting consistency is essential.

Moreover, combining these techniques, static replacement, arguments, optional values, and layered formatting, demonstrates that even simple LaTeX documents can achieve both clarity and typographic refinement with minimal effort once macros are properly structured.

8.4 Redefining Existing Commands

In LaTeX, many commands come predefined with specific behaviors. However, there may be times when you want to modify the functionality of these existing commands to suit your document's needs. Redefining commands in LaTeX can help you customize the behavior of commands without having to create entirely new ones. This section explores how to safely redefine existing LaTeX commands and offers best practices for doing so.

8.4.1 How to Redefine a Command

While defining your own commands in LaTeX is extremely useful for building structure and flexibility into your documents, there are times when it becomes necessary to modify the behavior of commands that are already defined, either by LaTeX itself or by a package you have included. In such cases, LaTeX provides the `\renewcommand` macro, which allows you to redefine an existing command's behavior safely and explicitly.

The syntax of `\renewcommand` is almost identical to `\newcommand`. The key difference lies in its intent: Where `\newcommand` is used to define something that does not already exist, `\renewcommand` is used to alter the behavior of something that does. This distinction is important. Attempting to use `\newcommand` to redefine an existing command will result in a compilation error, while `\renewcommand` will carry out the redefinition without issue.

The general form of the command is:

```
\renewcommand{\commandname}
{new definition}
```

Let us consider a simple example where we change the behavior of the `\today` command. By default, `\today` produces the current date in a format like "April 2, 2025." But you might prefer a numerical format such as "2025-04-02" for consistency across formal or technical documents. This change can be made easily using `\renewcommand`.

Redefining an Existing Command (\today)

LaTeX Code:

```
\documentclass{article}
\renewcommand{\today}
{2025-04-02}

\begin{document}
Today's date: \today
\end{document}
```

Output:

Today's date: 2025-04-02

In this example, we have redefined `\today` to no longer depend on the system clock. Instead, it now consistently prints the hardcoded string "2025-04-02." This can be useful when producing final versions of documents with fixed dates, such as certificates, reports, or archived records.

When redefining commands, it is important to proceed with caution. Overriding standard LaTeX commands can affect other parts of your document or interfere with packages that depend on them. Therefore, you should only use `\renewcommand` when you are certain that you want to change a command's behavior globally. In more advanced scenarios, it is sometimes safer to use conditional checks or to limit redefinitions to local environments, a topic we will explore in dedicated subsections.

For now, the key idea is that `\renewcommand` gives you the ability to adapt LaTeX to your preferred formatting and workflows by selectively modifying commands you already rely on. It is a fundamental tool in customizing LaTeX beyond its default behavior, offering both control and flexibility when used responsibly.

8.4.2 Redefining the Section Heading Command

LaTeX provides default styling for sectional commands such as `\section`, `\subsection`, and so on. These default styles, while functional, may not always suit the typographic goals of every document. For instance, in shorter reports, custom resumes, exam templates, or handouts, the large, bold section headings can appear overly dominant or out of place. In such cases, it can be desirable to redefine the sectioning commands to better align with the tone and visual hierarchy of the document.

The command `\renewcommand` allows us to redefine existing LaTeX macros, and it can be used to change the formatting of `\section`. By default, `\section` not only prints the section title but also manages automatic numbering and placement within the table of contents. Redefining it directly will bypass these features unless we handle them manually.

For simpler documents where such features are unnecessary, you can redefine the `\section` command to use plain formatting instead. Below is an example where the section heading is redefined to appear in bold and slightly enlarged font, omitting the default numbering and spacing.

Redefining the `\section` Command

LaTeX Code:

```
\documentclass{article}
\usepackage{amsmath}
\usepackage{xcolor}

% Redefining commands
\renewcommand{\section}[1]
{\textbf{\large #1}}
```

```
\begin{document}

\begin{verbatim}
\begin{document}
    \section{Introduction}
    This is a redefined section
    heading.
\end{document}
\end{verbatim}

\end{document}
```

Output:

Introduction

(This heading appears without numbering, followed by body text.)
This is a redefined section heading.

In this definition, the command accepts one argument, namely the title of the section, and formats it using `\textbf` to make it bold and `\large` to increase its size slightly. A manual line break (`\par`) and some vertical spacing are added to visually separate the title from the subsequent text.

It is important to note that this redefinition disables automatic numbering and table of contents registration, which are integral features of LaTeX's native sectioning commands. If your document relies on those features, redefining the command in this way may not be appropriate. Instead, packages like `titlesec` offer more fine-grained control while preserving internal LaTeX logic.

That said, for shorter or highly customized documents, redefining `\section` manually offers quick and effective control over the appearance of headings, giving the author more aesthetic flexibility without requiring external packages or complex configuration.

8.4.3 Redefining Commands with Arguments

Many built-in LaTeX commands dynamically generate content using internal arguments or counter values. While creating custom commands with arguments is useful, it is equally important to understand how to redefine existing commands that rely on such dynamic inputs. This allows you to customize document behavior in ways that align with stylistic or regional requirements.

One common example is the `\today` command, which automatically prints the current date in the format "April 2, 2025." Although this format is suitable for general use, formal reports, letters, academic theses, or localized documents often require alternative date formats. Redefining `\today` is an elegant solution when consistent formatting is needed throughout the document.

Let us first redefine `\today` to display the date in a common European format, day, month name, year, using italic styling for emphasis:

Basic Redefinition of `\today`

LaTeX Code:

```
\documentclass{article}
\usepackage{datetime}
% provides \monthname

\renewcommand{\today}{%
  \textit{\day~\monthname~\year}
}
```

```
\begin{document}
Today is \today.
\end{document}
```

Output:

Today is 2 April 2025.

Now let us consider a more compact, international-style numeric format (YYYY-MM-DD), which is common in academic publishing and metadata standards:

ISO-Style Date Format (YYYY-MM-DD)

LaTeX Code:

```
\documentclass{article}

\renewcommand{\today}{%
\number\year-\number\month-\number\day
}

\begin{document}
Date: \today
\end{document}
```

Output:

Date: 2025-4-2

Note that `\month` and `\day` are counters and do not automatically include leading zeros. To enforce a two-digit format (e.g., "04" instead of "4"), you would need to manually write helper commands or use a package like `datetime2`, which provides date formatting macros.

Finally, suppose you want to include the day of the week in your date output, for example, "Wednesday, 2 April 2025." This can be achieved using the `datetime2` package with a custom format string:

Redefinition with Weekday Name

LaTeX Code:

```
\documentclass{article}
\usepackage[useregional]
 {datetime2}

\renewcommand{\today}{%
  \DTMnow % triggers update
  \DTMdisplaydate{%
    \the\year}{\the\month}
    {\the\day}{weekday=true}
}

\begin{document}
Today is \today.
\end{document}
```

Output:

Today is Wednesday, 2 April 2025.

This format is useful for official documents, meeting agendas, or publications where clarity and human readability are essential.

In each of these examples, the underlying logic of `\today` remains the same, and it retrieves values stored in internal LaTeX counters. However, by redefining how these values are displayed, you can customize the appearance of dates to meet your audience's expectations or match your document's tone. This technique, when used thoughtfully, offers a reliable alternative to manual date entry or external software formatting.

Redefining \today Conditionally Based on Language

When preparing multilingual documents, it is often desirable to format the date according to regional conventions, for example, using "2 April 2025" in English, "2. April 2025" in German, or "2 avril 2025" in French. Rather than manually switching date formats or redefining `\today` in each section, you can use the `babel` package to detect the active language and redefine `\today` accordingly.

This method provides an adaptive approach that maintains consistency and clarity when switching between different languages in the same document.

Language-Aware Redefinition of \today

LaTeX Code:

```
\documentclass{article}
\usepackage[english,french,german]
{babel}
\usepackage{datetime}
\newdateformat{englishformat}{%
  \ordinal{##1}~\monthname[##2]~##3}
\newdateformat{frenchformat}{%
  ##1~\monthname[##2]~##3}
\newdateformat{germanformat}{%
  ##1. \monthname[##2] ##3}
\makeatletter
\renewcommand{\today}{%
\ifx\languagename\@undefined
 \englishformat\today
\else
\ifx\languagename\relax
\englishformat\today
\else
\ifx\languagename\stringenglish
```

```
\englishformat\today
\else\ifx\languagename\stringfrench
\frenchformat\today
\else\ifx\languagename\stringgerman
\germanformat\today
\else
\englishformat\today
\fi\fi\fi\fi\fi}
\makeatother
\begin{document}
\selectlanguage{english}
Today is \today.
\selectlanguage{french}
Aujourd'hui, c'est le \today.
\selectlanguage{german}
Heute ist der \today.
\end{document}
```

Output:

- In English: 2nd April 2025
- In French: 2 avril 2025
- In German: 2. April 2025

This example uses the `datetime` package to define different date formats for each language. It also takes advantage of `babel's` language tracking mechanism via `\languagename`. By wrapping the logic inside `\makeatletter` and `\makeatother`, we gain access to internal control sequences that allow the date formatting to switch based on the currently selected language.

While the conditional structure may appear verbose, it is robust and adaptable to additional languages. With this setup, every instance of `\today` will automatically render in the correct language, eliminating the need to manually manage regional styles across the document.

This approach is especially useful for international research reports, multilingual policy documents, or compiled proceedings where content appears in more than one language and clarity of time-related data is essential.

8.4.4 Redefining Formatting Commands

LaTeX provides a set of well-established commands for text formatting, such as `\emph` for emphasis, `\textbf` for bold, and `\textit` for italics. These commands follow traditional typographic conventions and are sufficient for most documents. However, in certain contexts, such as educational handouts, user manuals, or stylistically unique publications, you may find the default behavior either too subtle or inconsistent with your design preferences.

Fortunately, LaTeX gives authors the flexibility to redefine these formatting commands using `\renewcommand`. This allows you to preserve the semantic structure of your content while customizing its visual output. One of the most commonly customized commands is `\emph`, which is typically used to emphasize a word or phrase via italics.

Suppose you want emphasized text to appear both italicized and underlined to draw stronger attention to it. Rather than changing every instance of emphasis manually, you can redefine the behavior of `\emph` globally as follows:

Redefining `\emph` to Italicize and Underline

LaTeX Code:

```
\documentclass{article}
\usepackage{amsmath}
\usepackage{xcolor}
% Redefining commands
```

```
\renewcommand{\emph}[1]
{\textit{\underline{#1}}}
\begin{document}
\begin{verbatim}
\begin{document}
This is \emph{important} text.
\end{document}
\end{verbatim}
\end{document}
```

Output:
This is *important* text.

In this redefinition, the argument to `\emph` (represented as `#1`) is wrapped in both `\textit` and `\underline`, combining the effects of slanted and underlined typography. Since `\emph` is meant to indicate conceptual emphasis, this redefinition does not change its intended usage but rather adjusts its appearance for clarity or emphasis strength.

It is important to understand that `\emph` behaves contextually in default LaTeX: When used within already italicized text, it switches to upright. Redefining it as above disables this intelligent behavior. If you wish to preserve that alternation while adding your own styling, a more sophisticated approach using conditionals or font detection would be needed.

The ability to redefine formatting commands provides a powerful tool for visual control, especially in template creation or institutional branding. However, caution is necessary. Overriding commonly understood behavior may confuse collaborators or impact document accessibility, so it is best reserved for scenarios where typographic clarity outweighs convention.

8.4.5 Redefining Mathematical Commands

Mathematical typesetting is one of LaTeX's greatest strengths, and many of its symbols and operators, such as summation, product, integrals, and limits, are finely tuned for clarity and spacing. However, in some documents, particularly where inline mathematics plays a central visual role (such as in educational handouts or presentations), authors may want to enhance the visibility or consistency of specific mathematical symbols.

Redefining mathematical commands allows you to override LaTeX's default behavior for those symbols. This is useful when you need to ensure that an operator always appears in a specific style, regardless of whether it is used in inline math or display math mode.

A common example is the summation symbol, produced by the command `\sum`. In display math mode (e.g., equations set on their own line), the summation symbol appears larger and its limits (e.g., upper and lower bounds) are placed above and below the symbol. However, in inline math mode (within a paragraph), LaTeX shrinks the symbol and places the limits beside it to preserve line height. While this is typographically sound, it may not always match your design intent.

You can redefine the `\sum` command to always appear in display style, even within inline math, so that it remains prominent and visually consistent.

Redefining `\sum` to Always Use Display Style

LaTeX Code:

```
\documentclass{article}
\usepackage{amsmath}
% Force \sum to use display style
```

```
\renewcommand{\sum}{\displaystyle\sum}
\begin{document}
The sum is \( \sum_{i=1}^{n} i^2 \).
\end{document}
```

Output:

The sum is $\displaystyle\sum_{i=1}^{n} i^2$.

In this redefinition, `\sum` is wrapped with the `\displaystyle` command. As a result, when used in inline math mode (such as within a sentence), the symbol will appear in its full-size, display-style form, complete with vertically stacked upper and lower limits. This may improve legibility or visual impact in contexts where mathematical expressions are central to the discussion, such as when teaching or emphasizing structure in a printed formula sheet.

However, this approach also has drawbacks. Enlarging display-style symbols inside text can disrupt line spacing and may make paragraphs appear uneven. For this reason, it is best used selectively, either for documents with minimal body text or when visual clarity takes precedence over typographic compactness.

Redefining mathematical commands like this illustrates how LaTeX can be adapted beyond its default styles to accommodate the specific needs of a publication. This technique can also be applied to other mathematical operators, including `\prod`, `\lim`, and `\int`, depending on your goals for spacing and readability.

8.4.6 Safely Restoring Commands

Redefining commands in LaTeX grants considerable control over document styling and structure, but with that control comes responsibility. Once a command is redefined, its original functionality is lost—unless you take proactive steps to preserve it. In longer or modular documents, you may want to apply a custom behavior for only a portion of the text and then revert back to LaTeX's default behavior. To do this safely, LaTeX provides a robust and low-level tool: the `\let` command.

The `\let` command allows you to create a direct copy of an existing macro before changing it. Unlike higher-level commands such as `\newcommand` or `\renewcommand`, `\let` does not redefine or reformat anything, it simply assigns one command to another. This makes it ideal for preserving original versions of LaTeX commands prior to customization.

Let us walk through a practical scenario. Suppose you want to redefine the `\section` command so that it produces large, bold titles without numbers. But later in the document, perhaps after a title page or custom preface, you wish to return to LaTeX's standard numbered section headings. Here is how you can achieve that safely and cleanly:

Temporarily Redefining and Restoring `\section`

LaTeX Code:

```
\documentclass{article}
\usepackage{xcolor}

% Save the original definition
\let\origsection\section

% Apply custom styling
\renewcommand{\section}[1]{%
  \textbf{\large #1}
  \par\vspace{1ex}
```

```
}

\begin{document}

\section{Custom Heading}
This heading is bold and large,
but unnumbered.

% Restore the original
\let\section\origsection

\section{Default Heading}
This heading uses the standard
 format.

\end{document}
```

Output:

- The first heading appears in bold, large text without a section number.
- The second heading is formatted using LaTeX's original style, including automatic numbering.

This pattern, backing up a command before redefining it, is especially useful in custom templates, packages, or documents that require local variations in formatting. For instance, you may want to redefine `\emph` for a single chapter or create alternative section headings for appendices. With the `\let` technique, you gain the flexibility to make these changes safely and reversibly.

It is also important to note that `\let` performs a direct copy at the macro level. This means that the saved version will not be affected by any subsequent redefinitions. In other words, you truly preserve the original form of the command at the point in time where `\let` is applied.

Full LaTeX Example

Advanced Customization Example

LaTeX Code:

```
\documentclass{article}
\usepackage{amsmath}
\usepackage{xcolor}

% Redefining commands
\renewcommand{\section}[1]
{\textbf{\large #1}}
% Redefine section headings
\renewcommand{\today}
{\textit{\day~\monthname~\year}}
% Custom date format
\renewcommand{\emph}[1]
{\textit{\underline{#1}}}
% Custom emphasis:
italics + underline
\renewcommand{\sum}
{\displaystyle\sum}
% Force larger summation symbol

\begin{document}

\section{Introduction}
This is a redefined section
heading.

Today is \today.

Here is some \emph{important}
text.

The sum is
\( \sum_{i=1}^{n} i^2 \).

\end{document}
```

Output:

Introduction

This is a redefined section heading.
Today is July 7, 2026.
Here is some *important* text.
The sum is

$$\sum_{i=1}^{n} i^2.$$

Exercises for Chap. 8: Packages and Custom Commands

8.1 Introduction to LaTeX Packages

1. *Installing and Using Packages*: Write a LaTeX document that uses at least three different packages (e.g., `amsmath`, `graphicx`, `hyperref`). Explain the purpose of each package and how it enhances your document.

2. *Package Documentation*: Choose any LaTeX package and read its documentation. Write a short explanation of one feature or command provided by the package that you found useful.

3. *Handling Package Conflicts*: Write a LaTeX document where you intentionally load two conflicting packages. Identify the conflict by compiling the document and describe how to resolve the issue by adjusting the package order or using package options.

8.2 Common Packages for Mathematics, Graphics, and Formatting

1. *Typesetting Equations with `amsmath`*: Write a document using the `amsmath` package that includes at least three different mathematical environments such as `align`, `gather`, and `multline`. Include numbered and unnumbered equations.

2. *Inserting Graphics with `graphicx`*: Load the `graphicx` package and insert an external image (e.g., a JPEG or PNG file). Use `\includegraphics` with optional arguments to scale, rotate, and crop the image.

3. *Customizing Text with `xcolor` and `fontspec`*: Use the `xcolor` package to apply color to section titles, text, and mathematical symbols. If using XeLaTeX or LuaLaTeX, combine it with `fontspec` to load a custom font and apply font styling to a paragraph.

4. *Improving Tables with `booktabs`*: Create a table using the `booktabs` package. Include `\toprule`, `\midrule`, and `\bottomrule` to give the table a professional appearance.

5. *Mathematical Symbols and Operators with `mathtools`*: Extend your `amsmath` document by loading the `mathtools` package. Use it to align matrices, define paired delimiters, and typeset a piecewise function using `cases`.

6. *Combining Multiple Packages*: Create a mini document that includes an aligned equation (using `amsmath`), a figure (using `graphicx`), a colored title (using `xcolor`), and a formatted table (using `booktabs`). This should demonstrate the power of combining packages for a polished layout.

8.3 Creating and Using Custom Commands

1. *Creating Basic Commands*: Write a LaTeX document where you define and use at least two custom commands. For example, create a command to format a frequently used term in bold or italic.

2. *Custom Commands with Arguments*: Define a LaTeX command that accepts an argument. For example, create a command that formats text in a colored box and allows you to specify the color.

3. *Advanced Custom Commands*: Write a LaTeX document where you define an advanced custom command with optional arguments. For example, create a command that adds an image with optional width and caption parameters.

8.4 Redefining Existing Commands

1. *Modifying LaTeX Defaults*: Write a LaTeX document where you redefine the `\section` command to change its font size and style. Test the new behavior by creating multiple sections.

2. *Customizing Environments*: Redefine the `\itemize` environment to use a different bullet symbol. Apply this redefinition in a document and compare it to the default behavior.

3. *Preserving Original Commands*: Redefine a command while preserving its original behavior using `\renewcommand`. For example, redefine `\emph` to add color to the emphasized text while keeping the italics.

Chapter 9

Questions Designed for Interviews

Abstract: Interviews and viva-voce examinations, whether for academic, research, or professional roles, often aim to test not only a candidate's factual knowledge but also their conceptual understanding, clarity of expression, and ability to apply theoretical ideas to practical situations. This chapter is designed to support candidates preparing for such assessments, especially those focused on LaTeX, scientific writing, technical documentation, or typesetting tools.

Keywords: LaTeX interview questions, Technical interview preparation, Commonly asked LaTeX questions, LaTeX coding interviews, Viva-voce examinations, Interview-style problems

This chapter contains a carefully curated collection of more than 100 interview-style questions along with their best

Md Aquib, *Fundamentals of LaTeX*, University Texts in the Mathematical Sciences,
https://doi.org/10.1007/978-981-96-9318-4_9

possible answers. These questions have been framed with close attention to what an expert examiner might typically ask in an oral examination or technical interview. They cover a range of difficulty levels, from basic familiarity with LaTeX syntax and structure, to more advanced topics such as package development, custom class creation, mathematical typesetting, and graphical capabilities using packages like `tikz` and `pgfplots`.

Each question is presented clearly and concisely, followed by a thoughtfully crafted response that reflects what an ideal candidate might articulate. The answers not only provide accurate information but are also phrased to demonstrate confidence, clarity, and awareness of best practices in the use of LaTeX. This makes the chapter not just a revision guide but a training ground for mastering the art of presenting technical knowledge during a live discussion.

Furthermore, many of the questions are accompanied by small code snippets or usage examples where applicable, to ensure that explanations are practical and contextual. The chapter also includes tips on how to approach open-ended or opinion-based questions, how to handle follow-up queries gracefully, and how to steer the conversation toward your strengths during an interview.

Whether you are preparing for an academic defense, a research position, a teaching role, or a publishing-related job, this chapter aims to equip you with the insights and confidence necessary to perform at your best. It is particularly useful for postgraduate students, early-career researchers, technical authors, and anyone who expects to discuss their knowledge of LaTeX and its ecosystem in a formal evaluative setting.

Recommended Responses and Justifications

1. *What is LaTeX and how does it differ from a typical word processor like Microsoft Word?*
   LaTeX is a high-quality typesetting system designed for producing technical and scientific documentation. Unlike WYSIWYG word processors like Microsoft Word, where the user directly interacts with the visual layout, LaTeX allows users to focus on the content structure and logic. The document formatting is handled by predefined styles, ensuring consistency and high-quality output. In LaTeX, users write plain text files with markup commands, which are later compiled to generate a fully formatted document.

2. *Can you describe the basic components of a LaTeX document?*
   A LaTeX document is structured into three main parts:

   - *Preamble*: This includes the `\documentclass` declaration and optional packages. It sets up the overall document structure, layout, and styles.
   - *Document Body*: The main content of the document goes here, enclosed between `\begin{document}` and `\end{document}`.
   - *Environment Blocks*: These are specific constructs, like `itemize`, `equation`, and `figure`, that structure elements in the document.

3. *Why is LaTeX widely used in academic and scientific fields?*
   LaTeX is the go-to tool for academic and scientific writing because it excels at handling complex mathematical formulas, bibliographies, and large documents with intricate structures. The precise control

over formatting and typesetting ensures that documents meet publication standards. Additionally, LaTeX's ability to handle cross-referencing, tables of contents, and indices automatically makes it indispensable for research papers, theses, and technical books.

4. *What are some advantages of using LaTeX for document preparation?*
   LaTeX offers several advantages:

   - *Professional Quality*: LaTeX generates high-quality, professional documents that conform to academic publishing standards.
   - *Consistency*: Styles and formatting are consistent throughout, as they are defined globally in the document.
   - *Complex Mathematical Typesetting*: LaTeX excels in rendering complex mathematical formulas and structures.
   - *Automated References and Cross-referencing*: Bibliographies, citations, and cross-references are automatically handled with packages like `biblatex` and `hyperref`.
   - *Open Source and Customizable*: LaTeX is free and highly customizable, with a vast range of packages for different fields.

5. *How does LaTeX ensure consistency in formatting across large documents?*
   LaTeX enforces consistency by separating content from formatting. Once the formatting rules are defined in the preamble or through the document class, they apply uniformly across the entire document. This approach prevents manual formatting errors and

ensures that headings, tables, figures, and references all follow the same style.

6. *Can you explain the role of the document class in LaTeX?*
The document class (`\documentclass`) is the foundation of a LaTeX document, as it defines the overall layout and formatting rules. The most common classes are `article`, `report`, `book`, and `beamer`. Each class comes with its own predefined structures, such as chapter or section formatting, and can be customized further through options like font size, margins, and paper size.

7. *What is the purpose of the preamble in a LaTeX document?*
The preamble is the part of the LaTeX document that appears before
`\begin{document}`. It defines the document class, loads necessary packages, sets up custom formatting rules, and initializes any global settings for the document. The preamble ensures that everything is configured correctly before the content is typeset.

8. *How would you install and set up LaTeX on your system?*
Installing LaTeX involves downloading a LaTeX distribution such as TeX Live (for Linux/Windows) or MacTeX (for macOS). Once installed, you can use a LaTeX editor like TeXShop (macOS) or TeXworks (Windows/Linux) to write and compile LaTeX documents. Alternatively, Overleaf, a cloud-based LaTeX editor, allows users to write, compile, and share documents without installing any software locally.

9. *How do Overleaf and TeXShop differ in their approach to LaTeX editing?*
   Overleaf is a cloud-based LaTeX editor, allowing users to write, compile, and collaborate on LaTeX documents directly in the browser. It simplifies the setup process, making it accessible to beginners. TeXShop, on the other hand, is a local LaTeX editor for macOS. It provides more control over the local environment and is ideal for users who prefer offline work, but it requires installing a LaTeX distribution like MacTeX.

10. *What are some common LaTeX distributions and what purpose do they serve?*
    Common LaTeX distributions include:

    - *TeX Live*: A cross-platform distribution available on Linux, Windows, and macOS. It provides a complete LaTeX environment with all essential packages.
    - *MacTeX*: A version of TeX Live specifically packaged for macOS, including the TeXShop editor.
    - *MiKTeX*: A popular distribution for Windows, which allows users to install packages on-the-fly as they are needed.

    These distributions provide the LaTeX engine, necessary packages, and tools for compiling and managing LaTeX documents.

11. *How do you create sections, subsections, and paragraphs in LaTeX?*
    In LaTeX, sections and subsections are created using commands such as:

    - `\section{Section Title}`: Creates a section.

- `\subsection{Subsection Title}`: Creates a subsection.
- `\subsubsection{Subsubsection Title}`: Creates a subsubsection.

Paragraphs are created by simply leaving a blank line between blocks of text. LaTeX automatically indents paragraphs unless otherwise specified.

12. *Can you explain the differences between the* ***article****,* ***report****, and* ***book*** *document classes?*
The `article`, `report`, and `book` classes are predefined document classes in LaTeX, each designed for different purposes:

   - `article`: Ideal for shorter documents like research papers and articles. It supports sections and subsections but no chapters.
   - `report`: Suitable for longer documents like reports and theses. It introduces chapters in addition to sections and subsections.
   - `book`: Designed for books. It supports chapters, sections, and subsections and includes features like a title page, front matter, and back matter (e.g., bibliography, index).

13. *What LaTeX commands are used for text formatting (e.g., bold, italics, underline)?*
LaTeX provides several commands for text formatting:

   - `\textbf{text}`: Makes the text bold.
   - `\textit{text}`: Italicizes the text.
   - `\underline{text}`: Underlines the text.

14. *How do you control font sizes in LaTeX?*
LaTeX provides predefined font size commands that can be used to change the font size at any point in the document:

    - `\tiny`, `\scriptsize`, `\footnotesize`, `\small`, `\normalsize`, `\large`, `\Large`, `\LARGE`, `\huge`, `\Huge`.

    These commands can be used inline or globally in the preamble by specifying the font size in the `\documentclass` command (e.g., `\documentclass[12pt]{article}`).

15. *Can you explain how to create and customize itemized and enumerated lists?*
Itemized lists are created using the `itemize` environment, while enumerated lists are created with the `enumerate` environment:

    - `\begin{itemize}`: Creates a bulleted list.
    - `\begin{enumerate}`: Creates a numbered list.
    - Each list item is defined with `\item`.

    You can customize enumerated lists by specifying the numbering style (e.g., roman numerals or letters) or itemized lists by changing the bullet style using the `enumitem` package.

16. *How do you include special characters such as %, &, or $ in LaTeX?*
Special characters that have reserved meanings in LaTeX can be included in the document by preceding them with a backslash:

    - `\%`, `\&`, `\$`.

These characters are otherwise used for special commands or functions in LaTeX, so escaping them ensures they appear as regular text.

17. *What is the difference between inline and display math modes in LaTeX?*
In LaTeX, inline math mode is used to write mathematical expressions within the text, while display math mode is used for standalone equations:

    - *Inline math*: Enclosed by `$...$`, the equation is part of the text (e.g., $a^2 + b^2 = c^2$).
    - *Display math*: Enclosed by `\[...\]`, the equation is centered and displayed on a separate line.

18. *How would you write a simple fraction, square root, and exponent in LaTeX?*
In LaTeX, the following commands are used:

    - *Fraction*: `\frac{numerator}{denominator}` (e.g., $\frac{a}{b}$).
    - *Square root*: `\sqrt{argument}` (e.g., $\sqrt{x}$).
    - *Exponent*: Use the caret symbol `^`, followed by the exponent (e.g., x^2).

19. *Can you explain how to write a matrix using LaTeX?*
A matrix in LaTeX can be written using the `bmatrix` environment provided by the `amsmath` package:

```
\begin{bmatrix}
    a & b \\
    c & d
\end{bmatrix}
```

This produces a matrix with brackets:

$$\begin{bmatrix} a & b \\ c & d \end{bmatrix}.$$

20. *How do you align multiple equations in LaTeX using the* `align` *environment?*
The `align` environment, provided by the `amsmath` package, is used to align multiple equations:

```
\begin{align}
    a + b &= c \\
    d + e &= f
\end{align}
```

The `&` symbol is used to align the equations at a specific location, such as the equal sign.

21. *What is the purpose of the* `amsmath` *package in LaTeX?*
The `amsmath` package is an essential LaTeX package for handling advanced mathematical typesetting. It provides additional environments and commands for writing equations, matrices, multiline equations, and aligning equations. It ensures better formatting and flexibility when writing complex mathematical expressions.

22. *How do you create tables in LaTeX that contain mathematical expressions?*
To create tables with mathematical expressions, you can use the `tabular` environment along with math mode commands. For instance:

```
\begin{tabular}{c c c}
    $a^2$ & $b^2$ & $c^2$ \\
```

```
    $\frac{1}{2}$ & $\sqrt{x}$ & $y^n$
\end{tabular}
```

This produces a table where each cell contains a mathematical expression.

23. *How do you insert an image into a LaTeX document using the* `graphicx` *package?*
    To insert an image in a LaTeX document, you need to use the `graphicx` package. Here is an example:

    ```
    \usepackage{graphicx}
    ...
    \begin{figure}[h]
        \centering
        \includegraphics
        [width=0.5\textwidth]{imagefile.jpg}
        \caption{Example image}
        \label{fig:example}
    \end{figure}
    ```

    This inserts the image `imagefile.jpg` with half the text width. You can adjust the size using the `width` parameter and add a caption and label for referencing.

24. *What are the options for positioning figures and tables in LaTeX?*
    Figures and tables in LaTeX are typically placed using the `figure` and `table` environments, and the positioning is controlled by options such as:

    - `[h]`: Place the figure or table approximately "here" in the text.
    - `[t]`: Place the figure or table at the top of the page.

- `[b]`: Place the figure or table at the bottom of the page.
- `[p]`: Place the figure or table on a separate page dedicated to floats.
- `[!]`: Override LaTeX's placement constraints to place the figure exactly as specified.

25. *Can you explain how to create a table with multiple rows and columns in LaTeX?*
In LaTeX, you create tables using the `tabular` environment. For multiple rows and columns, you specify the number of columns and their alignment (left, center, right):

```
\begin{tabular}{|c|c|c|}
\hline
Row 1, Col 1 & Row 1, Col 2
& Row 1, Col 3 \\
\hline
Row 2, Col 1 & Row 2, Col 2
& Row 2, Col 3 \\
\hline
\end{tabular}
```

The & symbol separates columns, and \\ ends a row. The **hline** command adds horizontal lines between rows.

26. *What is a floating figure or table, and why is it used in LaTeX?*
Floating figures or tables are elements that are not strictly positioned "in line" with the text but are instead allowed to "float" to the best possible position on the page. This is especially useful when ensuring that figures or tables fit nicely within the page layout and do not interrupt the flow of text. Floats are managed through the `figure` and `table` environments.

27. *How do you reference figures and tables in the text using the `\ref` command?*
To reference figures or tables, you first label them using the `\label` command inside the `figure` or `table` environment. Then, you use the `\ref` command to reference them in the text:

```
See Figure \ref{fig:example} for more
details.
```

The `\ref` command will insert the figure or table number, which is automatically updated by LaTeX.

28. *What is the `TikZ` package used for in LaTeX, and how does it differ from `PGFPlots`?*
`TikZ` is a powerful LaTeX package used for creating complex diagrams, illustrations, and flowcharts programmatically. It allows users to draw shapes, lines, nodes, and more with precise control. `PGFPlots`, on the other hand, is built on top of `TikZ` and is specialized for plotting 2D and 3D graphs. While `TikZ` is more general purpose, `PGFPlots` is focused on data visualization and graphing.

29. *How do you add citations in LaTeX using the `biblatex` package?*
To add citations using the `biblatex` package, you first need to load the package and specify a bibliography backend (like `biber`). Then, create a `.bib` file with the references. Here is a basic setup:

```
\usepackage[backend=biber]{biblatex}
\addbibresource{references.bib}
...
According to \cite{author2020},
this theory is valid.
\printbibliography
```

This example cites a reference and prints the bibliography at the end of the document.

30. *What is the difference between numeric and author-year citation styles in LaTeX?*
In the numeric style, references are cited using numbers (e.g., [1], [2]) that correspond to entries in the bibliography. In the author-year style, the citations include the author's last name and the publication year (e.g., Smith 2020). The choice of citation style is set using options in the `biblatex` package, for example:

```
\usepackage[style=numeric]{biblatex}
\usepackage[style=authoryear]{biblatex}
```

31. *How do you manage multiple references in LaTeX and ensure they appear in order?*
When citing multiple sources at once, you use the `\cite` command with multiple keys, separated by commas:

```
\cite{author2019,author2020,author2021}
```

LaTeX will automatically sort and display the references in the correct order according to the bibliography style.

32. *Can you explain the difference between referencing sections and referencing figures in LaTeX?*
Referencing sections and referencing figures in LaTeX are similar in syntax but different in intent. Sections are referenced using `\label` within the section command and `\ref` to reference them:

```
\section{Introduction}\label{sec:intro}
See Section \ref{sec:intro}.
```

Figures are labeled similarly within the `figure` environment. The difference lies in the context—sections refer to parts of the text, while figures refer to images or graphical content.

33. *How do you create an index in LaTeX using the* ***makeidx*** *package?*
    To create an index, you first need to load the `makeidx` package and mark entries in the document with `\index{term}`. The index is generated using `\makeindex` and displayed with `\printindex`. Here is an example:

    ```
    \usepackage{makeidx}
    \makeindex
    ...
    \section{Introduction\index{Introduction}}
    ...
    \printindex
    ```

    This will create an index for the term "Introduction."

34. *What is the purpose of the* ***glossaries*** *package in LaTeX?*
    The `glossaries` package is used to create glossaries and lists of acronyms in LaTeX documents. It allows for easy management of terms and their definitions, which are automatically formatted and listed. The package provides commands to define terms, acronyms, and print them in the document. For example:

    ```
    \usepackage{glossaries}
    ```

```
\newglossaryentry{latex}{name=LaTeX,
description={a typesetting system}}
...
\printglossary
```

This example creates and prints a glossary of terms.

35. *How do you modify page margins in LaTeX using the **geometry** package?*
The `geometry` package allows you to set custom page margins in LaTeX. You can modify margins by specifying them directly in the preamble:

```
\usepackage[margin=1in]{geometry}
```

This sets all margins (top, bottom, left, right) to 1 inch. You can also customize specific margins:

```
\usepackage[top=2in, bottom=1in, left=1.5in,
right=1in]{geometry}
```

36. *Can you explain how to create custom headers and footers in LaTeX using the **fancyhdr** package?*
The `fancyhdr` package provides control over headers and footers in LaTeX. To use it, load the package and then define the header and footer content:

```
\usepackage{fancyhdr}
\pagestyle{fancy}
\fancyhf{}
\fancyhead[L]{Chapter Title} % Left header
\fancyhead[R]{\thepage}
% Right header with page number
\fancyfoot[C]{Confidential}
% Centered footer
```

This example creates a custom header with the chapter title on the left, the page number on the right, and a centered footer with "Confidential."

37. *How do you generate a table of contents in LaTeX, and how does it update automatically?*
LaTeX automatically generates a table of contents using the `\tableofcontents` command. This command should be placed where you want the table of contents to appear:

```
\tableofcontents
```

LaTeX updates the table of contents based on the sections, subsections, and other heading commands (like `\chapter` or `\section`) as the document is compiled. Each time the document is compiled, the table of contents reflects any changes made.

38. *What is the difference between footnotes and endnotes in LaTeX, and how do you implement both?*
Footnotes in LaTeX are placed at the bottom of the page where they are referenced, while endnotes are collected at the end of the document. To create footnotes, you use the `\footnote` command:

```
This is a footnote.
\footnote{This is the footnote text.}
```

To create endnotes, you need the `endnotes` package:

```
\usepackage{endnotes}
...
Text with endnote\endnote{Endnote text.}
\printendnotes
```

The `\printendnotes` command generates the list of endnotes at the end of the document.

39. *How do you create a multicolumn layout in LaTeX using the `multicols` package?*
The `multicols` package allows you to create a multicolumn layout. Load the package and use the `multicols` environment to divide text into columns:

```
\usepackage{multicol}
...
\begin{multicols}{2}
This is the first column.
This text will be distributed across
two columns.
\end{multicols}
```

This example splits the text into two columns. You can specify any number of columns by changing the argument to the `multicols` environment.

40. *What is the `beamer` document class used for in LaTeX?*
The `beamer` document class is used for creating presentations in LaTeX. It allows for structured slide creation, including sections, subsections, bullet points, and animations. Unlike regular LaTeX documents, `beamer` produces slides in PDF format with customizable layouts, themes, and transitions.

41. *How do you structure a `beamer` presentation with sections and subsections?*
In `beamer`, sections and subsections help structure the presentation and can be used for navigation:

```
\section{Introduction}
```

```
\subsection{Motivation}
\begin{frame}{Title of Slide}
Content of the slide.
\end{frame}
```

The \section and \subsection commands organize the presentation into clickable sections and subsections in the navigation panel.

42. *How do you customize the theme and colors of a* **beamer** *presentation?*
    The beamer class provides predefined themes and color schemes that can be easily applied. To set a theme, you use the \usecolortheme and \usetheme commands:

```
\usetheme{Madrid}
% Sets the theme to Madrid
\usecolortheme{beaver}
% Sets the color theme to beaver
```

    You can further customize colors using \setbeamercolor to adjust individual elements like headers, footers, and blocks.

43. *How do you insert images and tables into a* **beamer** *presentation?*
    Images and tables are inserted in beamer using the same commands as in standard LaTeX:

```
\begin{frame}{Image Slide}
\includegraphics[width=0.5\textwidth]
{imagefile.jpg}
\caption{Example image}
\end{frame}
```

```
\begin{frame}{Table Slide}
\begin{tabular}{|c|c|}
\hline
Row 1, Col 1 & Row 1, Col 2 \\
\hline
Row 2, Col 1 & Row 2, Col 2 \\
\hline
\end{tabular}
\end{frame}
```

This example demonstrates how to insert an image and a simple table into a `beamer` slide.

44. *What are overlays in **beamer**, and how are they used for animations?*
Overlays in `beamer` are used to control the visibility of slide elements, such as bullet points or images, at different times during the presentation. This creates an animation-like effect where content appears incrementally:

```
\begin{frame}{Example Slide}
    \begin{itemize}
        \item<1-> First item
        \item<2-> Socond item
        \item<3-> Third item
    \end{itemize}
\end{frame}
```

In this example, each bullet point appears one by one as the presenter progresses through the slide. The numbers in angle brackets (e.g., `<1->`) specify the slide steps at which the items appear.

45. *How do you load and use LaTeX packages? Provide an example of a useful package.*
To load a package in LaTeX, you use the `\usepackage` command in the preamble of the document. This tells LaTeX to load the specified package and make its features available throughout the document. For example, the `graphicx` package is used for inserting images:

```
\usepackage{graphicx}
% Loads the graphicx package for including
images
```

Once the package is loaded, you can use its commands, such as `\includegraphics` to insert an image.

46. *How do you create a custom command in LaTeX? Provide an example.*
You can create a custom command in LaTeX using the `\newcommand` command. This allows you to define shortcuts or frequently used code:

```
\newcommand{\vect}[1]{\mathbf{#1}}
% Define a command to typeset vectors in
bold
```

In this example, `\vect` is defined as a command that typesets its argument in boldface. You can now write `\vect{x}` to produce a bold x.

47. *Can you explain how to redefine an existing LaTeX command and why you might want to do this?*
You can redefine an existing LaTeX command using the `\renewcommand` command. This is useful when you want to change the default behavior of a command without creating a new one:

```
\renewcommand{\thefootnote}
{\fnsymbol{footnote}}
% Changes footnote numbering to symbols
```

In this example, the `\renewcommand` changes the footnote numbering style to symbols instead of numbers. Redefining commands is helpful for customizing document elements like headings, footnotes, or captions.

48. *What are some essential packages for writing research papers in LaTeX?*
    Several essential packages are commonly used when writing research papers in LaTeX:

    - `amsmath`: For advanced mathematical typesetting.
    - `biblatex`: For managing citations and bibliographies.
    - `graphicx`: For including images and graphics.
    - `hyperref`: For creating hyperlinks and clickable cross-references.
    - `cleveref`: For automatically handling cross-referencing.

    These packages provide essential tools for creating professional academic documents, handling complex mathematics, images, and citations.

49. *How do you write an algorithm or pseudocode in LaTeX using the* `algorithm2e` *package?*
    The `algorithm2e` package is used for writing algorithms and pseudocode in LaTeX. You load the package and then use the `algorithm` environment to write the algorithm:

```
\usepackage{algorithm2e}
...
\begin{algorithm}
\SetAlgoLined
\KwIn{Input parameters}
\KwOut{Output result}
\While{condition}{
    execute the statement\;
}
\caption{Sample algorithm}
\end{algorithm}
```

This example defines a simple algorithm with a while loop, and the `\caption` command adds a title to the algorithm.

50. *How can you customize theorem styles in LaTeX using the* `amsthm` *package?*
The `amsthm` package provides an easy way to define and customize theorem-like environments. To customize a theorem style, first load the package and then define the theorem:

```
\usepackage{amsthm}
\newtheoremstyle{mystyle}% Custom style name
    {3pt}% Space above
    {3pt}% Space below
    {\itshape}% Body font
    {}% Indent amount
    {\bfseries}% Theorem head font
    {.}% Punctuation after theorem head
    { }% Space after theorem head
    {}% Theorem head spec
\theoremstyle{mystyle}
\newtheorem{theorem}{Theorem}
```

In this example, a custom theorem style is defined where the theorem body is italicized and the theorem heading is bold. The `\newtheorem` command creates the actual theorem environment.

51. *How do you manage large documents in LaTeX using the `subfiles` package?*
The `subfiles` package is useful for managing large documents by dividing them into smaller, manageable parts (e.g., chapters). Each part can be written as a separate file and compiled individually:

```
\usepackage{subfiles}
...
\begin{document}
\subfile{chapter1.tex}  % Includes chapter 1
\subfile{chapter2.tex}  % Includes chapter 2
\end{document}
```

Each `subfile` can be compiled on its own, making it easier to work with large documents such as books or theses. The `main` document includes the individual parts as subfiles.

52. *How do you define a new environment in LaTeX, and what are some common use cases for doing so?*
You can define a new environment in LaTeX using the `\newenvironment` command. This allows you to create custom environments for specific tasks:

```
\newenvironment{example}[1][Default Title]%
{\textbf{#1}: } % Begin code
{}              % End code
```

This example creates an `example` environment with an optional argument for the title. You can use this for adding examples, notes, or custom boxes. Common use cases include defining environments for proofs, remarks, or structured content.

53. *What are some common errors in LaTeX, and how can they be resolved?*
Common LaTeX errors include:

    - *Missing* `\begin` *or* `\end`*: This happens when you forget to close or open an environment. The error is resolved by ensuring that every* `\begin{}` *has a corresponding* `\end{}`*.*
    - *Undefined control sequence*: This occurs when you use an unknown command or forget to load a required package. You can fix this by loading the appropriate package or correcting the typo.
    - *Mismatched braces*: This happens when the number of opening { and closing } braces does not match. To resolve this, check the syntax carefully and ensure that all braces are paired correctly.
    - *Overfull/Underfull* `hbox`: This warning indicates text that overflows the page margins or has too much white space. You can fix this by adjusting line breaks or margins.
    - *Misplaced alignment tab (&)*: This error occurs when you use the `&` character outside of tabular or alignment environments. Ensure that `&` is used only within environments like `tabular`, `align`, or `matrix`.

54. *How can you optimize the compilation process for large LaTeX documents?*
To optimize the compilation process for large documents, you can:

- *Use the* `\includeonly` *command: This allows you to compile only specific sections or chapters during editing, which speeds up the compilation process.*

```
\includeonly{chapter1.tex}
% Only compiles chapter 1
```

- *Use* `latexmk`*: This tool automates the compilation process, only recompiling the parts that have changed. It also handles bibtex or biber runs automatically.*
- *Disable images temporarily*: During the drafting phase, you can use a placeholder for images by disabling the `\includegraphics` commands.
- *Use a lighter bibliography style*: For large bibliographies, using a lighter bibliography style or minimizing bibliographies during drafting can save time.

55. *What are some best practices for writing clean, efficient LaTeX code?*
Best practices for LaTeX include:

- *Organize the preamble*: Group package imports, define commands, and manage settings at the beginning of the document.
- *Use custom commands*: Define frequently used symbols or code as custom commands to avoid repetition and improve readability.

- *Use comments*: Add comments in the code to explain sections or complex logic. This helps with readability and future modifications.

  ```
  % This section deals with formatting the
  abstract
  ```

- *Avoid hardcoding layout changes*: Instead of using commands like `\vspace` or `\hspace`, rely on LaTeX environments and packages (e.g., `geometry` for margins).
- *Keep large projects modular*: Break large documents into smaller subfiles or chapters using `\input` or `subfiles`.

56. *How do you use Git to collaborate on LaTeX documents with others?*
    Git is a version control system that allows multiple collaborators to work on the same LaTeX project. Here is how you can use it:

    - *Initialize a Git repository*: In the project folder, run `git init` to start a repository.
    - *Commit and track changes*: Use `git add` to stage files and `git commit` to save versions. Track changes over time and revert if necessary.
    - *Branching and merging*: Create separate branches for each contributor to avoid conflicts. Merge changes back into the main branch once edits are complete.

      ```
      git checkout -b feature-branch
      % Create a new branch
      ```

    - *Remote repositories*: Use services like GitHub or GitLab to host the repository online. This enables remote collaborators to clone the project, contribute, and push changes.

- *Resolve conflicts*: Git provides tools for resolving merge conflicts, which are especially useful when multiple collaborators edit the same file.

57. *What is Overleaf, and how does it facilitate collaboration on LaTeX documents?*
Overleaf is a cloud-based LaTeX editor that allows real-time collaboration on LaTeX documents. It facilitates collaboration by:

    - *Real-time editing*: Multiple collaborators can edit the same document simultaneously, with changes instantly visible to all participants.
    - *Version control*: Overleaf tracks changes and allows users to revert to previous versions or compare different versions of the document.
    - *No installation needed*: Overleaf works directly in the browser, so users do not need to install LaTeX locally.
    - *Easy sharing*: Projects can be shared with others via a link, and different permissions (e.g., read-only or edit access) can be assigned.
    - *Integration with GitHub*: Overleaf integrates with GitHub, enabling synchronization between Overleaf projects and Git repositories.

58. *How do you create comments in a LaTeX document, and why are they useful?*

In LaTeX, comments are created by placing a percent sign (%) at the beginning of the line or before a specific piece of text:

```
% This is a comment in LaTeX
```

Everything following the % on that line is ignored during compilation. Comments are useful for adding notes, explanations, or temporarily disabling certain parts of the code. They help improve readability, document the code, and allow for easier troubleshooting.

59. *Can you explain the difference between* `\include` *and* `\input` *in LaTeX?*
The `\include` and `\input` commands are used to include external files in a LaTeX document, but they have key differences:

    - `\input{filename}`: Inserts the content of `filename.tex` directly into the main document. This command can be used anywhere in the document and allows for flexible file inclusion.
    - `\include{filename}`: Similar to `\input`, but it starts on a new page and adds a `.aux` file for each included file. It is typically used for larger sections like chapters. `\include` also works with `\includeonly`, allowing selective compilation of specific parts of the document.

60. *What is the purpose of the* `\maketitle` *command in LaTeX?*
The `\maketitle` command generates a title for the document using information specified in the preamble (such as `\title`, `\author`, and `\date`). It automatically formats and displays the title page:

```
\title{My Document}
\author{John Doe}
\date{\today}
\maketitle
```

This command ensures that the title is consistently formatted according to the document class in use.

61. *How can you modify the document font size in LaTeX?*
To modify the overall font size of a document, you specify the font size in the `\documentclass` command:

```
\documentclass[12pt]{article}
```

This sets the base font size for the entire document (common values are 10pt, 11pt, and 12pt). You can also change the font size locally using the following commands:

```
{\small Small text} {\large Large text}
```

LaTeX provides predefined sizes such as `\tiny`, `\scriptsize`, `\small`, `\large`, `\huge`, etc.

62. *What are environments in LaTeX, and how do you create one?*
Environments in LaTeX define special blocks of content, each with specific formatting or functionality. They are created using the `\begin{}` and `\end{}` commands. For example, the `itemize` environment creates a bullet list:

```
\begin{itemize}
    \item First item
    \item Second item
\end{itemize}
```

Environments are commonly used for lists, figures, tables, equations, and more. You can also define custom environments using `\newenvironment`.

63. *How does LaTeX handle different languages? Provide an example of adding support for another language.*
LaTeX supports typesetting in multiple languages through the `babel` package, which provides correct hyphenation, character sets, and typographic conventions. To include a specific language, load `babel` in the preamble:

```
\usepackage[spanish]{babel}
```

This switches the language to Spanish. For documents that require multiple languages, you can load multiple options:

```
\usepackage[english,french]{babel}
\selectlanguage{french} % Switch to
French
```

LaTeX will handle hyphenation and other formatting rules according to the selected language.

64. *Can you explain the difference between `\newcommand` and `\renewcommand`?*
`\newcommand` is used to define a new custom command in LaTeX. If the command already exists, LaTeX will throw an error:

```
\newcommand{\myname}{Dr. LaTeX}
```

`\renewcommand` is used to redefine an existing command:

```
\renewcommand{\thefootnote}{\alph{footnote}}
% Change footnote format
```

`\renewcommand` is useful for modifying the behavior of predefined LaTeX commands without causing errors.

65. *What is the purpose of the **hyperref** package, and how does it enhance document navigation?*
The `hyperref` package is used to create hyperlinks and clickable cross-references within a LaTeX document. It enhances document navigation by linking sections, equations, figures, and citations. It also adds metadata such as document title and author to the PDF. For example:

```
\usepackage{hyperref}
\hypersetup{colorlinks=true,
linkcolor=blue}
```

This creates clickable links for cross-references (e.g., `\ref`, `\cite`) and generates a clickable table of contents.

66. *How do you add line numbers to a LaTeX document?*
To add line numbers, you can use the `lineno` package:

```
\usepackage{lineno}
\linenumbers
```

This command adds line numbers to the entire document. You can also limit the numbering to specific sections by using `\linenumbers` and `\nolinenumbers` commands within the document.

67. *Can you explain how to define a custom LaTeX counter and use it in a document?*
    In LaTeX, you can create and manipulate custom counters using the `\newcounter` command. After defining the counter, you can increment, reset, or display its value:

    ```
    \newcounter{examplecounter}
    \setcounter{examplecounter}{5}
    % Set initial value to 5
    \stepcounter{examplecounter}
    % Increment the counter
    \theexamplecounter
    % Display the counter value
    ```

    This defines a custom counter `examplecounter`, sets its value, increments it, and displays the current value in the document.

68. *How do you write a system of linear equations in LaTeX?*
    A system of linear equations can be written using the `align` environment or the `array` environment. Here is an example using `align`:

    ```
    \begin{align}
    2x + 3y &= 5 \\
    ```

```
4x - y &= 1
\end{align}
```

This aligns the equations at the equals sign, making them easy to read.

69. *What is the* **align** *environment used for in LaTeX, and how is it different from the* **equation** *environment?*
The `align` environment, provided by the `amsmath` package, allows multiple equations to be aligned at a specific point, such as the equals sign. Each equation is aligned using `&` and ends with \\. The `equation` environment, on the other hand, is used for single equations and does not support alignment:

```
\begin{align}
a &= b + c \\
d &= e + f
\end{align}
```

In contrast, the `equation` environment is for one standalone equation:

```
\begin{equation}
a = b + c
\end{equation}
```

70. *How do you create a case-based piecewise function in LaTeX?*
You can create a case-based function using the `cases` environment:

```
f(x) =
\begin{cases}
x^2 & \text{if } x \geq 0 \\
-x  & \text{if } x < 0
\end{cases}
```

This defines a piecewise function where different expressions are applied based on the value of x.

71. *How do you label and number equations in LaTeX?*
To label and number equations, use the `\label` command inside the `equation` or `align` environment and reference it using `\ref`:

```
\begin{equation}
E = mc^2 \label{eq:energy}
\end{equation}
Refer to Equation \ref{eq:energy}.
```

LaTeX automatically assigns a number to the equation, which can be referenced elsewhere in the document.

72. *Can you explain the purpose of the* `split` *environment in LaTeX for writing long equations?*
The `split` environment is used inside the `equation` environment to break long equations into multiple lines, with alignment at a specific point (usually an equals sign):

```
\begin{equation}
\begin{split}
a + b + c &= d + e + f + g \\
&+ h + i + j
```

```
\end{split}
\end{equation}
```

This format allows the equation to be written on multiple lines while maintaining alignment.

73. *What is the difference between* **`\frac`** *and* **`\dfrac`** *in LaTeX?*
    `\frac` and `\dfrac` both create fractions, but `\frac` uses the smaller, inline fraction style, whereas `\dfrac` uses the larger display style:

    ```
    \frac{a}{b}  % Inline fraction
    \dfrac{a}{b} % Display fraction
    ```

    `\dfrac` is typically used in display math mode for larger, more prominent fractions.

74. *How do you write Greek letters, such as alpha and beta, in LaTeX?*
    Greek letters can be written in LaTeX using the following commands:

    ```
    \alpha \beta \gamma \Gamma \Delta
    ```

    Lowercase Greek letters like alpha, beta, and gamma are written using the corresponding names (e.g., `\alpha`), while uppercase Greek letters use the same names but are capitalized (e.g., `\Gamma`).

75. *How do you create inline math expressions in LaTeX? Provide an example.*
    Inline math expressions are written by enclosing the mathematical content between dollar signs `$...$`. For example:

```
The formula for the area of a circle is
$A = \pi r^2$.
```

This generates an inline equation, $A = \pi r^2$, as part of the text.

76. *Can you explain how to use the* `cases` *environment for conditional equations in LaTeX?*
The `cases` environment is used to define conditional equations where different results are provided based on the value of a variable:

```
f(x) =
\begin{cases}
x^2 & \text{if } x \geq 0 \\
-x  & \text{if } x < 0.
\end{cases}
```

This format produces a piecewise function that applies different expressions based on the condition.

77. *How do you insert mathematical accents like hats or tildes in LaTeX?*
Mathematical accents such as hats or tildes can be added using the following commands:

```
\hat{x}, \tilde{y}.
```

This places a hat ($\hat{x}$) or a tilde ($\tilde{y}$) over the variable. Other accents include:

- \\`bar`: $\bar{x}$
- \\`vec`: $\vec{x}$

78. *How do you create side-by-side figures in LaTeX?*
To create side-by-side figures in LaTeX, you can use the `minipage` environment:

```
\begin{figure}
\begin{minipage}[b]{0.45\textwidth}
\centering
\includegraphics[width=\textwidth]
{image1.jpg}
\caption{First image}
\label{fig:image1}
\end{minipage}
\hfill
\begin{minipage}[b]{0.45\textwidth}
\centering
\includegraphics[width=\textwidth]
{image2.jpg}
\caption{Second image}
\label{fig:image2}
\end{minipage}
\end{figure}
```

This places two figures side by side, each occupying 45

79. *Can you explain how to use the `subfigure` package to create subfigures in a LaTeX document?*
The `subfigure` package allows you to create subfigures within a single figure environment:

```
\usepackage{subfigure}
...
\begin{figure}
\centering
\subfigure[First image]
```

```
{\includegraphics[width=0.45\textwidth]
{image1.jpg}}
\subfigure[Second image]
{\includegraphics[width=0.45\textwidth]
{image2.jpg}}
\caption{Subfigures example}
\label{fig:subfigures}
\end{figure}
```

This creates two subfigures labeled “First image” and “Second image,” each with its own caption.

80. *What are some ways to control figure and table placement in LaTeX?*
LaTeX allows you to control figure and table placement using placement specifiers:

    - `[h]`: Place the figure “here.”
    - `[t]`: Place the figure at the top of the page.
    - `[b]`: Place the figure at the bottom of the page.
    - `[p]`: Place the figure on a dedicated page for floats.
    - `[!]`: Override LaTeX’s default constraints for placing floats.
    - `[H]`: Force LaTeX to place the image where it in document.

    You can combine these options, for example, `[htbp]` to allow LaTeX flexibility in placing the figure.

81. *How do you adjust the width and height of images inserted into a LaTeX document?*
To adjust the width and height of an image, you use the `\includegraphics` command with the `width` and `height` options:

```
\includegraphics[width=0.5\textwidth,
height=0.3\textheight]{imagefile.jpg}
```

This resizes the image to 50

82. *Can you explain how to create multipage tables in LaTeX using the **longtable** package?*
The `longtable` package is used to create tables that span multiple pages. Unlike `tabular`, `longtable` automatically handles page breaks:

```
\usepackage{longtable}
...
\begin{longtable}{|c|c|c|}
\hline
Header 1 & Header 2 & Header 3 \\
\hline
Row 1 & Data 1 & Data 2 \\
\hline
\end{longtable}
```

The `longtable` environment will split the table across pages as needed.

83. *How do you rotate a figure or table in LaTeX?*
You can rotate a figure or table using the `rotatebox` command from the `graphicx` package:

```
\usepackage{graphicx}
...
\rotatebox{90}{\includegraphics
[width=0.5\textwidth]{image.jpg}}
```

This rotates the image by 90 degrees. You can also use the `sideways` environment from the `rotating` package to rotate an entire figure or table.

84. *How can you format table columns to be centered, left-aligned, or right-aligned in LaTeX?*
In LaTeX, you can control the alignment of table columns using:

- `l`: Left-aligned column
- `c`: Centered column
- `r`: Right-aligned column

For example:

```
\begin{tabular}{|l|c|r|}
    Left & Center & Right \\
\end{tabular}
```

This creates a table with left, center, and right-aligned columns.

85. *What is the `tabularx` package used for in LaTeX, and how does it differ from the standard `tabular` environment?*
The `tabularx` package allows you to create tables with columns that automatically adjust their width to fit the page:

```
\usepackage{tabularx}
...
\begin{tabularx}{\textwidth}{|X|X|X|}
    Column 1 & Column 2 & Column 3 \\
\end{tabularx}
```

The `X` column specifier automatically stretches to fill the available space, unlike the standard `tabular` environment where column widths are fixed.

86. *Can you explain how to create and customize captions for figures and tables in LaTeX?*
You can add captions to figures and tables using the `\caption` command:

```
\begin{figure}
    \includegraphics
    [width=0.5\textwidth]
    {image.jpg}
    \caption{This is a custom caption}
    \label{fig:custom}
\end{figure}
```

You can also customize the caption format using the `caption` package:

```
\usepackage[font=small,labelfont=bf]
{caption}
```

This sets the caption text to be small and the label to be bold.

87. *How do you create a table with merged cells (spanning rows or columns) in LaTeX?*
To create a table with merged cells, you can use the `\multicolumn` and `\multirow` commands (the latter requires the `multirow` package):

```
\usepackage{multirow}
...
\begin{tabular}{|c|c|c|}
\hline
\multirow{2}{*}{Row span}
& Column 1 & Column 2 \\
& Column 3 & Column 4 \\
```

```
\hline
\multicolumn{2}{|c|}{Column span}
& Column 5 \\
\hline
\end{tabular}
```

`\multicolumn` merges multiple columns, while `\multirow` merges rows.

88. *How do you create a glossary or list of acronyms in LaTeX?*
To create a glossary or list of acronyms, you can use the `glossaries` package. First, load the package and define your terms or acronyms:

```
\usepackage{glossaries}
\makeglossaries
\newglossaryentry{latex}
{name=LaTeX, description={A document
preparation system}}
\newacronym{NASA}{NASA}{National
Aeronautics and Space Administration}
```

Then, to print the glossary and acronyms:

```
\printglossary  % Prints the glossary
\printglossary[type=\acronymtype]
% Prints the acronym list
```

Use `\gls{}` to reference the terms or acronyms in the text.

89. *What is the purpose of the `\footnote` command, and how is it used in LaTeX?*

The `\footnote` command is used to add footnotes in LaTeX documents. Footnotes appear at the bottom of the page where they are referenced:

```
This is a sentence with a footnote.
\footnote{This is the footnote text.}
```

LaTeX automatically numbers the footnotes and formats them at the bottom of the page.

90. *How do you modify the spacing between paragraphs in LaTeX?*
To adjust the spacing between paragraphs in LaTeX, you can use the `\setlength` command to modify the `\parskip` length:

```
\setlength{\parskip}{1em}
% Increases space between paragraphs
```

This adds additional space (1em) between paragraphs. You can adjust the value as needed.

91. *What are some ways to change the page numbering style (e.g., roman numerals) in LaTeX?*
You can change the page numbering style using the `\pagenumbering` command. Common styles include:

- `\pagenumbering{arabic}`: Standard numbering (1, 2, 3)
- `\pagenumbering{roman}`: Lowercase Roman numerals (i, ii, iii)
- `\pagenumbering{Roman}`: Uppercase Roman numerals (I, II, III)

The command resets the page counter and applies the specified numbering style.

92. *How do you set up different page numbering styles for different sections (e.g., roman numerals for the preface and arabic for the main text)?*
    To set different page numbering styles for different sections, use the `\pagenumbering` command:

    ```
    \pagenumbering{roman}
    % Preface uses Roman numerals
    ...
    \clearpage
    \pagenumbering{arabic}
    % Main text uses Arabic numerals
    ```

    This changes the page numbering style at specific points in the document, allowing different styles for different sections.

93. *Can you explain how to create a table of figures or table of tables in LaTeX?*
    A table of figures or a table of tables can be created using the `\listoffigures` and `\listoftables` commands:

    ```
    \listoffigures
    % Generates a table of figures
    \listoftables
    % Generates a table of tables
    ```

    These commands automatically generate lists based on the `\caption` commands associated with figures and tables.

94. *What is the* **geometry** *package used for in LaTeX, and how does it help customize page layout?*
The `geometry` package is used to customize the page layout by allowing precise control over margins, page size, and orientation. You can specify custom dimensions using the following:

```
\usepackage[margin=1in]{geometry}
% Set all margins to 1 inch
```

You can also customize individual margins or change page size and orientation.

95. *How do you create a custom title page in LaTeX that differs from the rest of the document layout?*
You can create a custom title page by using the `titlepage` environment:

```
\begin{titlepage}
    \centering
    {\Huge My Custom Title}\\[1cm]
    {\Large Author Name}\\[3cm]
    \today
    \vfill
\end{titlepage}
```

The title page can have its own layout, distinct from the rest of the document, and does not affect the main formatting.

96. *What is the difference between single-column and multicolumn layouts, and how do you implement both in LaTeX?*

Single-column layouts use the full page width for text, while multicolumn layouts split the page into multiple columns. To implement a multicolumn layout, use the `multicols` package:

```
\usepackage{multicol}
\begin{multicols}{2}
    Text split into two columns.
\end{multicols}
```

This divides the text into two columns. For single-column layouts, simply do not use the `multicols` environment.

97. *How do you create section numbering that includes both chapter and section numbers (e.g., 1.1, 1.2, etc.)?*
To create section numbering that includes both chapter and section numbers (e.g., 1.1, 1.2), you need to use the \`numbering` commands. This is typically the default behavior for `book` and `report` document classes, but it can be manually set using:

```
\renewcommand{\thesection}{\thechapter.
\arabic{section}}
```

This creates numbered sections like 1.1, 1.2, etc., where `9` refers to the chapter number.

98. *How can you create cross-references between different parts of a document using* \`label` *and* \`ref`*?*
You can create cross-references by labeling parts of the document with \`label` and referring to them with \`ref`:

```
\section{Introduction}
\label{sec:intro}
...
As discussed in Section \ref{sec:intro}, ...
```

The `\label` command assigns a label to a specific section, equation, figure, or table, and `\ref` retrieves the number associated with that label.

99. *What is the **enumitem** package, and how does it improve the customization of lists in LaTeX?*
The `enumitem` package provides advanced customization for lists in LaTeX. It allows you to adjust list spacing, labels, and item formatting more easily than with default list environments:

```
\usepackage{enumitem}
\begin{enumerate}[label=\alph*),
start=5]
    \item Item 1
    \item Item 2
\end{enumerate}
```

In this example, the list starts from the fifth item and uses alphabetical labels.

100. *How do you use the **subfiles** package to manage large LaTeX projects, such as a book or thesis?*
The `subfiles` package allows you to divide large projects into smaller, manageable subfiles, which can be compiled independently or as part of the main document:

```
\usepackage{subfiles}
...
```

```
\subfile{chapter1.tex} % Include Chapter 1
\subfile{chapter2.tex} % Include Chapter 2
```

Each subfile can be compiled on its own, making it easier to work on individual chapters or sections.

101. *Can you explain the role of the log file in debugging LaTeX errors?*
The log file (`.log`) contains detailed information about the LaTeX compilation process, including warnings, errors, and the actions taken during compilation. It helps in debugging by pointing out syntax issues, missing files, or incorrect commands:

    - Error messages: Indicate the location of errors and provide suggestions for resolution.
    - Overfull/Underfull boxes: Warn about content overflowing margins or excessive white space.

102. *How do you define custom environments in LaTeX, and why would you need to do this?*
Custom environments are defined using the `\newenvironment` command. They are useful for creating reusable blocks of formatted content, such as custom examples, remarks, or definitions:

```
\newenvironment{example}[1][Example]
{\par\noindent\textbf{#1:} }
{\par\noindent}
```

This defines an `example` environment that adds a label and formats the content as an example.

103. *What is `latexmk`, and how does it improve the efficiency of compiling large LaTeX documents?*

`latexmk` is a build tool for LaTeX that automates the compilation process. It detects which parts of the document need to be recompiled and runs the necessary commands (e.g., `pdflatex`, `bibtex`, `biber`) automatically:

```
latexmk -pdf main.tex
```

This command compiles `main.tex` and manages bibliography and index processing efficiently.

104. *How do you generate a list of references or bibliography at the end of a LaTeX document using* ***biblatex****?*
To generate a bibliography with `biblatex`, load the package and specify the bibliography file:

```
\usepackage[backend=biber]{biblatex}
\addbibresource{references.bib}
...
\printbibliography
```

This will generate a list of references at the end of the document, based on the `references.bib` file.

105. *How does version control (e.g., using Git) help in collaborative LaTeX projects?*
Version control using Git allows multiple collaborators to work on the same LaTeX project simultaneously. It tracks changes, facilitates collaboration, and helps resolve conflicts:

    - *Branching*: Different collaborators can work on separate branches without affecting the main document.

- *History tracking*: Git tracks every change made, allowing you to revert to previous versions if needed.
- *Merge conflicts*: Git detects when two collaborators make conflicting changes and provides tools to resolve these conflicts.

106. *How do you incorporate external files (such as figures or data) into a LaTeX document using the* **`\include`** *or* **`\input`** *commands?*
The `\include` and `\input` commands incorporate external files into a LaTeX document:

    - `\include{filename}`: Includes `filename.tex` on a new page and adds an `.aux` file.
    - `\input{filename}`: Includes `filename.tex` without adding an `.aux` file or starting a new page.

    Both commands are used for modularizing content such as chapters, figures, or data.

107. *How can you add hyperlinks and bookmarks within a LaTeX document using the* **`hyperref`** *package?*
The `hyperref` package creates clickable hyperlinks and bookmarks in LaTeX documents:

```
\usepackage{hyperref}
...
\section{Introduction} \label{sec:intro}
See Section \ref{sec:intro} for
more details.
% Creates a clickable link to the
section
```

You can also create clickable URLs with the `\url` or `\href` commands:

```
\url{http://example.com}
% Adds a clickable link
\href{http://example.com}{Click here}
% Creates a link with custom text
```

The package also generates bookmarks in the PDF file for easier navigation.

Bibliography

1. A collaborative, continuously updated guide covering fundamental and advanced LaTeX topics. LaTeX Wikibook. Available online at: https://en.wikibooks.org/wiki/LaTeX

2. American Mathematical Society: An essential reference for handling complex mathematical environments in LaTeX. User's Guide for the `amsmath` Package. Available online at: https://www.ams.org/publications/authors/tex/amslatex

3. Downes, M.: A must-have reference for typesetting mathematical notation in LaTeX. In: Short Math Guide for LaTeX. American Mathematical Society, Providence (2002). Available online at: https://www.ams.org/arc/tex/short-math-guide.html

4. Downes, M.: A systematic guide to mathematical typesetting, including spacing, delimiters, and multi-line equations. In: A Guide to LaTeX Math Mode. American Mathematical Society, Providence (2017)

5. Eijkhout, V.: A deep dive into TeX internals, covering macro programming and advanced typesetting techniques. In: TeX by Topic: A TeXnician's Reference. Addison-Wesley, Boston (1992)

Md Aquib, *Fundamentals of LaTeX*, University Texts in the Mathematical Sciences,
https://doi.org/10.1007/978-981-96-9318-4

6. Flynn, P.: A comprehensive collection of frequently asked questions about LaTeX, TeX, and related tools. The UK TeX FAQ. Available online at: https://texfaq.org

7. Goossens, M., Rahtz, S., Mittelbach, F.: An in-depth guide to including and manipulating graphics in LaTeX. In: The LaTeX Graphics Companion. Addison-Wesley, Boston (1997)

8. Gratzer, G.: A detailed exploration of mathematical typesetting, including AMS-LaTeX and theorem environments. In: More Math into LaTeX, 5th edn. Springer, Berlin (2016)

9. Gratzer, G.: An encyclopedic reference covering LaTeX for mathematical and scientific writing. In: Texts and Math into LaTeX, 6th edn. Springer, Berlin (2023)

10. Knuth, D.E.: The classic reference for TeX, providing deep insights into document preparation and typesetting. In: The TeXbook. Addison-Wesley, Boston (1986)

11. Knuth, D.E.: A fundamental text on TeX's default font system and typography principles. In: Computer Modern Typefaces. Addison-Wesley, Boston (1986)

12. Kopka, H., Daly, P.W.: A user-friendly introduction to LaTeX, covering both basic and advanced document preparation. In: A Guide to LaTeX: Document Preparation for Beginners and Advanced Users, 4th edn. Addison-Wesley, Boston (2003)

13. Kottwitz, S.: A modern beginner-friendly introduction, covering document creation, formatting, and customization. In: LaTeX Beginner's Guide. Packt Publishing, Birmingham (2011)

14. Lamport, L.: The foundational text by Leslie Lamport, the creator of LaTeX, introducing core concepts and usage. In: LaTeX: A Document Preparation System, 2nd edn. Addison-Wesley, Boston (1994)

15. Lehman, P.: A reference manual for handling bibliographies and citations in LaTeX. The `biblatex` Package Documentation. Available online at: http://www.ctan.org/pkg/biblatex

16. Mittelbach, F., Goossens, M.: A comprehensive guide detailing advanced LaTeX usage, including fonts, layouts, and automation. In: The LaTeX Companion, 2nd edn. Addison-Wesley Professional, Boston (2004)

17. Moore, R., Oetiker, T.: A guide to using LaTeX for web publishing, including PDF and HTML conversions. In: LaTeX for the Web. Addison-Wesley, Boston (2000)

18. Oetiker, T., Partl, H., Hyna, I., Schlegl, E.: A widely used introductory document covering the essential aspects of LaTeX. The Not So Short Introduction to LaTeX2e. Available online at: https://tobi.oetiker.ch/lshort/

19. Tantau, T.: The definitive manual for the TikZ package, covering advanced diagramming and graphical representations. The TikZ and PGF Packages. Available online at: http://mirrors.ctan.org/graphics/pgf/base/doc/pgfmanual.pdf

20. Tantau, T.: The official guide for Beamer, covering slide design, animations, and professional presentations. User Guide to the Beamer Class. Available online at: http://www.ctan.org/pkg/beamer

21. Voss, H.: A comprehensive resource for creating high-quality vector graphics using PSTricks. In: PSTricks: Graphics and PostScript for TeX and LaTeX. Available online at: http://www.ctan.org/pkg/pstricks

The manufacturer's authorised representative in the EU is Springer Nature Customer Service Centre GmbH, Europaplatz 3, 69115 Heidelberg, Germany. If you have any concerns regarding our products, please contact ProductSafety@springernature.com

Printed and bound by CPI Group (UK) Ltd, Croydon, CR0 4YY
21/09/2026
02219988-0018